An Introduction to Budc

An Introduction to Buddhist Psychology and Counselling

Pathways of Mindfulness-Based Therapies

5th edition

Padmasiri de Silva

Research Fellow, Faculty of Philosophical, Historical and International Studies, Monash University, Australia

Fifth edition published 2014 by
PALGRAVE MACMILLAN

Third edition © Padmasiri de Silva 2000
Fourth edition © Padmasiri de Silva 2005

Palgrave Macmillan in the UK is an imprint of Macmillan Publishers Limited, registered in England, company number 785998, of Houndmills, Basingstoke, Hampshire RG21 6XS.

Palgrave Macmillan in the US is a division of St Martin's Press LLC, 175 Fifth Avenue, New York, NY 10010.

Palgrave Macmillan is the global academic imprint of the above companies and has companies and representatives throughout the world.

Palgrave® and Macmillan® are registered trademarks in the United States, the United Kingdom, Europe and other countries.

ISBN 978-1-137-28754-0   ISBN 978-1-137-28755-7 (eBook)
DOI 10.1057/9781137287557

A catalogue record for this book is available from the British Library.

A catalog record for this book is available from the Library of Congress.

To Our Renowned Meditation Guru
Ven. Uda Eriyagama Dhammajiva Thero

To My Family
Memory of my beloved parents & beloved wife, Kalyani
Our sons, Maneesh, Adeesh and Chandeesh &
their wives, Harini, Ananga and Sharron
Our grandchildren: Ishka Yugani, Ashan, Keisha and Jed

Contents

Preface   ix

Acknowledgements   xiv

Part I   Introducing Buddhist Psychology

1   Buddhist Psychology and the Revolution
    in Cognitive Sciences   3

2   Basic Features of Buddhist Psychology: An Overview   9

3   The Psychology of Perception and Cognition   23

4   The Psychology of Motivation   31

5   Emotions: Western Theoretical Orientations
    and Buddhism   46

6   Personality: Philosophical and Psychological Issues   68

7   Mental Health and Sickness   78

8   Mental Well-being   82

9   Mind–Body Relationship and Buddhist Contextualism   93

10 Towards a Holistic Psychology: Blending Thinking
    and Feeling   97

11 Buddhism as Contemplative Philosophy, Psychology
    and Ethics   108

Part II   Pathways of Mindfulness-Based Counselling

12 Nature of Counselling and Theoretical Orientations
    in Psychotherapy   119

13 Mindfulness-Based Therapeutic Orientations   126

14 Exploring the Content and Methodology
    of Buddhist Meditation   141

15 Stress Management and the Rhythms of Our Lives   147

16 The Logic of Sadness and Its Near Allies: Depression, Melancholy and Boredom   154

17 Understanding and Managing Grief: When the Desert Begins to Bloom   170

18 The Concept of Anger: Psychodynamics and Management   177

19 Addictions, Self-Control and the Puzzles Regarding Voluntary Self-Destruction   187

20 Pride and Conceit: Emotions of Self-Assessment   202

21 The Culture of 'Generosity' and the Ethics of Altruism   216

Guidelines for Readers   227

Further Reading   232

Notes   235

References   254

Index   265

Preface

The Emotional Rhythms of Our Lives

In a very basic sense, this work is an introduction to Buddhist psychology and counselling and especially mindfulness-based counselling. The first edition of the book on Buddhist psychology emerged in 1979, when only the early pioneering studies of Rhys Davids and, a little later, Rune Johanson's writings, focused on the psychology of *nirvāna*, comprised the literature on the subject. I did not in any way anticipate that this was going to continue as far as 2005 with three more editions with additional chapters. I am grateful to Palgrave Macmillan for their continuing interest in this book and the editor of the 'The Library of Philosophy of Religion', Professor John Hick, who initially invited me to write this work during his sabbatical as a Visiting Fellow at the Philosophy Department at Peradeniya University. In fact, recently he wrote to me to say that this book was one of the most successful books in the series. I am sure that he would be gratified to see that the work has emerged with a new lease of life as a book on Buddhist psychology and counselling. I am grateful to the teachers and students in the universities and institutes where the book has been used and also to a large number of Buddhist scholars, as well as to the continuing interest shown by the 'general reader'.

However, this book, especially the counselling dimensions of the work, has been nourished by my early difficult experiences, which were followed, as the years passed, with joy, contentment and fulfilment in my work and life. Thus, while I am more than happy about its acceptance into academia, this book has an undercurrent of what I refer to as the 'rhythms of our emotional lives'. It represents an authentic, existential and experiential strand in my life, which went through a deeply disturbing shattering phase in 1994 (see Chapters 16 and 17 on 'Sadness' and 'Grief') but culminated in the deepest insights of self-knowledge – of anger, fear and anxiety, loneliness and mild depression, with an emerging calm, equanimity, tremendous empathy, compassion and insights with the ability to understand the conflicts and tensions of my clients in counselling. The Buddha advised his son Rahula to look at his mind in the way that one looks at a mirror, as a pathway for self-knowledge, but in my counselling sessions the client's mind was a mirror to let me see my own 'emotional rhythms' in their mind and body. As Ervin Yalom says, the client and the therapist are fellow travellers – as they begin to understand the difficult encounters in life: going through shattering conflicts, anger and anxiety but gradually experiencing calm and contentment and insight into the nature of one's predicament. Chapter 11 focuses on the nature of the contemplative paths in therapy, which opens up new horizons in the life of both the therapist and client. Academia and the publishing worlds have given me a framework to reach a large number of readers, and Part II springs from authentic rhythms of my emotional life. T.S. Eliot has presented fine insights in his method of transforming a number of disorganised experiences into a beautiful format, something very personal into a universal message.

An Introduction to Buddhist Psychology has commanded a keen readership for over three decades. During the last two decades, courses on Buddhist psychology have been introduced in some universities, in departments of religion and philosophy, in the West; and, in the second wave of interest, Buddhist courses in psychology and new courses in counselling and therapy have emerged. In countries such as Thailand and Sri Lanka they now occupy an important place in Buddhist studies. Due to the emergence of a number of mindfulness-based therapies, the general readership for books on Buddhist psychology has increased and the book has evolved: new chapters were added to each edition. The following points summarise the significant facets of this book.

First, the present book brings together the elements of what may be described as mindfulness-based counselling, and so it covers both Buddhist psychology and counselling. This new dimension emphasises the practical value of Buddhist psychology. Secondly, a number of mindfulness-based therapeutic traditions have emerged in the West during the last two decades. There are chapters in Part II that introduce both the nature of counselling and the mindfulness-based therapeutic traditions, including the therapeutic method I have developed, Mindfulness-based, Emotion-focused (EFT) Therapy. Thirdly, for many years I have been immersed in 'emotion studies': Part I, Chapter 5 discusses emotions at length, and in Part II, against the background of therapy and counselling there are specific chapters on grief, sadness/depression, anger, conceit/pride, greed/addictions and presentation of some positive emotions, generosity, compassion, emotional balance and equanimity. A chapter on 'Thinking and Feeling' offers a

Buddhist perspective to try to resolve a Western debate on the nature of emotions: physiologically oriented theories vs cognitive theories of emotions. In fact, a sub-theme that reverberates in this book may be described as 'the emotional rhythms of our lives'. Fourthly, the book is a blend of material on the psychology of Buddhism from the original Buddhist sermons, structured according to the main topics in the discipline of psychology such as cognition, motivation, emotion, personality, health and well-being. My training in the philosophy of the mind at the University of Hawaii and during a Fulbright fellowship at the University of Pittsburgh have formed the way I handle basic concepts such as motivation and subliminal activity, emotions, intentions and volition and, in general, the fourfold cognitive, affective, volitional/conative and attentional dimensions of the mind. The charting out of different emotion profiles like grief, sadness, depression, anger, addictions and generosity is also partly facilitated by my training in the philosophy of the mind. Fifthly, many years of study, training and practising as a professional counsellor, which may be described as 'Buddhist Psychotherapy' has been a basis for the section on counselling in the book. Sixthly, Chapter 1 on Buddhism and the cognitive sciences defines the emerging interest in the Buddhism–cognitive sciences interface. Seventhly, Buddhism has also been described as 'contemplative science' and Chapter 11 is completely devoted to an analysis of Buddhism as contemplative philosophy, psychology, ethics and education, and in several other chapters there is a discussion of Buddhist psychology in the context of the current interest in 'moral psychology'. Eighthly, there are also new features in the new edition. Throughout my years of studying and teaching there has been a visible interdisciplinary spectrum running through formal studies in philosophy with philosophy of the mind as a speciality, Buddhist studies, counselling and psychology and a professional training in emotion studies. This background has given the present work an enriching flavour by illustrating the relevance of Buddhism to the contemporary world and, as Robert H. Thouless says, the surprising relevance of a message coming down twenty-six centuries.

In general, it can be said that there is a demand for Buddhist psychology texts integrating some of the more recent developments in counselling at the level of university courses, for Western-trained therapists integrating mindfulness practice to their work and a sophisticated group of readers interested in these new trends. Chapter 1 positions Buddhist psychology beyond its early philosophical beginnings grounding to be within the new revolution in cognitive sciences, which seeks new points of interaction with the areas of cognition, motivation and emotions.

One of the problems for a project of this sort is striking a balance between the popular demands for reading material in Buddhist psychology for those who are more focused on the practical uses of Buddhist psychology and counselling in routine life, and the demand of serious academic scholarship, authenticity of the sources in the original sermons of the Buddha, and very crucial, clarity and authenticity of meditation guidance. Meeting the demands of academic scholarship and authenticity of the material presented is crucial for a book of this sort, as I have maintained through all the previous editions. However, acting on some useful suggestions from readers I have included a glossary of Pāli terms, and made their usage in the main text as functional as far as is possible. Footnotes of reference to the discourses cannot be avoided but shall exercise some care where I introduce quotations from the Buddhist texts, especially with the aim of making the context lively and re-creating the spirit of the Buddha's sermons. The general flow and the tenor of the writing should make the reader aware that knowing some of the Pāli terms are useful, for instance, a term like *dukkha* (suffering, a world inundated with sorrow, lamentation, grief) and also the more modern rendering as 'stress': Another example would be the Buddhist rendering of 'good and bad', which is different from the Western-oriented usage, and the meaning of terms like '*kamma*', which has at least two dimensions: being related to the notion of re-birth and intentional action focused on the 'present'. These concepts become important in understanding the moral psychology in Buddhism, a dimension of psychology increasingly become relevant today. Also, Part II on Buddhist counselling psychology would be closer to the demands of the general reader interested in practical issues.

My long years of practice under the guidance of meditation guru from the forest hermitage in Meethirigala, Venerable Uda Eriyagama Dhammajiva, has added a new sense of depth to my understanding in unravelling the message in some of the *suttas*. The framework of this book has been enriched by this experience and guidance, for instance, as seen in Chapter 8 on mental balance and equanimity.

My acquaintance with the philosophy of the mind over several decades has sharpened my conceptual tools and the need for clarity and focus in my writings. I always remember with gratitude some wonderful seminars on the philosophy of the mind during my postgraduate studies at the University of Hawaii. Many readers have commented on the clarity and focus found in the *Introduction to Buddhist Psychology*. The chapters on counselling in Part II provide a practical dimension to the theory presented in Part I. Themes like addictions, stress management and grief counselling have been worked through with mostly successful clients.

Acknowledgements

First I would like to record a deep sense of thanks to our publisher Palgrave Macmillan for the sustaining interest in my work on Buddhist psychology for well over two decades and crowning this interest with the present volume with nine new chapters and the rest of the book greatly revised. I wish to also thank those on the editorial staff who reviewed the project proposal for this new book and also suggested certain creative ideas to improve the quality of the work, as well as the integration of different chapters into a well-knit book. I wish to thank Nicola Jones of the Palgrave-Macmillan editorial staff for coordinating the progress of the work at different stages.

I have worked with a number of copy editors over the years for a number of books, but Alec McAulay stands out as the editor par excellence. At a difficult juncture in the progress of the text and the proofs he restored in my mind full confidence that we could make some smooth progress, and carry it through till the book is ready for printing. I wish to express my most sincere thanks to Alec McAulay.

I greatly appreciate the assistance received from Professor G. Somaratne, an eminent scholar in Pali studies, for helping me with the Pali diacritical marks.

Part I
Introducing Buddhist Psychology

1
Buddhist Psychology and the Revolution in Cognitive Sciences

Cognitive science is a child of the 1950s, the product of a time when psychology, anthropology and linguistics were redefining themselves and computer science and neuroscience as disciplines were coming into existence. Psychology could not participate in the cognitive revolution until it had freed itself from behaviourism, thus restoring cognition to scientific respectability. By then, it was becoming clear in several disciplines that that the solution to some of their problems depended on solving problems traditionally allocated to other disciplines.[1]

James further speculated that the stream of consciousness may be a different type of phenomenon than the brain, one that interacts with the brain while alive, absorbs and retains the identity, personality, and memories constitutive in this interaction, and can continue without the brain. While James is still widely respected among contemporary cognitive scientists, his views on the origin and nature of consciousness have been largely ignored or rejected.[2]

Today, the early stages of the Jamesian dream are being realised. Renowned Buddhist scholars have joined psychologists, cognitive scientists and neurologists in integrating the methodologies of Buddhism to a specific discipline, which, following Alan Wallace, may be described as 'contemplative science'. This emerging framework has located both Buddhist psychology and counselling practices within this contemporary convergence of contemplative practices and the cognitive sciences. While I shall trace below these stages in the interface between Buddhism and cognitive science, Wallace feels that the cognitive sciences have *yet to undergo a complete revolution*, overcoming the domination of scientific materialism and devise rigorous and precise introspective methods for observing mental phenomena.[3]

What is referred to as the cognitive revolution in the sciences has gone through several phases. The first phase was marked by the work of Ivan Pavlov, and later by J.B. Watson, who considered psychology to be the science of behaviour, and whose focus was on 'visibles', 'audibles' and 'tangibles'. Later, B.F. Skinner asserted that the mind does not exist, and psychology was concerned merely with behaviour dispositions. Mental events were not visible and objective evidence was available only in the realm of publicly observable behaviour. Though the psychologist William James was interested in the study of consciousness, the domination of behavioural psychology meant that it was assumed that such a project did not have any scientific respectability.

The emergence of cognitive psychology in the 1960s was the first step towards the scientific study of consciousness. The next phase in the cognitive revolution was marked by new research in cognitive psychology, neuroscience, linguistics, molecular genetics and artificial intelligence. Harvard University established cognitive studies as a part of the curriculum, and Carnegie-Mellon developed information-processing psychology. As cognitive studies developed, these projects received financial support from the Sloan Foundation in 1976. The relevance of these new interdisciplinary sciences for a dialogue between Buddhism and cognitive sciences was articulated by a scientist of the calibre of Francisco Varella, and this line of thinking appeared to be a revival of interest in the insights of William James. While the scientific study of consciousness achieved legitimacy there were a few obstacles to the extending of these interests to the development of a Buddhist psychology. It took some time for Buddhist scholarship to break away from traditional scholasticism, and Francisco Varela was a pioneer who was instrumental in holding a conference on 'Buddhism and cognitive sciences' with a grant from the Sloan Foundation. This conference was held at the Naropa Institute in Colorado and, while teaching a summer course in Buddhist psychology, I had the good fortune to participate. The Naropa University now has a comprehensive degree and postgraduate programme in Buddhist psychology, and staff there are undertaking advanced research. Varella emphasised the point that Buddhism can potentially have an influence on modern science, at the research level in the study of the mind as well as on the epistemological foundations of some of the sciences such as physics. The life sciences that have developed over the years since the Naropa conference on Buddhism and cognitive sciences have a special focus on the study of mind, cognition, emotions or affect, and especially the new frontiers of neuroscience such as affective neuroscience. The meeting ground of science and Buddhism provides the background to the resurgence of interest in Buddhist psychology. The experientially based technology of meditation has generated the use of mindfulness as a therapeutic tool, and its impact on mental and physical well-being is of current interest and research. Thus, it has become important to explore the study of consciousness in the Buddhist meditative tradition and this study over the years, along with the interest among some neuroscientists, culminated in the groundbreaking discovery of the concept of 'neuroplasticity' by Richard Davidson and a discussion of its relevance to Buddhist psychology in several conferences of the Mind and Life Institute.

Richard Davidson argued for neuroplasticity, the ability of the brain to develop throughout life, and presented data suggesting that meditation practice could produce beneficial plasticity in the brain's affective centres, inhibiting destructive emotions while fostering positive ones.[4]

More recent works such as *The Mindful Brain*, by Daniel J. Siegel indicate that mindful awareness has been scientifically proved to enhance our physical, mental and social well-being.[5] At the very heart of this synthesis of science and mindfulness practice is the idea that our awareness of our ongoing experience creates a kind of attunement within ourselves and with others that can harness the specific social and emotional circuits of the brain. Such findings not merely help us to transform our lives and deepen our connections with others and ourselves but also these developments in contemplative neuroscience have given a great deal of confidence to those who have extended mindfulness techniques to different types of Western therapies, ranging from cognitive-behaviour therapy to psychodynamic, humanistic and Gestalt therapy. Chapter 13 in this book is devoted to describing and analysing number of mindfulness-based therapeutic traditions in the West and, therefore, gives a bird's-eye view of these dominant traditions today. All of the chapters in Part I illuminate the Buddhist psychology that, in the background, gives nourishment to these therapeutic traditions, as well as the practical application of mindfulness practice and Buddhist insights to specific problem areas such as stress management, anger management, grief counselling, depression and addictions.

The emergence of the Mind and Life Institute has led to a series of conference and related publications from 1987 onwards, and the Dalai Lama has given the necessary guidance throughout the series of meetings. In the field of Buddhist psychology I have constantly found their contributions to emotion studies and related issues very valuable: emotions and health; destructive emotions; mindfulness and compassion, and the treatment of depression; altruism, ethics and compassion; attention, memory and mind; mind–body connection; neuroplasticity; and contemplative science. Going beyond the mind, the exploration of epistemological questions in quantum physics and Eastern contemplative science has been a noteworthy contribution. Since 1987, dialogues between Buddhism and the cognitive sciences under the aegis of the Mind and Life Institute have explored a vast territory and have been a catalyst in the emergence of Buddhist psychology with a new face. They have also helped to restore the brain into the context of the body and its impact on the immune, autonomic and endocrine systems. Candace Pert's thesis concerning the body being a second brain has thrown new light on the links between the body, brain and mind in emotions.[6] On the practical side of counselling and therapeutic systems, mindfulness-based techniques have been integrated into stress-reduction therapy, cognitive-behaviour therapy, psychodynamic therapies, humanistic and Gestalt therapies, and also into the work I have done in developing mindfulness-based EFT (Emotion-focused Therapy), as well as Cultivating Emotional Balance (CEB), which is a broad based education programme. The Naropa University stands out in developing an entire degree programme in Buddhist psychology.

It must be stated that, from the perspectives of Buddhism as a liberation quest, while research in the sciences referred to above may certainly increase the relevance and credibility of Buddhist psychology and therapy in modern times, and, therefore, offer some kind of rationale for those who come to the Buddhist faith from outside as well as those who are serious practitioners, an understanding of the relevance of science has not been embraced by many of the monks who follow the traditional Buddhist path and who have become perfected ones or achieved higher stages on the way. But yet, today, for practitioners among both laymen and monks, this encounter with the fresh breeze of discoveries in psychology, therapy and neurology has helped to draw them to the practical path of ethics and the practice of meditation. In my personal life as a Buddhist and a therapist, I find that they are two mutually enriching dimensions. Needless to say, it is the deeper practice of Buddhism that helps our absorbing interest in Buddhist psychology to go beyond academic boundaries.

Evan Thompson observes that contemplative mental training and critical phenomenological and philosophical analysis of the mind form the cornerstone of Buddhist practice, and it may be considered more as a repository of contemplative and phenomenological expertise rather than being just an object of scientific study.[7] I hope that studying the biographies of the outstanding monks in the Buddhist contemplative tradition will open up a new chapter in this revival of the Jamesian heritage.

The place of 'moral psychology' in Buddhism will be referred to again in Chapter 2. Briefly, the links between psychology and morality in the context of the new scientific writings energised thinkers to move forward: consider, for instance, the work of Lawrence Kohlberg, who became popular because of the interviews he had with children on moral dilemmas, for example, the famous question – should Heinz steal a drug to save his wife's life? Antonio Damasio's book *Descartes' Error*[8] showed that morality and rationality were dependent on the proper functioning of emotional circuits in the prefrontal cortex. Daniel J. Siegel says in his book, *The Mindful Brain*:

> Of related 'neural note' is the finding of an active role of the middle prefrontal cortex in morality. This same region is active as we imagine ethical dilemmas and as we initiate moral action. We come to our sense of ourselves and of others, and a sense of right action and morality, through the integrative circuitry in our neural core.[9]

Siegel recommends the four great factors of curiosity, openness, acceptance and love – COAL:

> Just as attuning to oneself and approaching experience with COAL is a natural flow of being mindfully aware, so is the attuning to the larger world of living beings with a loving stance inherent in this reflective immersion in our deeper selves. This journey is a part of the path to dissolving the delusion of separateness.

He says thus we see 'right action' not as a mere judgment, but 'as a moral direction which has a deep universal structure'.

Thus the emerging links between Buddhist ethics and moral psychology is an important dimension of the interface between Buddhism and the cognitive sciences. Chapter 5 on emotions examines in detail the impact of the cognitive sciences on emotion studies, which maintains that understanding emotions illuminates the understanding of 'intelligent systems'.

The most recent developments that have led to the emergence of moral psychology have been presented by John M. Doris:

> Starting in late 1960s, the increasing influence of philosophical naturalism and cognitive science, particularly in epistemology and

philosophy of mind, set the stage for an interdisciplinary study of morality in philosophy, while in psychology, the demise of behaviourism enabled empirical investigation of an increasing variety of topics, including those that had been previously under the ambit of philosophical ethics. Since the early 1990s, such inquiry increased exponentially, and by the twenty-first century's inception, not only were philosophers and psychologists sampling the empirical and theoretical riches available in their sister disciplines, they had begun to collaboratively produce research aimed at illuminating problems that had previously been treated within the borders of individual fields.[10]

He says that what has emerged is not a new field, as moral psychology has been in existence in a number of fields, but a *resituated* discipline which straddles disciplinary boundaries.

2
Basic Features of Buddhist Psychology: An Overview

Though the interface between Buddhism and cognitive science emerged during the last three decades of the 20th century, as far back as 1940, the Cambridge psychologist Robert H. Thouless commented on the relevance and importance of Buddhist psychology: 'Across the gulf of twenty-five centuries we seem to hear in the voice of the Buddha the expression of an essentially modern mind'.[1] The discourses of the Buddha are very rich in their use of psychological terminology and psychological analysis, but this facet of the doctrine was badly neglected until the pioneering work of C.A.F. Rhys Davids.[2] Rune Johanson's *The Psychology of Nirvana*[3] has also emerged as an important contribution. *An Introduction to Buddhist Psychology* (de Silva, first published in 1979, 4th edition in 2005), performed a useful function for those teachers involved in developing courses on Buddhist psychology and for the large numbers of 'general readers', who were merely interested in the topic.[4] As the traditional teaching of Buddhist philosophy widened, interest in Buddhist ethics and psychology had an important impact on the new curriculum. This book adds a new component to these widening interests in Buddhist psychology including Buddhist contributions to counselling issues, for which I draw from my experience in professional counselling as well as my research into counselling issues. While there are important contributions to Buddhist therapy and counselling which this book will address, it also has a unique mission in presenting the basic issues and concepts in Buddhist psychology with an extensive supplement on Buddhist counselling together with the points of interaction between Buddhist psychology and counselling.

One of the important requirements in understanding Buddhist psychology is to have some understanding of the Buddha's basic doctrines, the ethics, the theory of knowledge, and the theory of reality along with the concept of the mind. This background material is briefly presented in this chapter. Also, a good grasp of the psychology of Buddhism will enrich the understanding of the different facets of Buddhism. The Buddha's deep understanding of the psychology of the mind was one of his lasting contributions. There are particularly strong links between psychology and ethics, and there is an implicit moral psychology in Buddha's discourses. The recent interest in moral psychology, with its implications for Buddhist ethics, is important, and this chapter will discuss what is described as 'ethical realism'. Along the Buddhist path to liberation, the cultivation of the good and the purification of the mind go together. Also, some of the important psychological terms in Buddhism have ethical overtones. What we consider as Buddhist perspectives on therapy and counselling are rooted in the psychology of Buddhism. Therefore, a book on Buddhist psychology and counselling would involve the integral relationship between the psychology and counselling dimensions of Buddhism. The Buddha also developed the social ethics of Buddhism emphasising the importance of harmony in the family and society. The Buddha recommended the development of the socially valuable qualities of self-control (*dama*), mental calm (*sama*) and restraint (*niyama*). In the discourses of the Buddha there is a detailed analysis of the reciprocal relations between family members, the development of a work ethic and family economics. This chapter also briefly deals with the Buddhist theory of knowledge, the theory of reality and it provides a short review of the Buddha's critique of current philosophical theories including rationalism, scepticism, materialism, hedonism, theism, different versions of determinism and indeterminism. In the *Brahma-jāla Sutta* he mentions 62 theories, because at that time there was a rich philosophical culture of contending theories.

In this chapter, there will be only a very brief reference to the therapeutic and counselling perspectives of Buddhism because Part II is devoted to this. The central problem areas in Part I are cognition, motivation, emotion, personality, the mind–body relationship, thinking and feeling, as well as the concepts of mental health and well-being. Part II introduces the nature of counselling, the development of mindfulness-based therapies in the West and specific counselling issues such as grief counselling, stress management, anger management, depression, addictions, self-esteem, self-identity and the positive emotions of compassion and generosity. Depathologising of negative emotions such as depression, anger, fear, anxiety, vanity and arrogance takes a central place based on my own development of mindfulness-based EFT (Emotion-Focused Therapy).

There will also be a short introduction to the primary sources for studying Buddhist psychology. A concluding section on the Buddhist architecture of the mind provides a background to the chapters on cognition, motivation and emotions.

Ethics and Psychology

The doctrine of the Buddha clearly accommodates the interlacing of the ethical and psychological aspects of behaviour. Closest to this in the history of Western ethics is Aristotle's *Nicomachean Ethics*. The development of virtue is not a mere blind adherence to rules but the development of a certain type of skill (*kusala*). Virtue has to be developed by the cultivation of good habits and continuous self-analysis.

Buddhist ethics is not limited to the analysis of ethical concepts and theories but also recommends a way of life and patterns of conduct. This practical orientation in Buddhist ethics is well grounded in an understanding of the psychological factors that obstruct as well as promote the living of a virtuous life. The four right exertions are important, as they sum up the process of moral discipline: exertion for the non-arising of unskilful qualities that have not arisen; abandoning unskilful qualities already arisen; exertion for the arising of skilful qualities not yet arisen; and the development of skilful qualities already arisen. The cultivation of the good and the purification of the mind go together. There are clear ethical overtones in the use of the Buddhist psychological roots of motivation: greed, hatred and delusion as *akusala roots* and generosity, love and wisdom as *kusala* roots. The Buddhist ethics is also guided by an understanding of human nature, and moral action is grounded in a psychology of motivation and emotions. This quality is described by contemporary philosophers as 'ethical realism'.

Buddhist Social Ethics

Since the well-known claims of Max Weber denying the presence of a Buddhist social ethic, there has been a misunderstanding among academic circles that Buddhism has no vibrant social dimension:

> Salvation is an absolutely personal performance of the self-reliant individual. No-one, and particularly no social community can help him. The specific asocial character of genuine mysticism is here carried to its maximum.[5]

The Buddha's sermons deal with a wide array of social issues ranging from the celebrated *Sigālovāda Sutta*, which is a type of charter for a family ethic, a critique of the caste system and provides detailed advice for the householder about economic activity. In fact, the Buddhist resources for economics encouraged E.F. Schumacher to write his inspiring thesis on economics *Small Is Beautiful*.[6] There is a range of sermons to the kings on state craft with an ethical basis. On the spiritual side, it is said, 'protecting oneself, one protects others, and protecting others one protects oneself'. The monks were also organised as a coherent group and among the householders friendship based on spiritual interests have been encouraged. King Asoka is often cited as the embodiment of someone who practised state craft on Buddhist principles, expanding this into a multi-religious society. The Buddha also says that in contexts of social disputes, one can find the origin of discord within oneself. Buddhist psychology helps us to understand the roots of good and bad social change. The Buddha recommends the socially valuable psychological qualities of self-control (*dama*), mental calm (*sama*) and restraint (*niyama*).[7] The Buddha gives a realistic picture of human beings: they are capable of both good and evil, and a morally conducive family and social environment may have a good impact on secular, moral and spiritual qualities.

Theory of Knowledge

As a prince in the sixth century BCE, Siddhartha was caught up in the intellectual ferment of the time – of ascetics, seers and philosophers of a wide variety: materialists, hedonists, theists, sceptics, nihilist and determinists. The Buddha offered an analysis of different philosophies, their weaknesses and strengths, and the *Brahma-jāla Sutta* (the network of theories,[8] stands out as a pre-eminent source for this analysis. As K.N. Jayatilleke (1963) has shown in detail, there were three main types of thinkers dealing with the nature of knowledge: traditionalists, who depended on the authority of the scriptures like the Vedas; rationalists, whose guide was reason and rational speculation; and contemplatives, who upheld extra-sensory perception and intuitive knowledge. The Buddha said that he belonged to the third group, although he did not completely reject oral tradition and logical reasoning. However, he also had reservations on the existing practitioners of the third group, as there were some who had mistaken beliefs based on meditative experiences.[9] As explained by Bhikkhu Analayo, the parable of the elephant and the seven men indicates that direct personal knowledge may reveal only a part of reality.[10] In fact, the *Sutta-nipāta* presents a very mature perspective on the excesses of mere philosophical debates in the *Kalaha-vivāda Sutta*.

Theory of Reality

Buddhism accepts a certain kind of order in the universe, which has a number of dimensions: the realm of physical laws (*utu-niyāma);* biological laws (*bīja-niyāma*), psychological laws (*citta-niyāma*) and laws pertaining to spirituality (*dhamma-niyāma*). These patterns of causal laws are neither deterministic nor indeterministic but present themselves as probable tendencies rather than inevitable consequences. Though man's actions may be conditioned or constrained by these laws he is not determined by any one of them. In general, the Buddha opposed all forms of determinism, whether it is natural determinism (*svabhāva-vāda*), theistic determinism (*issara-nimmāṇa-vāda*), karmic determinism (*pubbe-kata-hetu-vāda*), or any other philosophy in which these facets may be combined.

In general, the Buddhist theory of causation offers a *via media* between the extremes of determinism and indeterminism. According to strict determinism, the present and the past are unalterable but the Buddha upholds a concept of freewill according to which an individual may, to a certain extent, control the dynamic forces of the past and present and also the course of future events. Man has free will (*atta-kāra*) and personal endeavour (*purisa-kāra*) and is capable of changing both himself and the environment. This concept of possibility and flexibility for actions gives a framework for man's actions and behaviour in the realms of psychology, therapy, morality and spiritual commitments. The Buddha also made an analysis and a breakdown of the central metaphysical theories that prevailed in the *Brahma-jāla Sutta* (network of theories). There were, in fact, six prominent thinkers with whom the Buddha had debates and discussions: Makkhali Gosāla, who was a theist, and upheld the view that the world was created and guided by the will of God; Ajita Kesakambali, a materialist, who maintained that man was annihilated at death and there was as such no base for leading a virtuous life; Sañjaya Belaṭṭhaputta, a sceptic, who believed that certain basic notions like the belief in an after-life and moral responsibility could not be rationally demonstrated or verified; Pūraṇa Kassapa, a natural determinist and so unable to see any meaning in distinguishing between good and bad; Pakudha Kaccāyana, who attempted to describe the nature of reality in terms of discrete categories and is referred to as a categoralist; and, finally, Nigaṇṭha Nātaputta, a relativist, who saw some truth in every point of view.

The critical evaluation of such theories belongs to two branches of philosophy referred to as epistemology and metaphysics (or better termed 'theory of reality'). This analysis is relevant to locating human behaviour in morality, psychology and therapeutics. Another important analysis of the underlying concept of reality in Buddhism is the several facets of the 'lawful nature of the universe': physical laws (*utu-niyāma*); biological laws *(bīja-niyāma)*; psychological laws (*citta-niyāma);* moral laws (*kamma-niyāma*); and laws pertaining to spiritual phenomena (*dhamma-niyāma*). This analysis is not found in the *Suttas,* but in the commentaries. Nonetheless, this fits in with broader Buddhist perspectives on the causal patterns in the universe.

Central to the Buddhist analysis of reality are the basic realities of impermanence (*anicca*); suffering/stress (*dukkha*); and non-self (*anatta*). The philosophical perspective on the existence of a 'self' will be taken up in detail in the chapter on 'personality'. The Buddhist position offers an interesting middle position between the eternalist, who upheld a permanent self, and the materialist, who upheld that there was nothing beyond an aggregate of material particles. By the upholding of karmic consequences and the concepts of accountability, responsibility and free will, the Buddha went beyond the materialist. The doctrine of impermanence goes against the belief in an unchanging soul. Buddhist psychological analysis in terms of the five aggregates illuminates the perspectives on the nature of the 'self'. As Mark Epstein says in the work, *Psychotherapy Without the Self,* 'The Buddha did not dispute the relative reality of the conventionally appearing self. But he did not insist that we give the relational self an absolute status that it does not possess'.[11] While the Buddha offers a number of arguments relevant to the debates of current thinkers, it is through the contemplative approach of insight meditation that one may get a more lasting understanding of the existence of a 'self'. The psychological and therapeutic dimensions have been presented with great clarity by Epstein in a number of books.

Sources for the Study of Buddhist Psychology

Part I of this work is mainly concerned with the systematisation and interpretation of the psychological enquiries in early Buddhism, and so the primary sources are the discourses of the Buddha and sermons given by senior monks such as Sāriputta and Moggallāna, the closest of his disciples. There will be some reference to other traditions where relevant. These discourses, which are in the Pāli language and also translated into English, fall into two major groups: the Sutta Piṭaka and the rules of discipline for the monks referred to as the Vinaya Piṭaka. There is a third primary source, which is the systematic development, analysis in the form of summaries and classifications referred to as the *Abhidhamma*. Although greatly valued for its psychological analysis it was the work of later systematisation. One of my central interests has been to develop a psychology of Buddhism based mainly on the *Sutta Piṭaka*. The *Vinaya Piṭaka*, although mainly devoted to the disciplinary rules that guide the monks, may have occasional discussions that have great value for the psychology and ethics of Buddhism.

The *Sutta Piṭaka* may be divided into five sections:

1. The *Dīgha Nikāya* (Dialogues of the Buddha)
2. The *Majjhima Nikāya* (Middle Length Sayings)
3. The *Saṃyutta Nikāya* (Kindred Sayings)
4. The *Aṅguttara Nikāya* (Gradual Sayings)
5. The *Khuddaka Nikāya* (Division of Small Works).

The material is presented in a simple and lucid way and it is also designed for the student who wishes to explore any questions in more detail: translations are cited in the Bibliography. A glossary of Pāli terms has been added to this edition and I have been economical in using Pāli terminology, so that the reader should be able get used to them. There are also terms such as *dukkha*, whose complex meaning cannot be captured a single word. Also, though the possession of some degree of sophistication regarding Buddhist doctrine may be an initial advantage, readers with an elementary understanding of Buddhism should be able to make their way through the chapters. For the reader who wishes to have do some background reading on Buddhist doctrines as an aid to understanding psychology, venerable Walpola Rahula's, *What the Buddha Taught* is ideal.[12] It is expected that many readers of this book will be interested in the emerging field of mindfulness-based therapies.

After having completed the Advanced Diploma in Counselling at Sophia College and practised as a professional counsellor for over six years I have developed a technique of mindfulness-based EFT (Emotion-focused Therapy) at the Springvale Community Center. This has enabled a mutual enrichment of my understanding of Buddhist psychology and counselling. Also, as my original training and PhD were in the areas of philosophy of the mind and East–West comparative philosophy (University of Hawaii), I have accumulated knowledge and experience that has undoubtedly enhanced this book. I sat down in the quiet setting of my home in Lexington Gardens Retirement Village to write this book with a feeling of accomplishing a mission. I have also had the stimulation of the academic atmosphere at Monash University. My years of acquaintance and practice, and time spent at retreats at the feet of the meditation guru, the Venerable Uda Eriyagama Dhammajiva of Meethirigala, Sri Lanka, have reinforced not only my writings but also improved my personal vision of peace and liberation, which are modest and simple steps on the path advocated by the Buddha. It is because of my personal conviction that the understanding and practice of the Buddha's guide to inner peace through structured meditation practice, and the deep delving into the practice of psychotherapy, is a mutually enriching journey that I have offered to write this book. Thus, while it nourishes readers with an academic interest, it is basically a guide to those who wish to enrich their personal lives and those of their fellow beings. Serious study of the concepts and ideas presented here in academia has added greatly to intelligibility, credibility, relevance and the liveliness of debates and discussions. Thus this work opens up the exciting path of the Buddha, both for the theory and practice of the 'mindful and compassionate' way, and shared wisdom independent of your position in upholding different philosophical and religious beliefs, and will, I hope, generate a healthy dialogue among different groups.

Guide to the Basic Problem Areas Examined in This Book

Regarding the Buddhist methodology and content of meditation practice, Chapter 12 is central to Part II of this book and may be read after Chapters 1 and 2. For those who are new to meditation practice, it may be meaningful to initiate the practice and continue it into your daily life. This practice is open to everyone, not just those who formally belong to the Buddhist practice, and the guidance of an experienced teacher is recommended. A very important idea that I recommend is to build up the 'The Enchantment of Being Your Own Therapist'.[13] In pursuit of this goal, it is necessary to understand your own mind in the spirit of what the Buddha recommended to his son Rāhula: to see his own mind, as if he is looking at a mirror. 'What do you think Rāhula? What is the purpose of a mirror? "For the purpose of reflection, Venerable sir". So too, Rāhula, an action with the body should be done after repeated reflection; an action by speech should be done after repeated reflection; an action by mind should be done after repeated reflection'. As a professional counsellor, I was stimulated to understand my own mind as I was opening up issues to clients, and getting them to see their own mind, 'as a mirror'.

Irvin Yalom, in his insightful work, *The Gift of Therapy*[14] says 'The therapist and the client are fellow travellers. There is no therapist and no person immune to the tragedies of existence.' As a client, a person needs to master 'deep listening', to slow down, relax, listen, respect the flow of life, to see mirror images emerging out of a busy life, which is stressful, intricate, and at times, chaotic. We move out of the 'hurrying syndrome' that dominates life.

I recommend readers, and especially students, to read this work not merely as an educational venture but as something that will open up your mind to the constant mirror images that rush past you in daily life. You can almost predict that anger is about to catch your mind, fear to drown your mind, and a sly feeling of jealousy is about to creep into your mind. At such times you should have that tremendous skill to 'step back' and make your own choice and respond without reactivity. As you mature you will be able to 'laugh at your own anger' and develop a good sense of humour, as some of my clients have done after several sessions of counselling.

Chapters 3–6, which discuss cognition, motivation, emotions and personality form the real hub of Buddhist psychology. Chapter 7, on issues of health and well-being, offers a useful background to Part II of this book. Chapter 8 on the body–mind problem gives an over-all background picture to link facets of Buddhist psychology discussed in earlier chapters. Chapter 9 contemplative philosophy, psychology and ethics gives the philosophical rationale for the chapter on med-itation and mindfulness-based therapies in Part II. Part II applies the theory, practice of counselling, and the application of mindfulness tech-niques to specific counselling issues such as stress, grief and anger management, depression, addictions, and issues of self-esteem pride and conceit. The chapter on Buddhist generosity opens up the mind to 'pos-itive emotions' inspired by the pioneer of positive psychology, Martin Seligman.

Buddhist Model of the Mind and Subliminal Consciousness

A brief summary of the Buddhist concept of mind, which forms the basis of the psychological dimensions of Buddhism, is invaluable. The Buddha denies the existence of any permanent entity, whether we describe it as mind or consciousness. What we refer to when we use the term 'mind' is really a psycho-physical complex (*nāma-rūpa*). nāma is used to refer to the four non-material aggregates (*khanda*): these are feeling (*vedanā*), sense impressions and concepts (*saññā*), voli-tional/conative activity (*saṅkhāra*), and consciousness (*viññāṇa*). the term *rūpa* refers to the four great elements: extension, cohesion, heat, and the material shapes derived from them. The mental and physical constituents form one complex, and there is mutual dependency of the mind on the body and the body on the mind. The law of dependent origination (*paṭicca-samuppāda*) presents the dynamic format of the structural picture just outlined.

In terms of the dynamic conditioned nature of mental phenomena, sense impressions conditions contact, contact conditions feelings, feelings condition craving and craving conditions grasping, and so on. According to the doctrine of non-self (*anatta*), there is no abiding substance, neither within nor outside the psycho-physical complex. The nature of the mind as a dynamic continuum is described by terms such as the stream of consciousness (*viññāṇa-sota*). It also contains levels below the threshold consciousness, a subliminal level functioning at three levels: the level of impulsive actions (*vītikkama-bhūmi*),; the level of thought processes (*pariyuṭṭhāna-bhūmi)*; and the level of dormant passions (*anusaya-bhūmi*). Chapter 4 on motivation gives a detailed account of such subliminal activity below the threshold of consciousness.

It is of great interest to note that *saññā* and *viññāṇa* represent cognitive activity, *vedanā* represents the root of the affective/emotional dimension, and *saṇkhāra* the volitional/conative dimension. While this three-dimensional or tripartite analysis is also found in Aristotle, in a deeper sense, all these facets are found in a compressed form in all states of consciousness and experience.

The four non-material groups (*nāma*) need some detailed clarification. *Vedanā* (feeling) is described as being of three types: pleasant, painful and neutral. Feelings are also classified as bodily and mental feelings. Pleasant feelings excite man's attachment to sensory/sensual objects and the latent subliminal tendency for sensuous greed (*rāgānusaya*); painful feelings excite latent subliminal anger and hatred (*paṭighānusaya*). The saint on the path has to eliminate the tendency for attachment to pleasant feelings, revulsion for painful feelings, and the tendency to ignorance as far as neutral feelings are concerned. *Saññā* is sometimes rendered as perception and in other contexts as conceptual activity, but it appears that both components are found in perceptual activity. There are references to six kinds of perceptual activity: visual consciousness arising from the eye and material shapes; auditory consciousness from the ear and sounds; olfactory consciousness from the nose and smells; gustatory consciousness from the tongue and tastes; bodily consciousness through body and touching; and mental consciousness derived from the mind and mental states. *Viññāṇa* has a number of contexts, but in this context, may be thought of as cognitive consciousness.

In relation to the wheel of dependent origination, *viññāṇa* is seen as the unbroken stream directed by the rebirth producing *kamma*. Here *viññāṇa* is the total consciousness, which includes the conscious as well as residual mental events of the individual. The term *saṅkhāra* also has this dual contextual usage. As one of the four mental aggregates, *saṅkhāra* may be rendered as volition/will, but as a link in the wheel of dependent origination as karmic formation. As acts of volition saṅkhāra and viññāṇa may be conscious or unconscious, and they include all reflexes and dispositions, these being of three kinds: kāya – bodily reflexes and dispositions as walking and breathing; vacī – verbal reflexes and dispositions; and mano – ideational reflexes and dispositions. There is also a third use of saṅkhāra to convey the idea that something is conditioned, like all phenomenal existence: all formations are impermanent (sabbe saṅkhārā aniccā). Thus it is necessary to emphasise that terms like viññāṇa and saṅkhāra have different contextual usages and here we have only looked at their role in Buddhist psychology.

Moral Psychology and Buddhist Ethics

Around the year 1990, a group of philosophers in the West, Ameli Rorty, Owen Flanagan, David Wong and others introduced the notion of 'ethical realism'. In looking at the great ethical traditions over the years through Aristotle, Kant and the Utilitarian traditions, they have shown the importance of the relevance of empirical psychology for normative ethics. Traditional ethics and their contemporary developments appear to show a deficiency in not integrating some facets of psychology into ethics:[15] 'Moral psychology straddles two fields. On one side, there is normative ethics. On the other, there is empirical psychology.' The discipline of psychology according to their analysis covers such topics as the analysis of the nature and function of cognition and reasoning, the emotions, temperament, conceptual and personality development and socially construed attributes.[16] They say that normative ethics is constrained by psychology. In defending their central thesis, they say that every traditional moral theory presupposes a theory of the structure of character and agency; proponents of each theory, while justifying their theory conceive morality in a way that can motivate agents and guide practical deliberation; and traditional moral theories have been criticised for being very utopian in their outlook. A number of articles in this work attempt to support the idea of constraining normative reflection by psychological knowledge.

A more recent work, *Experiments in Ethics*[17] illustrates the relevance of new developments in sciences dealing with human nature – including experimental and cognitive psychology, neuroscience, evolutionary theories and behavioural economics – to the way we arrive at moral judgments. Appiah compares the kind of ethics that does not receive any nourishment from these sciences to a 'waterless moat', which is the title of the introduction. It is a graphic metaphor that captures the essence of what is communicated in this work. He does some interesting research of his own, 'taking seriously that a certain array of distinct moral emotions may be a deep feature of human nature, and explores the concordance between our traditions of explicit moral reflection and these posited primitives'.[18]

The primary motivation and the starting point for Appiah's work is to foster the ethical facets of our personality: '... empirical psychology can help us to think about how to manage our lives, how to become better people', and equally important, 'Our ethical theories must acknowledge, the empirical facts about our mutable ways'.[19] Going beyond what we are with these mutable ways, 'it matters what kind of people we hope to be'.

Buddhism and Moral Psychology

In Buddhism, there is an integral and holistic approach in which the Buddhist analysis of the nature of things, the critique of philosophical theories, ethics and the psychology, and the theory of knowledge are interconnected. Psychology and ethics interact very clearly in the theory of motivation. The analysis of human behaviour as good and bad has different types of criteria according to context: violation of precepts and codes of conduct among householders and monks; the impact /consequences of the act on society and oneself. The roots of motivation and intention (*cetanā*) is the most important criterion for evaluating behaviour as good and bad or skilful and unskilful: roots of morally harmful behaviour are greed, hatred and delusion, where as morally appreciative behaviour have the roots in non-greed/generosity, non-hatred/compassion and non-delusion/wisdom. It is also said that the worst result of a bad action is the tendency to repeat it and the best result of a good action is also the tendency to repeat it. This point indicates that character-building is very crucial and here both the psychological and the ethical are interwoven. There is a fascinating symmetry between the roots of motivation, personality types and the distinction between negative and positive emotions (on moral and psychological grounds): greed is the basis of the personality type Erich Fromm described as those who wish to accumulate – the 'having type' as different from the 'being type'; it is a basis for addictions. Chapter 21 deals fully with the culture of greed vs the culture of generosity. Greed also feeds envy (comparison with others) and often takes the form of accumulating, cheating without transparency and, today, lies at the base of a collapsing economic order.[20] The second root generates reactivity and emotions of aversion: while anger, hatred and aggression are negative from both a moral and psychological perspective, sadness and grief are natural and may provide a base for positive activity. The chapter discussing the difference between sadness and depression will explore this complex issue. The Buddha describes a specific personality type where anger and reactivity dominates. The third root described as 'delusion' has many interpretations, but the one relevant in this context is 'identity confusion', whose base generates narcissistic emotions of conceit (*māna*), arrogance, vanity, inferiority feelings and shame. The chapter on personality will look at these emotions.

An important issue about morality in Buddhism is that it is part of a threefold-path of *sīla* (morality), *samādhi* (concentration/meditation) and *paññā* (wisdom). Thus, ethics are integrated to the liberation path. This introduces a new component of 'experientialism' rather than 'empiricism', which is based on the practice of mindfulness. Though empirical sciences do not use such a methodology, the product of recent research in neuroscience, such as the neuroplasticity thesis of Davidson and a whole tradition of work on the mindful-brain, has generated a veritable revolution in the relationship between ethics and psychology in Buddhism.

This new psychology of 'experientialism' (that uses empirical methods where necessary) has brought new frontiers of connection between morality and psychology in Buddhism:

> Of related 'neural' note is the finding of an active role of the middle prefrontal cortex in morality. The same region is active as we imagine ethical dilemmas and as we initiate moral action. We come to a sense of ourselves and of others, and a sense of right action and morality, through integrative circuitry in our neural core.[21]

Siegel also highlights social neural circuitry in reaching others: 'If mindfulness promotes the development of the resonance circuits, then we can imagine that we will become attuned to the internal lives of others as well as ourselves.' Thus there is a neural basis for compassion and the empathetic imagination. Siegel says that studies reveal the *participation of the middle pre-frontal cortex in the mediation of* morality. Antonio Damsio's celebrated work indicates that when there is damage to the pre-frontal cortex, there is also emotional disturbance at various levels: decreased emotional reactions, compromising of social emotions, deficiencies in making choices, planning in everyday routine, and deficiencies in human relationships. Briefly, Damasio's research indicate that that morals have a neurological functions, related to the genesis of emotions and, thus, he provided empirical evidence that 'affect' has an impact on decision-making.

3
The Psychology of Perception and Cognition

Perception

This chapter examines the role of perception, thinking and, very briefly, extra-sensory perception, in the psychology of Buddhism. There are many philosophical and knowledge-related words in the vast array of cognitive terms but as an aid to both the student and the general reader, I am focusing on three concepts: *saññā* (perception), *vitakka* (thinking) and *paññā* (wisdom) along with a few refreshing usages in the context of meditative experience. This is one way of bringing clarity and seeing the 'trees in the woods'. More than any other chapter in this book, some economy in the use of terms is necessary to guide the reader through a crucial part of Buddhist psychology.

The senses are the channels through which we come into contact with the external world. In addition to the sensory organs for vision, hearing, smell, taste and touch, the mind is also considered as a sense-door (*mano-dvāra*).The Buddha raises the question, 'what, brethren, is the diversity of elements'? The reply is as follows:

> The element of eye, of visible object, of eye awareness; the element of ear, sound, of ear awareness; the element of nose, of odour, of nose awareness; element of tongue, of taste, of tongue awareness; element of body, tangibles, of body awareness; element of mind, of ideas, of mind awareness; this, brethren, is called the diversity of elements.[1]

Buddhist meditative practice calls for a natural environment that is quiet, clean, and well-ventilated. The initial emphasis, before one focuses on the flow of the breath, is the importance of the sense doors and as one gets deeper in to the mindfulness of breath, one is free of any disturbance from sensory stimuli. When one is not engaged in meditation, it is equally necessary to be aware that the sensory doors are also avenues through which desires and passions are kindled. In addition to saying that there is a need to take care that sensory stimuli do not excite our desires, and thus get attached to them, the Buddha has also indicated through analysis that our perception of objects is embedded in our psychological make-up and conceptual apparatus. The Buddha does not deny the reality of the sensory process at a *conventional level* – the world of tables and chairs and trees. Thus, they are not illusions. But he says that our sensory knowledge is embedded in our categories, conceptual tools and the imagination. Meditative practice brings a great deal of refinement to sensory experience and helps the meditator to look at the sensory world with clarity of mind and at a deeper level with penetrative insight. The primary objects of meditation are the body (*kāya*), feelings and sensations (*vedanā*), states of consciousness (*citta*) and mental objects (*dhammā*). If during meditation, an external sensory object impinges strongly on the awareness so as to distract from the primary object, a useful procedure is that of labelling, noting and knowing: you must identify it as 'hearing' till the sound fades away, and then gradually bring your attention to the primary object. By labelling, naming or noting this sound it is easier to return to the primary object of meditation. Naming is called *vitakka* and knowing called *vicāra* (analytical mind): this process may also be applied to the defilements emerging within the mind. Thus Buddhist cognitive skills are developed through the practice of meditation and this phenomenology is considered as 'objective' within the Buddhist meditative tradition. The use of this technique for understanding physical behaviour, verbal behaviour and movements of the mind adds a sense of being refined and cultured, and will be referred to at a later point in this book.

The Middle Length Sayings present the process of visual perception as a product of three factors: an unimpaired sense organ, external visible forms and an act of attention. Here the term used for cognition is *viññāṇa*. This process is not only true of the eye (*cakkhu*) but also is similarly seen in the case of the ear (*sota*), nose (*ghāna*), tongue (*jivhā*), body (*kāya*) and mind (*mana*).

Sensory Consciousness and Meditation

During meditation, vigilance regarding the operation of the sense faculties is very important, as we mindfully observe sense impingements that pass across our consciousness. As the eye consciousness is shut out, ear consciousness needs to be guarded, and gradually the mind settles without any sensory impingements:

> When the breath becomes finer and the mind settles, we arrive at a consciousness unrelated to the senses. The mind is no longer running after sense impingements. This state of mind cannot discern good and bad or react to pleasure and disappointment. It is a state of mind that stays in the middle. You begin to understand ignorance, which gives way to the arising of wisdom. Although most yogis are able to reach this stage in their practice, very few are able to remain in such a state of mind with ease and patience and maintain the concentration that has been developed. At this stage we observe a preliminary or primordial form of consciousness, – one that cannot be experienced through the sense faculties. In Pāli, this consciousness is called *anindriyapatibaddha viññāṇa*, a consciousness that is unrelated to the senses faculties.[2]

When one reaches this stage and persists with continuous mindfulness, one is able to contemplate the operations of the mind and finally reach a stage of equanimity from where one directly observes the operations of one's consciousness.

If there were not this satisfaction that comes from the eye, beings would not lust for the eye. But inasmuch as there is satisfaction in the eye, therefore beings lust after it. 'If misery, brethren, pertained not to the eye beings would not be repelled by the eye. But in as much there is misery in the eye beings are repelled by it.'[3]

The subject of cognition and the vocabulary of different cognitive terms is an intricate area, and as this book is designed for the student, therapist and the general reader, I shall not digress into a scholarly and academic exposition, but keep the discussion as it falls within the chosen framework. Where people are admonished not to fall a victim to the senses as in the above warning, the Buddha uses a vocabulary of realism. When he is emphasising the point that perception and cognition are synthetic processes the analysis is different, and when his focus is the nature of extra-sensory perception, he enters another dimension of the process of cognition.

Rune Johanson emphasises the process of cognition as a synthetic process: 'Perception and thinking is in the ordinary person not altogether realistic and objective. There are usually some distortions from the needs (you exaggerate what you want to see).[4]

In the *arahant*, these unrealistic influences are not present that he sees the world as it is: 'Then, Bāhiya, thus must you train yourself: In the seen, there will be just the seen; in the heard, just the heard; in the sensed just the sensed, in the cognised, just the cognised'.[5] *The Madhupiṇḍika Sutta* has been the standard example of the distorting facets of the perceptual process, of conceptual proliferation:

> The conditioned character of the perceptual process is a central aspect of the Buddha's analysis of experience. According to the *Madhupiṇḍika Sutta*, the conditional nature of the average perceptual process leads from contact *(phassa)* via feeling *(vedanā)* and cognition *(saññā)* to thought *(vitakka)*, which can in turn stimulate conceptual proliferation *(papañca)*.[6]

Thus the original sense data gets distorted, and that is the reason for the Buddha instructing Bāhiya 'In the seen, there will be just the seen.'

It is in this context that the Buddha recommends cognitive training and with a penetrative understanding of the cognitive process one could make good progress on the liberation path:

> In this way, receptive and detached *sati* applied to the early stages of the perceptual process can make habitual reactions conscious and enable an assessment of the extent to which one is reacting automatically and without conscious deliberation. This also reveals the selective and filtering mechanism of perception, highlighting the extent to which subjective experience mirrors one's hitherto unconscious assumptions.[7]

Thus cognitive training, when practised as a part of *satipaṭṭhāna* (four-fold mindfulness training), helps the de-automatising of the causes of unwholesome cognitions.

Compared with current cognitive studies in Western philosophy these perspectives offer a new approach to studies of perception and cognition. *Vitakka* is the general term in the Suttas for what we popularly mean by the word 'thinking'. Without the prefix *(vi)* the word *takka* refers to logical and dialectical reasoning. *Vicāra*, a term used with *vitakka*, generally mean discursive thinking, but in the state of the first *jhāna*, it means focused reflection on the object of mindfulness. There are other cognitive states closer to the dimension of meditative reflection, such as *paccavekkhati, sati* and *sampajañña*. In the Buddha's advice to Rāhula to look at his mind as if one is looking at a mirror, the term *pacchavekkhati* is used. *Sati* (mindfulness) and *yoniso-manasikāra* (wise attention) capture the development of introspection with clarity and lucidity in meditative settings; other terms such as *anussati* are used for reiterated recollection and *sampajañña* for clear consciousness. By developing a sound mental culture the meditator prepares for the development of higher cognitive powers.

Thinking: *Vitakka*

Apart from the knowledge gained through the avenues of the sense organs, it is necessary to look at the psychology of thinking. *Vitakka* is the general term for 'thinking' but there are different contexts for its use. In the use of the term in the contexts of ethics, there are three unwholesome kinds of thought: sensuous thought (*kāma-vitakka*), hateful thoughts (*vyāpāda*) and cruel thoughts (*vihiṃsā*), and three wholesome kinds of thought: thoughts of renunciation (*nekkhamma*), of hatelessness (*avyāpāda*) and of not harming (*avihiṃsā*). The last three are also right thoughts in the eight-fold path. There is also thinking described as inference (*anumāna*) where a monk examines the moral consistency in his daily life).[8] A very good psychological import of the term is found in the *Vitakka-saṇṭhāna Sutta*, which addresses the five techniques of dealing with distracting thoughts: this is discussed under Buddhism and cognitive therapy here. There is also an attempt to locate thinking in terms of reflection or reasoning as opposed to book learning and meditative knowledge: *cintāmaya-paññā* (knowledge based on thinking), *sutamaya-paññā* (knowledge based on learning the *Suttas*) and *bhāvanāmaya-paññā* (knowledge based on mental development). A very complex use is *vitakka* in relation to *vicāra*: as the first factor of the first *jhāna*, *vitakka* means the mind aiming and 'sticking to an object' and *vicāra* the second factor in the first *jhāna* indicates the 'continuous rubbing against the object'. A very clear analysis of this point and other meditative experience is found in Venerable Sayadaw U. Panditha's *In This Very Life*.[9] This usage is very different from the other usages of the term *vitakka*. *Takka* refers to logical reasoning and in the three epistemological traditions discussed in Chapter 2 I have examined its usage.

The distorting role of thinking is examined in the celebrated *Sutta* referred to as the *Honey Ball Sutta* (*Madhupiṇḍika Sutta*). This Sutta also has a well-known analysis by Venerable Nanananda.[10]

Visual consciousness, your reverence, arises because of the eye and material shapes; the meeting of the three is sensory impingement;

feelings are because of sensory impingement; what one feels one perceives; what one perceives one reasons about; what one reasons about obsesses one; what obsesses one is the origin of number of concepts and obsessions which assail a man in regard to material shapes cognizable by the eye.[11]

As Nanananda says, here the ignorance of the person 'runs riot'; the proliferation of concepts that assails a person is captured in the Pāli term, *papañca*.

This sort of perspective is not alien to Western philosophical traditions such as 'idealism'. The important point in the Buddhist analysis is Buddhist contextualism. The Buddha often uses the language of 'realism', of tables, chairs and trees. Then he changes perspectives such as in the *Honey Ball Sutta*.

Paññā is a superior form of wisdom that emerges on the Buddhist path to perfection:

> *Paññā* as a stage in the Buddhist path to spiritual perfection is said to be developed on the basis of *sīla* (good conduct) and *samādhi* (mental composure). The difference between *paññā* and *viññāṇa* is that where as *viññāṇa* occurs quite passively in sense experience, *paññā* has to be cultivated with effort. *Paññā* is different from *viññāṇa* in the sense that it is a form of cognition which involves cognising the nature of things on the basis of a certain systematic training of the mind. The *paññā* perspective takes into account the known empirical facts and their multifarious relationships.[12]

As Premasiri notes, *paññā* is different from the types of knowledge upheld in traditions as Western empiricist and rationalist traditions, as *paññā* is a form of 'emancipating knowledge'. It certainly works as far as perceptual knowledge is concerned, for instance, in seeing change and impermanence, but converts this knowledge in relation to the Buddhist path of liberation. Change and impermanence can be seen at the 'perceptual' level, but what is described as 'emancipatory knowledge' is a higher level of discernment of the fact of change and impermanence.

Paññā is different as it is a higher form of knowledge that helps a person to liberate from the wheel of suffering, of birth and death. While *dukkha* (suffering), *anicca* (impermanence) and *anatta* (non-self) have interesting empirical and existential corollaries, *paññā* is qualitatively different because it is emancipatory knowledge. Premasiri concludes that this difference in the varieties of knowing between Western and

Buddhist traditions indicates 'not only difference in perspective and purpose but also differences in depth and intensity of vision'.[13]

As I have limited the analysis of cognition to the framework of Buddhist psychology in this book, I do not wish to go into the topic of extra-sensory perception in great detail. This topic has been examined in terms of the material in the Buddhist Pāli canon in great detail by K. N. Jayatilleke.[14] The six kinds of knowledge analysed by Jayatilleke are: psycho-kinetic activity;[15] clairaudience;[16] telepathic knowledge;[17] retrocognitive knowledge of past existences;[18] knowledge of the disease and survival of beings;[19] and knowledge of the destruction of defiling impulses.[20]

Of these types of knowledge, it is necessary to focus on three facets directly related to the awakening:

1. Recollection of past lives.
2. Insight into the death and rebirth of beings throughout the cosmos.
3. Insight into the ending of the mental defilements or fermentations (*āsava*) within the mind.

The first two insights were not exclusive discoveries of the Buddha, as there were Shamanic traditions across the world with seers who had these insights:

> The third insight, however, went beyond Shamanism into the phenomenology of the mind, i.e. a systematic account of phenomena as they are directly experienced. This insight was exclusively Buddhist, although it was based on the previous two. Because it was multifaceted, the Canon describes it from a variety of standpoints, stressing different aspects as they apply to specific contexts.[21]

When the Buddha later analysed the process of awakening, he breaks it into two facets: 'First there is the regularity of the *dhamma*, after which there is the knowledge of unbinding'.[22]

The first knowledge, the regularity of the *dhamma*, is the causal principle working in the universe and our minds, which is described as the Awakening. The second is the unbinding of it, which really proves the value of the first kind of knowledge. In fact Thanissaro says that 'true knowledge is gauged by how skilfully one can manipulate them'.[23] In exploring the causal principle it would be seen that *the basic causal factor is the mind, and in particular the moral quality of the intentions*. These intentions are expressed through thoughts, words and deeds resting on the rightness of views underlying them.

Our readers need to discern that these reflections give us an ideal framework for presenting Buddhist psychology and, due to the direct link between psychology and ethics in Buddhism, in this book there is a focus on what may be called the moral psychology of Buddhism. I have purposely repeated this point in several chapters to emphasise the importance of the emergence of the discipline of moral psychology among philosophers and psychologists. The therapeutic traditions, with their focus on non-judgmental awareness, have to yet develop a cautious and highly nuanced awareness, as to what is therapeutically effective. The importance of the therapist– client relationship needs to be emphasised as the road to successful therapy. It has been observed that a 'mindful therapeutic relationship between the therapist and the client is the road to success' – a point that has been presented as a clinically fertile idea recently by a group of therapists.[24] It is a point that has been emphasised in the humanistic tradition of Maslow and Rogers, and more openly integrating the mindfulness approach by Fromm.[25] I also wish to emphasise that perhaps the suspension of the critical faculty in a mindful way has an early exponent in Sigmund Freud:

> Freud's major breakthrough, which he refers to over and over again, in his writings, was his discovery that it was actually possible to suspend what he called the 'critical faculty'. This suspension of the critical faculty was, in fact, what made the practice of psychoanalysis possible for Feud. It is a feat that he accomplished with no outside help, one that he apparently taught himself without knowing that this was the attentional stance that Buddhist meditators had been invoking for millennia.[26]

4
The Psychology of Motivation

The term 'motivation' is a general term that covers three aspects of behaviour: states that motivate behaviour, behaviour motivated by these states, and the goals of such behaviour. All three facets may be regarded as stages in a cycle. Hunger as a motivational state would impel a person to seek food, appropriate behaviour, which is instigated by this need, would be the seeking of means to attain this end, and the alleviation of hunger would be the final goal. Then the motivational cycle terminates until the need for food emerges again. Terms such as need, want and drive refer to the inner condition of the organism that initiates and directs behaviour towards a goal, and have a more physiological quality about them. Terms such as desire, craving and motive have a greater *psychological* orientation compared with the *physiological* drives. Some of the goals are of a positive nature, which individuals approach; others have a negative nature, which individuals try to avoid. Where the motivating states have a clear physiological nature, the goals are relatively fixed, as in the need for sleep and food. When we move into the more psychologically oriented sources of motivation, there is flexibility, variation and complexity. If we consider the context of a starving man begging for food, we see a different kind of motivation to that of a wealthy person who is concerned with status, fame and the desire to be well-known: a more complex set of motives rooted in an attachment to his identity and self.

In general, theories of motivation are linked to a need to examine and explain a sense of puzzlement relating to some facets of human behaviour. In this chapter, we will focus on the framework within which the Buddha examined the nature of human motivation and tried to understand and find ways to alleviate human suffering (*dukkha*). The Buddhist psychology of motivation is directly concerned with the factors that lead to human unrest, tension, anxiety and suffering, in general. Thus, the Buddhist psychology of motivation is embedded in the desire to uncover the roots of human unrest and offer a positive path towards happiness.

The negativity/positivity distinction in relation to desires may be understood in terms of the quest for liberation from the wheel of suffering and of developing a way out of tension and unrest. The recluse seeking ultimate release from suffering aims at inner peace (*ajjhatta-santi*). The householder aims at righteousness and a harmonious life (*dhamma-cariya, sama-cariya*). In evaluating the householder's life moral precepts are very important, whereas the recluse has a more stringent moral code, which is often taken for granted in the practice of concentration and wisdom. Thus, ethical implications need to be contextualised.

During recent times, the concept of ethical realism has brought out interesting linkages between the psychology and the ethics of motivation that we need to integrate into our understanding of motivation concepts in Buddhism. In a study of the psychological foundations of happiness and well-being it has been observed: 'Human beings are powerfully driven by systems of desire, which become attached to material possessions and social status. The gap between these desires and what the world can yield is an enduring source of frustration'.[1] As the Buddha observed, 'To wish for something and not get it is suffering '(yam *p' iccham na labhati tam pi dukkham*).[2] Some desires that cannot be obtained may be given up; but others, which are insatiable, often break down into boredom and emptiness. Buddhism advocates voluntary simplicity and skilful management of needs. Recent studies in neurology also emphasise the linkages between morality and psychology and, in keeping with an important need to locate Buddhist psychology and ethics in the context of emerging sciences, Siegel says, 'Studies reveal the participation of the middle-prefrontal cortex in the mediation of morality' and also, when the middle prefrontal region is damaged, there is an impairment in moral thinking leading to a form of amorality.[3]

The basic springs of motivation are accordingly analysed in terms of the three wholesome roots (*kusala*) and three unwholesome roots; of the unwholesome roots, *lobha*, rendered as greed or lust, generates the positive 'approach desires', *dosa* generates the 'avoidance desires' in the form of hatred and resentment, and *moha*, rendered as delusion, creates confusion in the mind and is also associated with wrong intellectual views. Their opposites, generosity (*alobha*), compassionate love (*adosa*) and wisdom (*amoha*) lead to inner happiness at the individual level and harmony at the interpersonal level.

The Buddha also makes a detailed analysis of the concept of craving (*taṇhā*). Diverse forms of desires and craving emerge from time to time, find temporary satisfaction and again surge up seeking new and novel forms of satisfaction. In addition to the psychological/physiological roots of motivation, the discourses of the Buddha present a detailed analysis of craving that takes three forms – the drive for egoistic pursuits (*bhava-taṇhā*), the drive for sensuous and sexual gratification (*kāma-taṇhā*), and (*vibhava-taṇhā*) – avoidance desires like hatred, that find aggressive ways of destroying what is unpleasant, and which may result even in suicidal behaviour or forms of masochism. *Bhava-taṇhā* may be seen in terms of a legitimate self-preservation drive linked to basic survival needs such as thirst, hunger and sleep, or more complex forms of self-assertion, power, fame and various forms of endless acquisition. The drive for sensuous gratification goes beyond sexual gratification to the gratification of the senses, the need for diversions and an exposure to an unending source of sensory stimuli. They also have different contextual implications. If a layman goes to a retreat observing the ten precepts, it is necessary to understand the nature of hindrances. The need for diversions that excite the senses is a hindrance (*nīvaraṇa*), described *as kāma-cchanda*, and even minor movements of boredom with the meditation, anger at the meditation not working well (*vyāpāda*), unrest, agitation and worry (*uddhacca-kukkucca*), slothfulness (*thīna-middha*) and doubt (*vicikicchā*). Thus, the psychology and ethics of the motivation concept need to be contextualised. For instance, graphic similes in A V 193 describe how these states hinder the practice of meditation at a retreat or for the individual who practises regular meditation within the framework of an average householder. Sensuous desire is compared to water mixed with manifold colours; ill-will with boiling water; slothfulness with water covered by mosses; restlessness and agitation with water whipped by the wind; and sceptical doubt with turbid and muddy water.

Studies of human well-being focus on four levels of behaviour. This chapter concentrates on the *motivational level*: closely linked to this level is the *conative* level, which often refers to the attempt to discipline oneself through effort and, in ordinary language, is referred to as 'will power'. But it also works closely with motivation in adding the element of volition. In Chapter 9 on human addictions, the nature of the *conative* dimension will be illustrated. The second level is the *cognitive level*, with a focus on sensory perception and thinking. While the disciplining of the sensory channels needs to be carried out with good *attentional* levels, dealing with thought patterns is the subject of the *vitakka-saṇṭhāna Sutta*. The third is the *affective* level, and Chapter 5 on emotions deals with this in detail. A number of discourses deal with feelings and emotions and, one of which is the *Satipaṭṭhāna*, a guide to meditation. The fourth is the *attentive* level, which takes a central place in meditation practice and is the most important facet of human well-being. Thus, Chapters 3, 4, 5 and 7 on cognition, motivation, emotions, addictions and mindfulness practice have an integral standing in the psychology of Buddhism, and they are also related to issues of health, well-being and mental balance.

Subliminal Levels of Motivation

The question whether motives, desires and drives always operate at a conscious level is an important concern. Ever since the work of Sigmund Freud, the realm of unconscious desires has become a very important factor in human motivation. At a common-sense level, this concept indicates that we are not aware of the *real motives* that prompt a person to perform an action. A number of explanations may be given to make good sense of unconscious motivation. Our daily routine involves bits of behaviour into which several goals and desires are intertwined, and it is difficult to isolate a particular motive for any one action. Also, as our behaviour is basically habit-dominated, we are not always aware of specific motives, whereas in other areas we plan and make a choice. Freud gave a third reason in that motives fashioned in unpleasant circumstances tend to be forgotten or 'repressed'. Of course, he had a theory regarding certain traumatic events – that their recollection is repressed unconsciously. In writing early editions of *Buddhist and Freudian Psychology* I was influenced by the Freudian model of the unconscious in looking at the unconscious in Buddhism; however, I have recently changed my position.

In the discourses of the Buddha it is said that the excitement of a pleasurable feeling may arouse latent sensuous greed (*rāgānusaya*) and painful feelings arouse latent anger and hatred (*paṭighānusaya*). There are seven of these latent tendencies in total: sensuous craving, anger, conceit, erroneous opinion, scepticism, craving for existence, and ignorance. In the present context we are more interested in sensuality, aggression and conceit (*mānānusaya*). In general, the term *anusaya* indicates a dormant or latent predisposition working at a subliminal level, closer to threshold consciousness rather than at the level of buried traumatic experience.

In several editions of my book *Buddhist and Freudian Psychology*, (1973, 1978, 1992) I was inclined to regard these latent tendencies as similar to the Freudian concept of the unconscious. However, in the most recent issue of my book[4] I present a different perspective of the unconscious, which term I have replaced with the term 'subliminal' because I see these traits as closer to the conscious level rather than buried at a deeper level. I see them as more like 'sleeping' or dormant passions. Part of this new perspective rests on recent studies and, particularly, the work of neurologist Joseph Ledoux,[5] who analysed the emotion of fear. He cites the case of a man walking on a lonely forest track, who tramples a bundle of dry twigs. Without even looking, thinking that it is a rattle snake, he is about to run. In such a context the central nervous system is hijacked by the amygdala before it goes through the normal information process to the CNS (central nervous system). When such alarm bells ring the flight-or-fight response emerges. The dormant level of emotions is described as the *anusaya* level; the emotions may emerge as thought processes (*pariyuṭṭhāna*), at which level mindfulness may help the individual to restrain, or, if not, they may emerge as impulsive action (*vītikkama*). Keith Oatley, well known for his studies on emotion, says that we need to move away from Freud's archaeological metaphor of excavating the unconscious:

> The archaeological metaphor was one of Freud's favourites. Once one had brought to consciousness, one's disowned intentions to consciousness, it would be possible to take responsibility for them, and in that movement we can be free of their tyranny over us.[6]

There are thoughts which lie between the conscious and the unconscious, and instead of looking for buried conflicts, we should focus on the 'autopilot' within us, the incessant movement-to-movement flow of thought. Mark Epstein says: 'Yet in Buddhism – and even in more recent psychoanalysis – there has emerged a different model, one that is less about digging and more about opening. At the root of this difference lies an alternative view of the unconscious'.[7] In the *Greater Discourse to Māluṅkya*, the heretics say that as dormant passions cannot arise in the mind of an infant, the concept of such dormant passions is not possible. The Buddha replies that even in a baby boy a view regarding 'own body' is latent. A number of other latent 'leanings' are mentioned: leaning to attachment regarding sense pleasure (*kāma-rāgānusaya*); a leaning to malevolence (*byāpādānusaya*); a leaning to rite and rituals (*sīla-bbata-parāmāsa*); a leaning to perplexity (*vicikicchānusaya*); and the leaning to view of 'own body'.

Seven *anusaya*s are mentioned in the Dialogues of the Buddha:

1. Sensuous craving (*kāma-rāga*)
2. Anger (*paṭigha*)
3. Conceit (*māna*)
4. Erroneous opinion (*diṭṭhi*)
5. Scepticism (*vicikicchā*)
6. Craving for existence (*bhava-rāga*)
7. Ignorance (*avijjā*).

The stream-winner (*sotāpanna*) and the once-returner *sakadāgāmi*) still have five *anusaya*s: 1, 2, 3, 6, and 7. The never-returners (*anāgāmi*) are subject to three *anusayas:* 3, 6, and 7. Thus we see that conceit, craving for existence and ignorance are the most powerful. The concept of *anusaya* is also linked to the three forms of craving discussed below: *kāma-rāgānusaya* with the craving for sensual pleasures; *paṭighānusaya* with the craving for destructive and annihilationist urges; and *māna, diṭṭhi*, and bhava-rāgānusaya with the ego instinct.

Āsava

Some of psychological terms found in the sermons of the Buddha are described in imagery and metaphorical language; one such term is *āsava*. Two such metaphors are the intoxicating extract of a flower and a discharge from a wound. The *āsava* symbolises something that has been simmering in the mind for a long time, and this concept may be compared to the Freudian notion of the id, which again has been described as a 'cauldron of seething excitations'. The *āsavas*, which are mentioned, are *kāmāsava, bhavāsava, diṭṭhāsava* and *avijjāsava*. The *Sabbāsava Sutta* describes ways of mastering these influxes: by insight, restraint of the senses, avoidance, wise use of life's necessities, eliminating unclear thoughts, and development of the mind. The development of the mind is effective in keeping out corroding passions.[8]

The stream of consciousness (viññāṇa-sota)

It is important to note that 26 centuries ago the Buddha discerned the mind as a dynamic process: a stream of consciousness rather than a static entity. The term *saṃvattanika-viññāṇa*, translated as 're-linking consciousness', is used to refer to the survival factor that links one life and another. In general, consciousness is the influx conditioned by a causal pattern in a dynamic continuum. It is also referred to as a stream of becoming (*bhava-sota*). The evolving consciousness that continues maintains its dynamism because it is nourished by craving. There is a residuum from the psychological dispositions of the individual, which by its dynamic nature nourishes the continuation of the individual or of phenomenal existence in general. It is also said of the stream of consciousness of a living person that a part of it is present in this world (*idha loke patiṭṭhitaṃ*) and a part in the world beyond (*para-loke patiṭṭhitaṃ*). This stream of consciousness has a conscious and an unconscious component. The part of the stream of consciousness of which the individual is not aware may be the dynamic unconscious, comprised of the dispositions (*saṅkhāra*) that determine the character of the next birth.[9] Knowledge of this stream of consciousness, with a conscious and unconscious component, is only within the reach of those who have developed meditation to a very high degree. This direct knowledge is superior to any inferences based on reasoning. The *Sutta* also has a concept of *asampajāna-mano-saṅkhāra*, mental dispositions of which we have no awareness.[10] We can make sense of this concept by describing it as a process that does not come within normal consciousness and thus describable as subliminal consciousness (*anusaya*). Two other concepts often referred to are *ālaya-vigñāna* (store-house consciousness), which is a concept in Mahayana Buddhism, and *bhavaṅga-sota* (stream of existence), which belongs to the Abhidhamma literature.

Conative activity (saṅkhāra)

In the way that *vedanā* provides a base for looking at affective/emotional processes, and *saññā/vitakka* for cognitive processes, *saṅkhāra* gives us an entry into conative processes or the will. Though these distinctions are not absolute, they provide a useful perspective to understanding the role of key terms in Buddhist psychology and different facets of the mind.

Saṅkhāra has been defined as, 'motivated and purposeful activity which also has moral consequences'.[11] There are three psychological facets to the concept of *saṅkhāra*: deliberation, volition, and dynamism. The term '*cetanā*', with which the term *saṅkhāra* is used synonymously, suggests the notion of volition. The concept of *abhisaṅkhāra* brings out the element of dynamism that emphasises the meaning of *saṅkhāra* as karma formation: 'The wheel kept rolling so long as the impulse that set it moving lasted (*abhisaṅkhārassa gati*). Then it circled round and fell'.[12] This graphic image from the *Aṅguttara Nīkāya* captures the notion of momentum and dynamism that the concept of *saṅkhāra* indicates as a link in the wheel of dependent origination.

These conative dispositions are necessary, and as the Buddha described, following the Buddhist path is going against the current (*patisota-gāmi*). Right intention, effort, energy and persistence are qualities necessary to withstand the strength of defiling impulses. It is said that there are four kinds of effort: the effort to restrain the senses; the effort to abandon evil thoughts; the effort to develop such spiritual skills as mindfulness and investigation of the dhamma, zest, tranquillity and equanimity; and the effort to watch over and concentrate on repulsive objects that would destroy any emerging lust and greed.

The Psychology of Craving

The concept of craving (*taṇhā*) is hard to translate into the terminology of Western psychology for a number of reasons. Western psychologists have used theoretical constructs such as 'instinct', 'drive', 'motives', etc. as aids to explain behaviour, but the use of these terms in different systems of psychology is not uniform. Neither a 'drive' nor an 'instinct' is something concrete like a pen or a pencil: they are constructs associated with certain theories that attempt to explain visible forms of behaviour. There have been psychologists in the West interested in the primary determinants of human behaviour. The Buddha was not merely attempting to record certain regular patterns of human behaviour but was raising the question: 'Why do people behave in certain ways that contribute to their personal suffering?' and searching for basic motivation patterns in humans. Not only did the Buddha see certain regularities of behaviour in people but he also attempted to find their roots. Thus explaining human behaviour has a focus on a certain part of the law of dependent origination: contact conditions feeling, feeling conditions craving, and craving conditions clinging. The Buddha's focus was on the craving for sensual pleasures (*kāma-taṇhā*), egoistic pursuits (*bhava- taṇhā*) and the aggressive drive to destroy unpleasant objects, which may also be directed towards oneself (*vibhava-taṇhā*). In the context of meditation, the links between feeling and craving are important: 'This crucially important conditional dependence of craving and mental reactions to feeling probably constitute the central reason why feelings have become one of the four *satipaṭṭhānas*'.[13] The location of motivational concepts within the framework of a meditation setting is an important feature of a Buddhist perspective on motivation. In fact, in meditation settings, mindful awareness needs to be subtle to avoid any reactivity caused by unwholesome desires (*abhijjhā*) and discontent (*domanassa*), whereas wholesome desire (*chanda*), commitment and endurance, leads eventually to desirelessness. Craving and clinging also emerge in the everyday world, and meditation practice will gradually help a person to see through the traps in mundane life:

> Applied at a mundane level, the contemplation of the four noble truths can be directed to patterns of clinging (upādāna) to existence occurring in everyday life, as, for example, when one's expectations are frustrated, when one's position is threatened, or when things do not go as one would want. The task here is to acknowledge the underlying pattern of craving (tanhā) that has led to the building-up of clinging and expectations, and also its resultant manifestations in some form of dukkha. This understanding in turn forms the necessary basis for letting go off craving (tanhāya paṭinissagga). With such letting go, clinging and dukkha can, at least momentarily, be overcome.[14]

This analysis of craving indicates that there is a difference in the Buddhist framework for locating motivational concepts compared to its Western counterpart, and this quality also illuminates our orientation towards mindfulness-based therapy.

Kāma-taṇhā (craving for sensuous gratification)

The concept of kāma-tanhā has a very broad usage that goes beyond mere 'sexuality' as such; it is basically the craving for 'sensuous gratification' rather than 'sexual gratification'. The Suttas refer to two significant terms, pañca-kāma-guṇa and kāma-rāga: pañca-kāma-guṇa refers to five types of pleasure objects accessed by the eye, ear, nose, tongue and body, and kāma-rāga refers to the desires and passions of a sensual nature. Thus the term pañca-kāma-guṇika-rāga refers to the fact that in human beings there is a deep-seated proclivity for the enjoyment of the five senses. In a broader sense this proclivity may be understood in terms of what Freud described as the 'pleasure principle' – the natural proneness of man to seek pleasure and be repelled by pain. It is necessary to emphasise that this drive for pleasure goes beyond mere genital pleasure, and accounts for such manifestations as the craving for excitement and for constant diversion, moving from one object to another, which the Buddha described as tatra tatrābhinandini (finding delight now here, now there). Regarding the moral dimensions of pleasure, the Buddha has a specific perspective: legitimate pleasures obtained by the householder and (differently) the recluse. For the householder/layman an attempt is made to work out a via media between complete suppression of sexuality and complete permissiveness. Complete abstinence and celibacy is a requirement for the recluse. In general, restraint of the senses is the basic requirement for both the householder and the monk. There is an ethico-religious dimension that cuts across the critique of the pleasure principle, which is also based on psychological insights. From one standpoint the Buddha describes the ills besetting the pleasure principle, but from another he distinguishes pleasures obtained by legitimate means and illegitimate means fed by excessive *craving*, between perverted lust and harmless pleasures.

For the layman, there is a *via media*: sexual control, in the sense of perfect celibacy and abstinence, is limited to monks. There is, however, one thing common to both standpoints – the search for pleasure as the only ideal in life is not possible. A life of pure sensuality without any ethical considerations is what the Buddha condemns as *kāma-sukhallikānuyoga* (the way of sensuality). This is referred to as low, pagan practice and is compared with an equally pagan extreme, the way of self-mortification. The Buddha recommends the eightfold path as the middle way.[15]

It is against the background of the Buddha's analysis of human suffering that the deep-rooted instinct for sensuous gratification has to be analysed. The origin of suffering (*dukkha-samudaya*) and craving is a factor leading to re-birth (*pono-bhavika*) and is accompanied by lust and self-indulgence (*nandi-rāga*): it seeks temporary satisfaction 'now here, now there'(*tatra tatrābhinandini*).[16] The question is raised where 'craving takes its rise' and where 'it has a dwelling'. First, it is said that craving has its rise and dwelling in the material things that are pleasant and dear to us: in the senses of sight, hearing, smell, taste, touch and imagination. Apart from sensory stimuli, sensuality may invade feeling, perception, intentions, as well as conceptual and discursive thinking. Recent cognitive therapy has a focus on the 'auto-pilot' of thinking, and emotion-focused therapy looks at the initial excitement of feelings, where one can 'apply the brakes'. Regular practice of meditation brings out the restraint on the senses as well as mindfulness of the body, feelings and thoughts. This structure that emerges from the management of sensory stimulation may also be used to look at other forms of craving.

In the final analysis, it is not the sense organs or the impact of sense organs that is emphasised, but the persistence of desire and lust. The eye is not the bond of objects, nor are objects the bond of eye, but the desire and lust that arise as a result of these two. The concepts of *kāma-rāga* (sensuous passion), *kāma-upādāna* (sense clinging) and *kāma-āsava* (the canker of sense desire) refer to the persistence and upsurge of the craving for sense gratification. Clinging works on a deeper level as the subliminal proclivities (*anusaya*) are excited and such undercurrents continue to influence the emergence of lust and anger. The Pali word for craving, *taṇhā*, metaphorically implies the notion of thirst, which is temporarily quenched by temporary satisfaction. When obstructed desires become frustrated the deeper ramifications of a life devoted to pleasure as the dominant goal is that such persons become a victim of boredom. In a study comparing the Don Juan personification of the pleasure lover in Kierkegaard and the Buddhist depiction of the life of pure sensuality, I have shown that Soren Kierkegaard's depiction of the one-track pleasure lover and hedonist is a graphic description of the boredom that starts with a 'simple B' and ends with a capital 'B'.[17]

Self-preservation and ego-oriented behaviour

The ego-orientation has a number of sources, a cognitive root in eternalism (*sassata-diṭṭhi*), motivational roots in *bhava-rāga* and *bhava-taṇhā*, and also a subliminal base in *diṭṭhi-anusaya*. The craving for self-centred pursuits has its ideological roots in the dogma of personal immortality (*sassata- diṭṭhi*). We tend to believe in a pure ego existing independently of the psycho-physical process that constitute life, and it is assumed that this pure ego exists even after death.

The 'bias towards egocentricity', rooted in the belief of an abiding ego, manifests at various levels – linguistic, intellectual, emotional, ethical and so on. The acquisitive and possessive personality structure of the egocentric person has a threefold base in craving (*taṇhā*), conceit (*māna*) and false views (*diṭṭhi*). This erroneous concept of the self expresses itself in the linguistic form of craving, 'This is mine', conceit, 'This I am' and false view, 'This is my self'. These expressions may emerge in relation to a person's body, feelings, perceptions, dispositions and consciousness, making inroads into the five aggregates.[18] From the mutual nourishment of the intellectual and the affective roots of egocentricity emerge the diverse manifestations of egoistic behaviour – the desire for self-preservation, self-continuity, self-assertion and power, fame and self-display. It is important that on psychological and ethical grounds there is a difference between a healthy self-regarding attitude – looking after one's health, one's job and family – and self-aggrandisement and aggression. There are also self-transcending activities such as generosity, helping others in distress and spiritual activities.

It must be mentioned that the drive for self-preservation implies the need for fresh air, water, food and sleep, which are basic physiological drives. However, these natural physiological and biological functions may be distorted by destructive lifestyles, patterns of current consumption so that instead of basic needs, pseudo-desires spring up like mushrooms. It is because of these dangers that a monk's lifestyle is governed by certain *vinaya* rules. Unhealthy attitudes towards the acquisition of wealth, or the drive for power and status tarnish our ability to distinguish between needs and greeds.

Self-conceit can take three forms:' I am superior to others', 'I am equal to others', and 'I am inferior to others'. *Māna* as a fetter may vary from a crude feeling of pride to a subtle feeling of distinctiveness, which prevails till the attainment of arahatship (sainthood). Chapter 20, which deals with emotions of self-assessment, goes into great detail in describing Buddhist and Western perspectives on conceit, pride and humility.

The ego illusion may be seen by a breakdown into twenty components:

1–5:   ego as identified with corporeality, feelings, perception, disposition and consciousness;
6–10:   the ego as contained in them;
11–15:   ego is independent of them; and
16–20:   ego is their owner.

These forms of identification are fed by deep affective processes, and graphic examples of these identifications are available. For instance, a materialist would identify the self/ego with corporeality, a hedonist with feeling, a sensationist with perceptions, and a vitalist with the will. The corporeal overtones of the ego-illusion are described in the *suttas*: they regard the body as the self (*atta* in Pali, *ātman* in Sanskrit); they regard the self as having a body, body as being in the self, the self as being in the body.[19] In Freud's use of the myth of Narcissus, we find a person falling in love with the reflection of his body in water and obsessed with it.[20]

Self-annihilation and aggression

While *bhava-taṇhā* arises with a false conception of personality based on the dogma of personal immortality, *vibhava-taṇhā* emerges from the view that the physical and mental processes identified with the ego will be annihilated at death (*uccheda-diṭṭhi*). Though on a superficial analysis these two attitudes appear to be diametrically opposed, against the larger setting of the law of dependent origination, they are considered as merely the contrasting attitude of a man bound to craving.

I have presented a detailed comparison of Freud's concept of death instinct with that of *vibhava-taṇhā* in Buddhism elsewhere.[21] Though Buddhist psychology does not offer exactly the same analysis of *vibhava-taṇhā* as Freud does with the death instinct, there are both interesting parallels and differences. Buddhism accepts hatred (*dosa*) as one of the roots of human behaviour along with greed and delusion as the base for aggressive behaviour and as a reactive response. The root hatred moves people in situations of frustration and depression towards self-destructive behaviour. The addict who knowingly courts disaster by continuously falling a prey to alcohol, and the man who in the final act of a suicide exhibits the moment-to-moment ambivalence – 'to live' or 'court death', illustrate how people *flirt with the death instinct*. It is a vacillation between two facets of craving. The Freudian death instinct had many components, and one of them was what he called the 'repetition compulsion', the demonic path of the addict towards self-destruction. Aggression and self-hatred mingle with our love of life. The Buddha would consider the self-destructive urge as more 'reactive' than 'appetative' and in this context appears to be different from the Freudian position. Also, he would see *bhava-taṇhā* and *vibhava-taṇhā* as two sides of the same coin – contrasting attitudes of a man bound to craving. In fact, Freud was himself baffled by his own concept of the death instinct:

> So immense is the ego's self-love, which we have come to recognize as the primal state from which instinctual life proceeds, and so vast is the amount of narcissistic libido which we see liberated in the fear that emerges as a threat to life, that we cannot conceive how the ego can consent to its own destruction.[22]

Compared with the drive for sensuous pleasures and egoistic behaviour, the desire for annihilation is puzzling, and it has number of contexts which helps us to understand its complexity. It may arise with a care-free pleasure lover personified in Kierkegaard's image of Don Juan, who sees death as the end of life: a hedonist and materialist; a man full of anxieties and unending worries courting 'sweet death', and falls into the delusion of not seeing the continuity of life in a long *saṃsāric* journey; a man full of anger and hatred towards the world and himself, and turns towards self-hurt – the self-destructive urge is clearly manifest in this context.

The most significant context in relation to the concept of *vibhava-taṇhā* is found in the Middle Length Sayings:

> Those worthy recluses and Brahmins who lay down the cutting of (*ucchedaṃ*), the destruction (*vināsaṃ*), the disappearance (*vibhavaṃ*)

of the essential being, these afraid of their own body, loathing their own body, simply keep running and circling round their own body. Just as the dog that is tied by a leash to a strong post or stake keeps running and circling round that post or stake, so do these worthy recluses and Brahmins, afraid of their own body, simply keep running and circling round their own body.[23]

The three terms *uccheda*, *vināsa* and *vibhava* are used as synonyms, and the word *vibhava* connotes the idea of self-destruction. Even those who attempt to 'destroy' the essential being are assuming an ego which does not exist.

This context also exemplifies that apparently contradictory attitudes, such as on the one hand, narcissistic self-love, adorning and beautifying the body and, on the other hand, displays of disgust and anger towards the body are caught in the same vicious circles as the dog tied to the post. Venerable Nanananda says, about the eternalist and the annihilationist, that the 'former ran after his shadow', 'while the latter tries in vain to outstrip it, both equally obsessed to take it to be real'.[24] In fact, some people at the time misunderstood the implications of the concept of *nibbāna* and described the Buddha as a nihilist (*venayika*),[25] and a destroyer of growth (*bhûnahu*).[26] The Buddha was critical of both the 'narcissistic' character type dominated by love of the body and self-image and the 'nemessistic' type displaying aggression turned inwards.

Buddhism and suicide

The psychology of the craving for annihilation, which has been the main subject of the above analysis, helps us to understand the psychological roots of suicide to some extent. Now, it is necessary to understand briefly, on what other grounds Buddhism rejects suicide. The most important is that one cannot by violent means offset the consequences of *kamma*: 'He shakes not down the unripe fruit, but awaits the full-time of its maturity'.[27] Secondly, for spiritual reasons, one cannot force the maturity of one's actions: Venerable Kumāra Kassapa responds to this wrong view held by Pāyāsi, saying that it is like a woman who cuts open her belly to find out whether the child she hopes to have soon is a boy or a girl. Another criticism is the objection to extreme asceticism and physical torture, which the Buddha himself rejected when he chose the middle path between the way of sensuality and that of asceticism. The Jains accepted that 'vocal sins are destroyed through silence, mental restraint through respiratory restraint, bodily sins through starvation and lust crushed through mortification'.[28] The basic ethical grounds are clear as it is a violation of the first precept regarding the sanctity of life. There have been controversial contexts where suicidal impulses become transformed into dispassion and insight into the impermanent nature of things. Within the framework of the present work, it is difficult to critically appraise these controversial cases in a comprehensive manner. The case of Channa, Sappadissa, Vakkhali and Godhika provokes serious analysis.[29] Buddhism may have different cultural varieties and ritual expression but as Durkheim observed the Buddhist focus is on the liberation from suffering.[30]

Concluding Thoughts

Having discussed the psychological, spiritual and ethical boundaries of suicide, I wish to conclude by saying that the most significant insight of the Buddha was that *bhava-taṇhā* and *vibhava-taṇhā* are not opposites but rather like the two sides of the same coin. And Edwin Schneidman, one of the foremost suicidologists of recent times, thinks that the common internal attitude of suicides known to him may be described as one of ambivalence. He believes that though the dichotomous Aristotelian logic does not leave any room for ambivalence, in the context of suicide there is a situation that is both A and non-A.[31]

5
Emotions: Western Theoretical Orientations and Buddhism

The study of emotions has been neglected until the last three decades for several reasons. They have been considered as antithetical to our cognitive skills and a source of irrationality. It was assumed that emotions interfere with calm, voluntary, rational behaviour, and they are associated with ethically undesirable states that ought to be eliminated. Psychologically, emotions have been considered as states of agitation. In the area of academic research in psychology, emotions were relegated to the status of subjective phenomena incapable of verification. In general, in the psychologist's landscape of the study of behaviour and consciousness, emotions remained a poor relation compared with stimulus–response behaviour, perception, motivation and personality. However, recent work by Antonio Damasio (1994)[1] in emotion studies; by Joseph Ledoux (1996)[2] in neurology; by Paul Ekman (2003)[3] in biology and facial expression of emotions; by Daniel Goleman (1997)[4] in emotions, medicine and health, as well as his contribution to emotional intelligence and education (Goleman, 1996);[5] by brain, body and emotions in Candace Pert's thesis of the body as a 'second brain' (Pert, 1997)[6] and in philosophy (Robert Solomon, 2004a, b)[7] – all these contributions represent a veritable revolution in emotion studies. As well as these developments, projects carried out at the Mind and Life Institute produced several publications on emotion studies, among which was the ground-breaking neuroplasticity thesis concerning the impact of meditation practice on the brain by Richard Davidson.[8] More recent works, *Emotional Awareness*,[9] *The Mindful Brain*[10] and *Buddha's Brain*[11] bring out the contemporary conversation within which Buddhist perspectives on emotion studies have been located.

Another important concern is that there are certain emotions that have a 'negative' quality and others that have a 'positive quality'.

Though the reasons for this distinction may vary in different philosophical and religious traditions, as will be clarified later in this chapter, Buddhism would consider 'anger' as negative at the level of morality. However, in the deeper reaches of meditation practice, as is also reflected in my counselling practice, we may 'change gears' as we learn from our anger, bracketing qualities of good and bad and looking at it as an 'impersonal process', neither yours nor mine. In meditation practice we do not throw away our anger, greed, addictions and anxiety but convert them into fertile soil from which emerge therapeutic and meditational insights. We do not try to 'destroy' them, but embrace them and see their points of entry, staying for a while and passing away.

Rhys Davids, in a very early study of Buddhist psychology,[12] observed that there was an 'archaic silence' on the subject of emotions. In the earlier editions of my book on Buddhist psychology, I have responded to this query by including a comprehensive account of emotions in Buddhism. The present chapter goes beyond these early writings to integrate emotions as a central theme in Buddhist psychology.

Today, there is a pro-emotion consensus: emotions often provide information for making fast decisions about practical problems, contain information for rational deliberation and generate shifts in practical perception, such as in the experience of compassion in the role of a social worker. Emotional intelligence has been included in the curriculum of some schools, especially in the USA. In the area of counselling I shall describe the therapeutic importance of emotions in greater detail, especially in the development of what I describe as 'Mindfulness-based Emotion-Focused Therapy'.

First, this chapter will describe and analyse in detail Western theories of emotions and then present a comparative Buddhist perspective. Analysis of the short sketches of the emotions of fear, anger/hatred, grief/sadness and love which was in the third chapter of the earlier editions on motivation and emotions have been changed: there is a separate chapter on motivation and a long chapter on 'emotions'; specific chapters have been devoted to an analysis of 'emotion profiles' of anger, grief, sadness/depression, pride/conceit and greed/generosity. Also they are linked to the dimension of counselling. This project is continued in the section on counselling dealing with the management of stress, grief and loss, anger management, addictions and loneliness. Since my participation as a professional associate for two years in the East–West Center Culture Learning Institute project on emotion and culture, many decades ago, the study of emotions has become an abiding interest. The transition that took place from an academic philosophical

interest to an invigorating immersion in counselling provides a background to this work. Also, my long acquaintance with, and practice of,
meditation has added a new element to my exploration of the diverse
contexts on emotions in Buddhist sermons.

The concept of emotions

It is important to look at the history and etymology of the English word
'emotion'. The word is derived from the Latin, e + *movere*, meaning
to migrate or move from place to place. It was also used to describe
states of agitation or perturbations, and it is this metaphor that has
been popularly associated with the word. James Averill, the psychologist, says that the word 'passion' was the term used to refer to emotions
for approximately 2000 years, from the ancient Greeks to the middle
of the eighteenth century: it is derived from the Latin, *pati* (to suffer)
and also related to the Greek, *pathos*. The concept of emotions came to
be associated with passivity: 'At the root of these concepts is the idea
that an individual (or physical object) is undergoing or suffering some
change as opposed to doing or initiating change'.[13] Averill also upholds
that this 'experience of passivity is an illusion', and can be seen for what
really is the case, by widening the area of self-awareness and developing
greater insight into the sources of one's actions. The kind of metaphor
that dominates our everyday usage also tends to give a very passive picture of the emotions: 'drowned by sorrow', 'driven by anger', 'plagued by
remorse' or 'struck by a Cupid's arrow', when a person falls in love. Averill thus emphasises the need to break away from such passive metaphors
and see emotions as rules that guide human behaviour, and thus having
a great deal of richness and complexity.

While not denying the biological strand in emotions, he emphasises
the need to see them also as social constructions. According to Averill,
the passivity that we attribute to emotions is a kind of interpretation
we put on behaviour, which he calls 'self-attribution', which allows the
individual to abjure to some extent the responsibility for actions revolving on emotions.[14] He mentions three important insights in connection
with this. When we look at specific emotions, such as anger and love,
we see that the feeling of passivity is due to the lack of insight into
one's own actions. Secondly, due to the unusual emotional stimulation,
the cognitive structures that define the 'phenomenal self' or in Buddhist parlance, the 'conventional self' is lost. Thirdly, we tend to take
a small class of biological reactions, such as the startle reactions, as the
paradigm emotions. Averill observes that the paradigm emotions have a

rich complexity and a grammar of their own. When the reader becomes acquainted with the many emotion profiles presented in this study, this tremendous richness and the variety of their structure and mechanisms will be evident. He also comments that some of the cognitive structures in emotional settings are not completely secure and the anxiety regarding their impending collapse is evident. Buddhism accepts the distorting power of the ego attached to some of these affective structures.

It is also important to mention something very paradoxical: though Buddhism offers a very rich territory for emotion studies, both in the Pāli *Suttas* and the Tibetan counterpart, there is no generic term for emotions. However, the term *vedanā*, translated as hedonic tone (feeling), is the base for the affective dimension as compared with the cognitive, volitional and motivational facets of psychology.

Western Theories of Emotions

I will first present an analysis of the Western theories of emotions, and then the Buddhist perspectives in a comparative setting.

The most significant debate in the West has been between physiological arousal theories linked to the body, and cognitive theories focused on thought patterns, beliefs and appraisals. As an example let us reconsider the emotion story from Joseph Ledoux: a man walking on a forest track stumbles on a bundle of dry twigs and, even before his central nervous system tells him to find out what he has trodden on, he is struck by the *emergency bell of fight or flight*. He looks to find the quickest way of moving away from what he thinks is a rattlesnake. In this context, the physiological arousal of the heart beat and the invisible impact on the brain stand out as features of the emotion of fear. If he examines what he has trodden on under his boot and finds that it is only a few twigs he will calm down. In a normal setting, if he sees the snake at a distance the thought emerges that it is a danger, along with the belief that snakes are poisonous: these are clear cognitive features of the emotion. This second context brings out four important features of the emotion of 'fear': perceiving a certain situation or object, thought patterns, appraisals, and a 'desire' to save one's life, plus the physiological arousal. Physiological arousal is a necessary quality of these basic emotions such as anger, fear and sadness, but the meaning given to cognitive factors, as well as the motivational component of desire, are necessary for a normal or paradigm emotion.

Emotions can be more complex, such as the anger that emerges at the infliction of an injustice, where there is a moral aspect and feelings of retaliation. Sometimes anger directed at a superior under whom a person works would be mixed with feelings of fear, and the anger may become suppressed. Many emotions in routine life are located in a network of emotions such as the threat from Henry to Peter's emerging romance with Julia: jealousy is a blend of the love of one's partner, anger at the rival, fear and sadness at the possibility of losing Julia, ambivalence of love and hatred towards one's partner, and shame at the challenge to one's self-image. The remarkable way in which emotions interact is important, and in these contexts, the meanings given by cognitive components are also important.

Extreme anger may have a strong physiological impact and, in treatment situations, the brain and the body emerge as important foci of therapy and treatment. Social and cultural facets of certain emotions are relevant. The vital point is that while emotions affect the whole person, emergence and expression can be seen at various levels of emotional experience. Emotions are linked to the electrical activity of the brain, the visceral glandular system, the circulatory system and the respiratory system; their expression is also manifest in the psychological dynamics of our motives, drives and the physiology of basic needs of the organism. It is also closely related to the ways in which we respond to and evaluate external situations such as danger, threat or loss, and thus linked to our thoughts and beliefs and, lastly, there is the social and cultural context.

The feeling theory of emotions

One of the traditions in emotion studies considers 'feeling' to be the emotion. Though there are different versions of the feeling theory, their common stance may be described in the words of Alston:[15] 'What makes a condition an emotion, and what makes it the particular emotion it is, is the presence in consciousness of a certain felt quality which like sensory qualities (redness, smell of burning wood), is completely accessible in no other way.' The attraction of the feeling theory is that an emotion could occur without its typical overt expression, and thus one could be angry or afraid without anyone noticing it. Also, if it is an inner mental state rather than an inner bodily state, it is based on an immediate infallible knowledge of one's own thoughts and sensations that no one else has any claims to know. However, in spite of this attraction, the theory has been subjected to criticism by Lyons.[16] If a person was so inclined and has sufficient control, he or shecould inhibit possible overt manifestations, yet the tendency to overt expression is strong. Also, it has yet to be proved that someone can be angry without the activation of the internal bodily processes. The second claim about infallibility has been disproved by psychoanalysis, and that is that a personcould misinterpret and misidentify his or her own emotional states. The feeling theory of emotions has been subjected to critiques of a more general nature from analytic philosophers who have been influenced by Wittgenstein. They say that terms that have reference only to private experience do not have a place in the area of inter-subjective communication and thus they do not function in the realm of public discourse. Philosophers who have criticised the feeling theory also say that such an internal experience does not help us to make finer distinctions such as the difference between anger and sadness. Reference to the public world of events and objects is quite central to the experience of emotion.

For these reasons, both philosophers and psychologists have developed a more physiologically oriented feeling theory of emotions, especially the one developed by William James (1984). First, we will explain the nature of the physiological theories of emotions and attempt a comprehensive analysis of the William James theory of emotions and look at its strengths and limitations.

Physiological approaches to emotions

Emotions have broadly two dimensions. The first is a blend of the cognitive and appraisal aspect: there is a snake, a snake is a threat and snake venom is poisonous. This facet has been described as the 'cold' aspect of emotions, whereas the visceral side has been described as the 'hot'.

The human nervous system has two elements, the central and the peripheral nervous system. The latter is, in turn, is divided into the somatic and autonomic nervous system. The somatic nervous system is in charge of the reception and conduction of information. The activation of the autonomic nervous system is seen in the visceral muscles, the heart, veins, arteries, lungs and endocrine glands. It is, in turn, subdivided into the sympathetic and parasympathetic systems. The activation of the former leads to excitement, dilation of the pupils to enhance vision, rising of the skin hair, adrenal gland secretions, release of sugar from the liver, inhibition of digestive and excretory functions and constriction of the intestines. In general, the sympathetic system deals with the emergency reactions of 'flight' or 'fight'. The parasympathetic system moderates such arousal and results in secretion of tears and enhances digestive and excretory functions. William James, for instance, insisted that the quality of emotional experience rested on the sensory feedback of the actual effects of the autonomic nervous system on the viscera.

The importance of autonomic changes can be seen in the kind of metaphors used in routine life: 'red with anger', 'face looked pale and white', 'butterflies in the stomach', 'burning with fury'. Also, there are physiological changes in relation to emotions that are not necessarily upsets or disturbances. In emotions of joy, calm and tranquillity there is empirical evidence of the working of the parasympathetic nervous system, and this is very much seen in meditative experience and when listening to certain types of music.

Another important concern is the *subject's awareness* of these physiological changes. First, there are physiological changes of which we are aware and necessarily so, for example, dryness of the mouth and often increased constriction of the throat; then there are changes that we are not necessarily aware of such as the dilation of the pupils and pallor; and those that we may or may not be aware of, depending on the context, such as increased pulse rate, increased respiratory rate, flushing, sweating, muscular tension, increased muscle tone and increased level of motility in the gastrointestinal tract.[17] In general, we see that physiological changes are a central part of emotional experience. Regarding the question as to whether 'different patterns of ANS activity are associated with different emotions', there is a considerable controversy over this issue. It is a fact of experimental studies that the face and the body have links with emotional experience, and Paul Ekman's work on expressions on the face has demonstrated this facet of emotions, or what are called basic emotions, which have pan-cultural dimensions.[18] However, studies have not yet demonstrated such a close linkage.

The James–Lange theory of emotions

While William James is one of the psychologists who directed our attention to the role of physiology in emotions, in a more specific theoretical thrust he suggested that 'an emotion is the feedback from bodily changes',[19] a view he shared with the Danish psychologist C.G. Lange. According to James, certain stimulus situations generate specific bodily reactions such as the pounding of the heart and related visceral responses, and the perception of this physiological process is the emotion:

> Common sense says, we lose our fortune, are sorry and weep; we meet a bear and are frightened and run; we are insulted by a rival and are angry and strike. The hypothesis here defended says that this order of sequence is incorrect... that the more rational statement is that we feel sorry because we cry... angry because we strike, afraid because we tremble.[20]

Thus, for James the feeling in emotion is an effect of bodily changes and not their cause. We can, of course, think of a few examples that give some intelligibility to this theory. Imagine that you are walking down a long staircase and suddenly miss a step, stumble and immediately grab the handrails before you have had time to recognise a state of fear. Then you feel that first sense: the pounding of the heart, rapid breathing and trembling in the arms. As an overall theory of emotions, James–Lange has had many critics, but over the years the theory has reappeared like the phoenix from the ashes. In fact, during contemporary times this theory has re-emerged in a different form as the theory of somatic markers put forward by the neurologist Antonio Damasio[21] and the philosopher Jesse Prinz,[22] who describes emotions in terms of 'gut reactions'.

One of James's lasting contributions is that he was emphatic on the point that physiological arousal is an important ingredient of emotions, especially in basic emotions:

> I now proceed to urge the vital point of my whole theory. Which is this: if we fancy some strong emotion and then try to abstract from our consciousness of it all the feelings of its characteristic bodily symptoms, we find we have nothing left behind, no 'mind stuff' out of which the emotion can be constituted, and that a cold and neutral state of intellectual perception is all that remains.[23]

It is clearly found in this statement that it is the experience of bodily symptoms that gives emotional quality to our consciousness. Many philosophers in the cognitive tradition of emotion studies have neglected this point, although Lyons is an exception, as he presents both the legitimate claims of the cognitive and the physiological theories.[24]

Critics of the Jamesian theory of emotions

There have been number of critical points raised regarding the Jamesian theory of emotions:

1. Gerald Myers, who has written an excellent study of the life and work of James, observes: 'If James had worked out more clearly the link between an emotion and feeling, he might have avoided the unfortunate conclusion not only in the elaboration of the James–Lange theory, but in this very formulation of it'.[25] A similar criticism has been presented by Benett and Hacker. According to them it is necessary to distinguish between an emotion as an episodic emotional perturbation and a long-standing emotional attitude. The important point is that a person's judgment may be clouded not

only by the distress and agitation of the moment but also by long-standing resentments and jealousies, and, especially in the context of Buddhism, these dispositional dimensions are as important as the episodic reactions of the moment. They also add that motivational patterns over time have a complex relation to emerging emotions and feelings.[26]

2. The link between particular emotions and specific bodily feelings is a mystery that James did not resolve. Also, there is no single proto-type of emotions, though Paul Ekman's concept of basic emotions is useful in certain contexts. Yet, emotions such as hope, remorse, guilt, pride, compassion and gratitude offer conceptual complexi-ties, and our discussion of emotion profiles in Part II will present some of these conceptual features. In fact, Ekman's analysis of 'dis-gust' may not completely explain the Buddhist perception of disgust within its own conceptual terrain. However, it must be mentioned that Ekman's analysis of basic emotions has proved useful in my counselling sessions.

3. Above all, emotions are linked to volition, agency and making a choice, a point emphasised by the psychologist, James Averill and the philosopher, Robert C. Solomon.[27] It must be mentioned that William James recognises the importance of character and will in another context, though in his celebrated theory of emotions there was no place for the importance of volition: 'The faculty of volun-tarily bringing back a wandering attention over and over again is the very root of judgment, character and will'.[28] This passage which has been quoted with great admiration by the pioneer of mindfulness-based stress reduction, Kabat-Zinn,[29] and in my own writings on Buddhist contemplative ethics, strikes a kind of dissonance with James' theory of emotions.

4. James' neglect of the cognitive dimension of emotions was another weakness.

5. It appears that the clue to understanding James and his paradox-ical claims is that there appears to be an illicit logical movement from the position 'the emotional quality of an emotion is caused by physiology' to, 'Our emotions are caused by the bodily symptoms of emotions'.

Motivational strands in emotions

Issues about desire lie at the heart of major controversies in contem-porary theory of action and emotion. Yet this breadth of attention has been matched by a shallowness of scrutiny given to the notion of desire itself. Indeed, the more recent philosophical discussions of the nature of the mind and psychological attitudes show a neglect of desire, with belief showing as the paradigm of the intentional.

Marks also observes that desire is 'intentional' but in an interestingly different way from the way in which belief is 'intentional'. The term 'intentional' in this context may be described as 'directed towards', for instance, as an arrow released from a bow. Marks says that the preoccupation with *cognitivism* in emotion studies led to the neglect of the role of desires in emotions. In the history of emotion studies, Aristotle[30] and Spinoza[31] recognised the links between desire and emotions, and this linkage plays a central role in Buddhist psychology. This 'appetative' aspect of the mind, recognised by Aristotle, has its parallel in the nature of greed (*lobha*) in Buddhism. While greed or what is described as *lobha* in Buddhism, is the root of various forms of 'addictions', greed also feeds many negative emotions, including envy and covetousness (*abhijjhā*).

More recently, Anthony Kenny presents the linkage between desire and emotion clearly:

For the connection between emotion and behaviour is made by desire: one emotion differs from another because of the different sorts of things it makes one want to do. Fear involves wanting to avoid or avert what is feared; anger is connected with the desire to punish or take vengeance on its object. Love of one kind is linked with the desire to fondle and caress the loved ones and shame with the desire to conceal.... These connections are not contingent: a man who was unaware of them would not possess the concept of emotions in question.[32]

Lyons also accepts the significant role of 'desire' in emotions:

Most,though not all, emotions contain desires as part of their occurrent states, and with some emotions this appetitive aspect is part of their very concept. It is this aspect which explains how emotions can be cited as motives, and how behaviour can reveal the nature of emotions, for the desire generated by the evaluative aspect of emotions are the causes associated with emotion. The appetitive aspect, while it does mingle with the evaluative aspect can be separated at the theoretical level.[33]

The cognitive orientation

What may be described as a cognitive theory of emotions has been recognised since Aristotle. Being insulted by a person in front of an admirer and perceiving it as a bad action provides the cognitive element of anger; what Aristotle describes in his own way as the 'boiling of the blood' provides the physiological component of the emotion, and the desire for revenge would be the appetitive – or the desire-oriented – component of the emotion. Aristotle does not make a finer distinction between the purely cognitive aspect, in recognising the statement as an insult and evaluating it as a threat. Lyons defines a cognitive theory as follows: 'One that makes some aspect of thought, usually a belief, central to the concept of emotion'.[34] Such thought patterns *help us to distinguish one emotion from another* and that is one of the central features that makes this theory stand out from others. We also need to make a distinction between the factual component of an emotion, such as seeing a snake, and the evaluative component that it may be a danger to life. There have been many cognitive theories of emotion: the earliest was that of Robert C. Solomon (2004) that emotions are judgments. There have been attempts to explain an emotion as a logical entailment between a judgment and a response. Others wish to opt for a weaker form of cognitive theory closer to life.

In fact, Cheshire Calhoun says that only a small fraction of our beliefs are consciously articulated and the greater portion is a 'darker cognitive area', an unarticulated cognitive set that interprets the world.[35] She makes an insightful observation that we have 'doxic ailments' that misinterpret the world, ringing a familiar chord with the Buddhist concept of *moha* – wrong and illusory ways of seeing the world. This point will be explored in greater detail in the section on Buddhist perspectives on emotions.

Critics of the cognitive theory of emotions

A general point of criticism is that the cognitive theory of emotions (in spite of its variety) neglects other important facets of an emotion such as physiology and the role of desires in emotions. Joel Marks, for instance, observes, 'I shall call my opponents "cognitivists" because they champion belief over desires in the explanation of actions'.[36] Similar criticisms have been made about the neglect of the physiological factor[37] and neglect of feelings.[38]). However, there have been balanced accounts such as that of Lyons, where the cognitive factor has been integrated into the other components of an emotion. Robert C. Solomon, the most important pioneer of cognitive theories, also became receptive to a broader concept of emotions and, before his untimely death, brought out an edited volume on thinking about feeling in which he assembled the best minds in the Anglo-American traditions, which certainly is a landmark in the history of emotion studies.[39] I am greatly indebted to him for his interest in Asian studies on emotions and my own writings, and I published an article on the Buddhist perspective on the topic in a journal issue dedicated to his work,[40] as well as a chapter in the memorial volume for Solomon.[41] In addition, the chapter on thinking and feeling in the present work has a section on this theme, which was written as a tribute to Solomon, a pioneer in emotion studies.

> But what led me to an increasing concern about both the role of the body and the nature and role of bodily feelings in emotion was the suspicion that my judgment theory had been cut too thin, that in the pursuit of an alternative to the feeling theory I had ventured too far in the other direction. I am now coming to appreciate that accounting for the bodily feelings (not just sensations) in emotion is not a secondary concern and not independent of appreciating the essential role of the body in emotional experience[42]

The Buddhist perspective on the conflict between the cognitive theories and the physiological theories of emotions is to convert them into contrasting perspectives rather than conflicting theories (see Chapter 10 in this book).

Calhoun refers to the notion of the emotional inertia hypothesis, where one clings to an emotion in spite of cognitive evidence to the contrary. She says that though the cognitivist would like to 'deny brute emotions that lack an intelligible wellspring in belief', the phenomenon of emotional inertia is an observable phenomenon. It is deeper than the oft-quoted example of the 'fear of spiders' when you know that they are harmless. She, in fact, refers to 'dark cognitive sets' that function at a subliminal level and such 'doxic ailments', which incidentally have a parallel in Buddhist psychology, work beyond the logical entailment thesis of fact and entailment offered in the cognitive theories of emotions.[43]

The Buddhist Architecture of the Mind

Following the Greek philosopher Aristotle who presented a tripartite division of the mind, the Buddhist architecture of the mind may be described accordingly: perception/cognition (*saññā* and *viññāṇa*) representing the cognitive dimension of the mind; feeling (*vedana*) representing the affective dimension of the mind; and the *conative* or volitional dimension of the mind *(saṅkhāra)*.

Four Mental Aggregates and the body:

- Perception (*saññā*)
- Consciousness (*viññāṇa*)
- Feelings (*vedanā*)
- Volitional activity (*saṅkhāra*)
- The Body (*rūpa*)

Even though this traditional picture of the mind is useful, we need not place absolute reliance on it, as all four mental aggregates and the body may be present at a minute level in all states of consciousness. A crucial point in Buddhist psychology is the reciprocal relationship between the body and the mind, because Buddhist psychology avoids any Cartesian dualism or reductionism that attempts to reduce the mental into the physical or the physical into the mental. This latter feature helps us to have a more holistic perspective on emotions in Buddhism: Chapter 9, on the body–mind relationship, and Chapter 10, on an holistic perspective on emotions, develop this theme in detail. All five aggregates are inseparably associated with each other, and the mind and the body are seen as a dynamic continuum, associated with the interplay of causal factors.

The causality of what is described as 'dependent origination' gives more insight into the emergence of different psychological factors: for instance, sensory contact conditions feeling, feeling conditions craving and craving conditions clinging. Thus in addition to the 'structural perspective' of the mind and the body in terms of the five aggregates, there is the 'dynamic perspective' of the interplay of sensations, feelings, desires, volitions and dispositions. In terms of these schemes it is possible look at a particular context such as 'Why did Fred lose his temper?': his father refused to let him devote more time tor sports than his studies at his college, and his teacher did not give him a good credit for his essay, and so on. Both the lack of balanced desires and reactivity (anger) and a strong sense of ego are features that emerge when research is carried out into contexts of this sort. Thus, Buddhist psychology offers a rich potentiality for application to practical issues and the section on counselling unravels this quality in detail, providing examples and case studies. There are innumerable examples that show how the Buddha has opened up the minds of people with problems concerning their anger and reactivity, lack of concern for others, envy of the achievement of others, deep prejudices and the unexpected grief over calamities and the healthy ways that they have found of managing these issues. Many such contexts are found throughout the sermons of the Buddha. The present work explores and explains the deeply structured psychology behind these insights.

Another central perspective is that the Buddhist concept of the mind is supplemented by an analysis of mental activity at a subliminal level. Threshold consciousness is open to six sense doors through which stimuli reach us, as seeing, hearing, smelling, tasting, touching and, via the mind-door, conceptual and ideational activity, including memory. The ability to control the senses helps a person to stay unaffected by the inroads of sensory stimuli, but the mind is subject to subliminal pressures. In an earlier edition of *Buddhist and Freudian Psychology*[44] I developed the idea of an Unconscious in Buddhism influenced by Freud's theories and case studies, but recently I have realised that there is a difference between Buddhism and Freud. While Buddhism accepts the traumatic unconscious as depicted by Freud, the more significant layer of activity that lies close to our everyday consciousness, which I refer to by the term 'subliminal', is the dominant concern of Buddhism, and this view is developed in a later edition of my book.[45] I have moved away from the archaeological metaphor of 'digging in' the inaccessible and often traumatic layers of the psyche to a metaphor of 'opening up' thoughts and affects closer to ordinary life/threshold consciousness. Today, in mindfulness-based cognitive therapy (which is different from an alternative such as the Freudian psychodynamic view), the focus is on the moment-to-moment flow of thoughts, which is described as 'the auto-pilot' of mechanical responses. New research in neurology by Joseph Ledoux (1996), which I have already referred to in the example of the man whose boots crush a bundle of dry twigs while walking and is about to run, thinking it is a snake, explains how our normal rational consciousness may be hijacked by the amygdala, the instigator of impulsive activity. Such tendencies to fear or anger in another context may be explained as the excitement of dormant subliminal tendencies described by the Pali term *anusaya*. These dormant or lurking tendencies may be described by the metaphor of a neglected drain choked with accumulated mud and dust. Regular mindfulness practice and development of awareness can help us to be acquainted with these 'sleeping passions'. This dormant level or ground is referred to in Buddhist analysis as '*anusaya-bhūmi*'; sleeping passions may also lie at the level of our thoughts and thought patterns described as *'pariyuṭṭhāna-bhūmi'* or become fierce and ungovernable and result in impulsive actions (*vītikkama-bhūmi*).

The archaeological metaphor

The archaeological metaphor was one of Freud's favourites. Once disowned intentions are brought to consciousness, it would be possible to take responsibility for them, and in that movement we could be free of their tyranny over us.[46]).

The opening metaphor

However, in Buddhism – and even in more recent psychoanalysis – there has emerged a different model, one that is less about digging and more about opening. At the root of this difference lies an alternative view of the unconscious.[47]

These two contrasting metaphors convey the new perspective on the subliminal that I have developed instead of the Freudian unconscious. Epstein cites a beautiful Tibetan story that captures the essence of his graphic metaphor of 'opening'. A woman named Manibhadrā, who was engaged in advanced meditation, was carrying water from the village to her home and one day dropped the pitcher so that the water gushed out on to the ground. The broken pitcher worked as a powerful model for meditation for her, and she was suddenly liberated.[48] Here was the experience of jarring loose, breaking to pieces without falling apart.

Buddhism and Emotion Theories

The review of Western theories of emotions presented earlier in this chapter will help us to locate the Buddhist perspectives on emotion theories. It may seem strange but that there is no generic term for emotions and this fact is also true of the Tibetan Buddhist tradition, a point discussed in a dialogue between the Dalai Lama and Richard Matthieu[49]).

There is no word in Tibetan that can be translated as 'emotion' in English. However, if you speak of one category of emotion, such as negative emotions – *kleṣas*, or afflictions – then there are definitely six primary ones, but even here it is not precisely correct to use the English word *emotion*. The six prominent ones are ignorance, anger, pride, wrong views and scepticism or afflictive doubt.

The Dalai Lama thinks it is a little problematic to call ignorance an emotion, as it implies dullness or lack of clarity. In the early Buddhist

Pāli *suttas*, greed (*lobha*) provides the base for addictions and attachment; hatred (*dosa*) provides the base for emotions of aversion/reactivity and for delusion/identity confusion; and *moha* is the base for what was referred to earlier in this chapter as 'doxic ailments'. Goleman throws some illumination on this concept: 'The dynamics of information flow within and amongst us points to a particular human malady: to avoid anxiety we close off crucial portions of awareness, creating blind spots. That diagnosis applies to both self-deception and shared illusions'.[50]

The Buddhist analysis of emotions considers the basic hedonic tone or feeling described by the Pāli term *vedanā* as the basis of the whole affective dimension, and such feelings may be pleasant, painful and neither pleasurable nor painful (neutral).

> It should be made clear that, in Buddhist psychology, 'feeling' is the bare sensation noted as pleasant, unpleasant (painful) and neutral (indifferent). Hence it should not be confused with emotion, which though arising from the basic feeling, adds to it likes and dislikes of varying intensity, as well as other thought processes.[51]

In Buddhist psychology an emotion may be considered as an interactive complex or construct emerging with the causal network of the five aggregates. Thus within this network it is possible to distinguish feeling, bodily sensation, desires, beliefs and appraisals as variables that go to make anger, fear, sadness and so on. Though there are variations in the Tibetan and early Buddhist tradition, both traditions consider negative ones as afflictive, causing suffering, and they are described as defilements. The concept of *saṅkhāra*, translated as volitional activity, provides the notion of intention and accountability, crucial in the task of moral criticism. Negative emotions are fed by the cognitive distortions rooted in the 'ego' and roots of greed and reactivity/anger. Emotions such as conceit and pride as related to a delusional sense of the self will be discussed in Chapter 20.

Feelings

Feeling arises when there is a meeting of three factors: the sense organ, object and consciousness. This interaction is described by the Pāli term *phassa*, which means 'contact'. It is sixfold and is conditioned by the five physical sense organs and the mind. In the sense of dependent origination,[52] contact conditions feeling and feeling conditions craving. Pleasant feelings, if not properly understood and managed, may turn into lust, greed and infatuation; painful feelings, if not properly understood and managed, may manifest as anger, destructive forms of fear, and depression; neutral feelings which are not properly understood and managed may lead to boredom. Pleasant feelings, which result in attachment to pleasant objects, can rouse a subliminal tendency towards greed (*rāgānusaya*); painful feelings can arouse latent anger and hatred (*paṭighānusaya*); and the delusion of the attachment to the ego may arouse the latent proclivity toward ignorance and conceit (*diṭṭhānusaya*).

As feelings are the gateway to more complex thinking and behaviour, which may be wholesome or unwholesome, the Buddhist practice of mindfulness gives a prominent place to the practice of mindfulness of feelings:

> This, therefore, is a crucial point in the conditioned Origin of Suffering, because it is at this point that Feeling may give rise to passionate emotions of various types, and it is therefore here, that one may be able to break that fatuous concatenation. If in receiving a sense impression, one is able to pause and stop at the phase of Feeling, and make it in its first stage of manifestation, the object of Bare Attention, Feeling will not be able to originate Craving. It will stop at the bare statement of 'pleasant', 'unpleasant' or 'indifferent'.[53]

By the practice of bare attention, the possible transition from feelings to negative emotions is watched with great vigilance. A very important point concerning both the psychology and epistemology of Buddhism is that concepts such as feelings are part of a synthetic process, and it is only by abstraction and analysis that we can speak of feelings as different from perception. However, in meditative practice, conscious awareness is kept on the primary object by noting and labelling and, thus, the transitions that take place in the stream of consciousness are discerned. So, the slowing-down process helps one to focus on feelings in their unalloyed form in meditative practice. Though in a sense, sensory consciousness, feeling and perception are inseparable,[54] the meditator understands the flow of dependent origination: visual consciousness arises because of eye and material shape; the meeting of the three is sensory impingement, and because of sensory impingement arises feeling.[55]

It was a characteristic feature of the wisdom of the Buddha that he did not push these distinctions too far so that he became trapped in metaphysical issues but he used them within a context: different contexts are seen through his pragmatism and the importance of practice.

This point may be illustrated by the way the Buddha intervened in a celebrated controversy among the monks about the exact number of feelings. He said that one way of analysing feelings is to speak of two feelings (bodily and mental); three feelings in another way (pleasant, painful and neutral); five types of feeling, the pleasure faculty, pain faculty, the joy faculty, displeasure faculty and the equanimity faculty; six feelings, in yet another way (related to the six sense organs and the mind); eighteen feelings, six accompanied by joy, six by displeasure and six followed by equanimity; thirty-six types of feelings, six joy of household life, six based on joy on renunciation, six types of displeasure in household life, six types of displeasure in renunciation by joy, six by displeasure, six accompanied by equanimity in household life and six on equanimity in renunciation; or a hundred and eight feelings, the above thirty-six feelings in the past, future and present.[56]

Thus from one point of view these distinctions are important, but from another standpoint they are mere 'designations' to be used in appropriate contexts. In this manner the Buddha brought sanity and pragmatism into Buddhist practice.

The *arahant* (perfected one) may be described as a person of refined sensibility going beyond the attachment-reaction process found in the ignorant worldling (*puthujjana*). The gross aspects of the cognitive process have been eliminated. The meaning of sensory contact (*phassa*) and the position of the perfected one have already been described with the Pali term (*phassa-nirodha*), where *nirodha* means 'extinction'. This means that although the perfected one does go through sensory experience it is not dominated by what is called 'the aroma of subjectivity' – appropriation of things as 'mine'.[57] When it is said that the perfected one is not assailed by 'contact', it does not mean that he is like a man who cannot hear, see or smell. If this were the case, a blind person or a deaf person would be perfected. However, it does imply a more refined and sensitive person. In describing a liberated monk, it is said that he is completely calmed and free; the sights, tastes, sounds, smells and touches which are normally 'longed for and loathed for' by the worldling do not disturb the *arahant*, and it is said that he is like a massive rock unmoved by the winds.[58]

The *arahant* may experience a painful feeling, as in the case when a bamboo splinter injured the Buddha. However, he only experiences the physical impact without the psychological reaction. It is said that the worldling is struck by two arrows, the bodily and the mental, but the *arahant* only one, the bodily.[59] This does not mean that Buddhist detachment should be identified with the destruction of emotions. On the contrary the Buddhist sage is capable of a wide range of rich and wholesome emotions.

Desire and craving

As has been clearly stated earlier, some of the motivational theories of emotions in the Western tradition see a close link between feeling and desire as well as desire and emotion. However, in recent emotion studies in the West, the strong focus on the cognitive factor has led to the relative neglect of desire. Joel Marks claims that desire is *intentional* but in an interestingly different way from belief.[60] These points should make the Buddhist analysis of the role of desire and craving in the generation of emotions a subject of current interest. In fact, in the Buddhist analysis, one of the dimensions for the moral criticism of emotions is their motivational base and related desires. According to the discourses of the Buddha, a person feels attraction (*sārajjati)* for agreeable objects and feels repugnance for disagreeable objects (*byāpajjati).* An individual thus possessed of like (*anurodha*) and dislike (*virodha*) approaches pleasure giving objects and avoids painful ones. Craving in turn conditions clinging *(upādāna).* The word *taṇhā*, is translated as 'craving',and its etymology suggests an unquenchable thirst. Clinging implies a strong bonding with the object: greedy possession or anxious obsession. A desire to destroy an unpleasant object is also paradoxically related to clinging. Though the word clinging (*upādāna*) refers to things we like, in a deeper sense it means entanglement with things we like or dislike. It is the notion of clinging that adds the element of adhesiveness to certain desires. An interesting distinction between appetitive emotions and possessive emotions has been made by C.C.W. Taylor[61]: the former emphasises the elements of appetite, greed and craving, and the latter, the elements of adhesiveness, fixation and clinging.

On the analogy of sexual desire or the simple physiological drive of thirst, it can be said that these desires are temporarily satisfied but they emerge from time to time, and it is an unending process, which is referred to in the Buddhist contexts as 'becoming'. On the one hand, there is strong fixation on the object of desire, but there is also a search for variety and change, finding 'delight in this and that, here and there' (*tatra tatrābhinandini*).

It must be noted that desire (*chanda*) as opposed to craving *(taṇhā)* is considered as virtuous or vicious depending on context. For instance, the word is associated with the desire to do the right thing and the zeal for righteousness.[62] It is considered as a vice, where there is a reference to the desires that generate evil: partiality, enmity, stupidity, and fear.[63] Compared with the term *desire, craving* has a negative connotation with a few exceptions, for instance where Venerable Ānanda says 'Dependent on craving is craving abandoned'.[64]

In general, when the issue of moral assessment emerges, the bases for moral assessment in Buddhist psychology should be looked at: the springs of behaviour and action are found in six roots, including greed *(lobha)*, which may manifest either as the craving for sensuous gratification or the craving for egoistic pursuits; hatred *(dosa)*, which manifests in aggressive and self-destructive behaviour; and delusion *(moha)*, which may be rendered in the present context as the existential confusion regarding the identity of a 'self'.[65] These bases of craving provide a framework to plot the negative emotions: attachment emotions such as greed, covetousness and addictions; emotions of aversion such as anger, indignation, resentment envy, self-hate and malice; and emotions of delusion involving different forms of conceit, pride, vanity, shame and the emotion of jealousy, which has other ingredient emotions such as love, hatred, ambivalence and shame feeding it. It is of great interest to note that in the context of the liberation path, the hindrances on the way to higher states of concentration also consist of negative emotions: sensuous desire *(kāma-cchanda)*, ill-will *(vyāpāda)*, dullness, boredom, torpor and languor *(thīna-middha)*, restlessless and worry *(uddhacca-kukkucca)*, and a cognitive factor, wavering, doubts and scepticism *(vicikicchā)*. This dimension is important, as one moves along the path of liberation the obstructing emotional and cognitive factors have a more refined nature than their more gross predecessors and are thus more complex and difficult to manage. On the positive side equanimity *(upekkhā)* provides emotional balance and equipoise; this factor is discussed in detail, in Chapter 8.

Emotions and the cognitive orientation

Buddhism has a strong cognitive orientation and this is exemplified in a celebrated sermon, the *Vitakka-saṇṭhāna Sutta*.[66] This sermon presents five techniques of dealing with intrusive thoughts and, perhaps as the ancient predecessor of the contemporary cognitive therapy, is focused on the 'autopilot' of repetitive thinking: 1. First is the method of getting the mind to focus on a 'different object'. Ideational activity *(vitakka)* associated with desire, aversion and delusion is to be eliminated by reflecting on a wholesome object. This is compared to a carpenter driving out a large peg with a small peg. 2. The second aims at scrutinising the perils of the harmful thoughts. This is compared to a man in the prime of life, who is fond of adornment of the body, seeing the disgusting sight of a carcass round his neck. 3. The third is the method of 'not attending' to the thoughts or letting go where unwholesome thoughts are eliminated by not attending to them. 4. Fourth is the uncovering of the causal roots of the bad thoughts. 5. If these methods fail will power should be used to restrain the unwholesome thoughts. It is said that by repeated practice, one could emerge as someone who has mastered these pathways of thought. In addition to unwholesome disposition of body and speech, unwholesome dispositions of the mind are the focus of meditative practice.

There are also cognitive distortions at the deeper level, influencing our daily routine thinking and behaviour due to the root of delusion. In fact an interesting parallel to this manner of looking at emotional distortions is cited by Cheshire Calhoun:

> Our cognitive life is not limited to clear, fully conceptualized, articulated beliefs. Instead, beliefs constitute only a small illuminated portion of that life. The greater portion is rather dark, an articulated framework for interpreting our world, which if articulated, would be an enormous network of claims not all of which would be accepted by the individual as his beliefs.[67]

I have discussed elsewhere[68] a comparison of the Buddhist concept of the cognitive unconscious in Buddhism and Sigmund Freud. What is necessary to keep in mind is that cognitive distortions may be found at the level of our routine life, as presented in mindfulness-based cognitive therapy. Also, a deeper layer of cognitive distortions are cited by Calhoun, that have some kind of parallel in the Freudian concept of the archaic irrational, symbolised in the term id, which is partly an inheritance from the philosopher Nietzsche. So we need to see levels of cognitive distortions or 'doxic ailments'.

The body and physiology in emotions

> Bhikkhus, just as various winds blow in the sky: winds from the east, winds from the west, winds from the north, winds from the north, winds from the south, dusty winds and dustless winds, cold and hot winds, mild winds and strong winds; so too various feelings arise in the body: pleasant feeling arises, painful feelings arise, neither-painful-nor-pleasurable feelings arise.[69]

Leslie Greenberg the founder of emotion-focused therapy says:

> People need to attend to whether the emotional experience felt in their bodies as hot or cold, a big ball or a small knot.... Thus if you begin to label the quality of and location of your feelings as 'hot sensations in my chest', to notice its intensity as 'moderate' and its shape as a 'round ball', then the torrents of emotion will subside.[70]

While the cognitive theories of emotion have a focus on thought patterns and appraisals, the body-based physiological theories, first presented by William James, are now enjoying a revival through the work of the neurologist Antonio Damasio and the philosopher Jesse Prinz.[71] It was William James who first described the body as the mind's sounding board, allowing the emotional signals to resonate as the sound of a guitar amplifies the sound of the strings: this means by suppressing some automatic bodily changes, and consciously making others, we gain emotional control. When we move, in Chapter 12, to counselling, it will become apparent that body-based therapies have acquired a new sense of importance today. In four-fold meditation techniques described as the *Satipaṭṭhāna*, the body, feelings, thoughts and the nature of phenomena are presented as frontiers for the establishment of mindfulness. It is clearly stated in the sermons of the Buddha that while both book knowledge of the various sermons, logical and rational understanding of concepts are useful, it is only the meditative experience and knowledge that leads to deeper understanding. What is recommended is the contemplation of the body through the body, and in all the four sections the road to deep understanding is experiential knowledge.

The body is also important as, apart from its place as a central component of an emotion, the 'breath' focus is the pathway for meditation. As the breath stands between voluntary and involuntary actions, this practice helps us to be aware of many actions that are, in normal circumstances, performed in an automatic and mechanical manner. Breathing is controlled by the autonomic nervous system and thus does not come within the average consciousness, unless we develop the awareness of breath as a special exercise. As we have a separate chapter in this work on the breath l only made a brief reference to this theme here.

Knowing the body through the body is described as a 'sixth sense' in addition to the knowledge through the senses.

6

Personality: Philosophical and Psychological Issues

It is necessary to make a distinction between the psychological perspectives of personality and the Buddhist philosophical concept of the human person, as in the discourses of the Buddha the material is intermingled and even interwoven. The term 'personality' has distinctive meaning within psychology, and the following rendering sums up the basic perspective: 'the study of the characteristic and distinctive traits of an individual, the stable and shifting patterns of relationships between these traits, the origin of the traits, and the ways, the traits interact to help or hinder the adjustment of a person to other people and situations'.[1] Such a study has two aspects: a structural aspect dealing with the traits and their relationship, and a dynamic aspect that deals with the motivational influence of traits upon adjustment. The facets of motivation and emotion already examined help to understand the dynamics of personality organization and adjustments.

The psychology of personality deals with aspects that are *characteristic* and *distinctive*. The psychology of Buddhism offers material for the study of personality types and traits, though these references are rooted in the ethical and religious quest of Buddhism, namely psychological qualities that have a bearing on the ethical and religious quest. There are references to personality types in the discourses of the Buddha, especially in the Aṅguttara Nikāya[2] and Dīgha Nikāya,[3] and a more systematic analysis in the work Human Types (*Puggala-paññatti*) and the Path of Purification (*Visuddhi-magga*).[4] The most dominant classification is based on the three negative roots of greed, hatred and delusion, and on the positive generosity, compassion/love and wisdom. There is an interesting passage that refers to ways of finding out the qualities of the character of virtue, integrity, fortitude and wisdom of another person: in living with a person one can fathom the quality of virtue; in having dealings with a person test his or her integrity; when one has a crisis in life, it is possible to test his or her powers of fortitude; and in having regular conversation test his or her wisdom.[5] This reference is significant, as it offers a kind of behavioural test to explore the personality of others. This is a sample of qualities of character discussed by the Buddha that are somewhat different from established studies of personality traits in modern psychology. It must be mentioned that, unlike Western psychology, personalities in a Buddhist context carry a lot of 'kammic flavour' emerging from past births. The following example indicates the character traits carried over from past births:

> In this case, Mallikā, a certain woman, is ill-tempered, of a very irritable nature. On very little provocation she becomes cross and agitated. She is upset and becomes stubborn, she shows temper and ill-will and displeasure. She is no giver of charity to recluse or brāhmin, nor gives food and drink, vehicle, flowers, scent, ointment, bed, lodging or light. Moreover she is jealous minded, she is jealous of other folk's gain, of the honour, respect, reverence, homage and worship paid to them. She is revengeful and harbour's a grudge. Such a one, if deceasing from that life, she comes back to this state of things, wherever she is born, is ill-formed, of a mean appearance and poor, having little of her own of small possessions, and is of small account.[6]

Philosophical Issues

In the discourses of the Buddha the philosophical and psychological aspects of the person concept are often intermingled, and it is by a process of dissection and abstraction that the material can be separated. The question has been raised as to how the concept of *anatta* (non-self), and *anicca* (impermanence) can be reconciled with a concept of 'persons'. There is some apparent tension in the use of the Pali term 'puggala', more oriented towards the description of the individual and 'reborn' persons as character types, and the context of an individual in a deep meditative setting – oriented towards discerning the impersonal qualities that emerge through the injunctions for self-control and self-knowledge and the 'realization of selflessness'.

> The term *puggala* refers to differences in character, ethical disposition, spiritual aptitude and achievement, and karmic destiny. There are many places in the canon where these topics are mentioned, but the most extensive treatments are found in the *Aṅguttara Nikāya* and in

a work of the *Abhidhamma* entirely devoted to the subject, *puggala-paññatti*.[7]

Collins describes the logic of the term *atta-bhāva* as a middle position between conventional usage and ultimate thinking:

> For Buddhism, conventional thinking presupposes unitary selves or persons who are in some way subject to a series of discrete births. Ultimate thinking refers solely to a collection of impersonal elements, the sequence of which provides continuity both within 'one lifetime' and in the process of 'rebirth'. The idea of *atta-bhāva* forms the bridge between these two.[8]

The important distinctions that Collins makes help us to clear potential philosophical blockages in locating the psychological concept of personality within the Buddhist analysis. The first is the issue about 'individuation' and second the concern about agency and accountability. It has been observed that a defensive pursuit of the doctrine 'selflessness' may result in a fear of 'individuation' and taking responsibility and being assertive. At the doctrinal level, there need not be a problem about individuation (*atta-bhāva*). The psychological wholeness and coherence of each person, as distinct from being split and fragmented, may vary. The concept of not-self (*anatta*) does not deny that each person has an individual character. The Buddhist concept of individuation leaves room for the diversity of character. The Buddha's broad-based analysis of personalities into the greed-dominated (*rāga-carita*), anger-dominated (*dosa-carita*) and delusion-oriented (*moha-carita*) is well known. There are references to personality types in the *Gradual Sayings*,[9] *Further Dialogues*[10] and the book on personality types.[11] The subject is also given a stimulating discussion in The Path to Purification. The Buddha respected this point in prescribing certain forms of meditation that suits the individual. As my meditation teacher, the Venerable Uda Eriyagama Dhammajiva, says, the recommended meditation exercises were 'not obtainable over the counter' but depended on the prescription of the Buddha. In looking at the five hindrances, the Buddha realised that the domination of each of these varies from person to person. There is also the variety of personalities and different routes taken by those who achieved perfection. According to Engler, the goal of freeing oneself from egocentric desires may result in the avoidance of anxiety-producing situations, taking responsibility and being in charge of one's life.[12] In doctrinal Buddhism, freedom, karmic correlation, and 'serial individuality' give meaning and direction to the notion of responsibility and the focus on mindfulness in daily life is important. In mindfulness-based therapy of addictions, for example, the therapist helps the client 'to take charge of his or her life'. It is necessary to clear these prejudices: Rubin for instance says, 'in throwing the bathwater of egocentricity, Buddhism eliminates the baby of human agency'.[13] He has thus missed the distinction between the conventional use of the self, which accepts agency and, in a more ultimate sense, accepting the full implications of the *anatta* doctrine. The tools of looking at the context and 'changing gears' when necessary helps the practising individual to understand some of the apparent paradoxes encountered in insight meditation.

There is a strong focus in Buddhist discourses on the morally worthy person and the primacy of character, as well as the discussion of such psychological issues as the nature of conflicts, frustration and anxiety: these topics will be discussed further later in this chapter. Along with the meditative practice on the individual as a complex of five aggregates, there is a great deal of rich material in what may be described as the Buddha's veritable counselling practice dealing with the diversity of people and their psychological issues.

The Buddha and the current philosophical climate

While I have clarified and cleared the Buddhist perspectives on the nature of the 'self', it is also useful to have some idea of the exact philosophical controversies at the time, which helps us to better understand the Buddha's analysis. Though the meditative experience is the ultimate test, the Buddha's philosophical analysis is very illuminating. One of the dominant views in the background is the belief in a self which is not identical with any of the five aggregates (*khandas*), taken severally or collectively. In this context, the Buddhist position is a middle position between the eternalist (*sassata-vāda*) upholding an eternal self and the annihilationist (*uccheda-vāda*) a temporary self, annihilated at death. According to the law of dependent origination, there is nothing that has an independent existence over these causal laws. The second point is that there is nothing that evades the law of impermanence. Thirdly, though the Buddhist position accepts an agent, this not a distinct thing from the five aggregates. The Buddha also presents the idea that if there is a permanent self, we should be in 'full control' of everything and the interlinks between the non-self, impermanence and suffering (*anatta, anicca, dukkha*) indicates that these realities limit any idea of having full control of things. A more detailed analysis of the points I have summarised is found in a very useful article presented in relation to number of Buddhist Suttas by Karunadasa:[14]

> If Buddhist philosophy seeks to show why the idea of self-entity is a wrong conception, its psychology shows how it comes to be, its ethics shows how it can be overcome and its final goal which is *Nibbāna* shows the final state where it is completely eliminated.

Though the Buddha does not accept a persisting susbstratum, the word 'person' is used in a conventional sense to 'distinguish one serial process from another'.[15] Now that the philosophical setting has been clarified, it is useful to link this picture with the Buddhist concept of personality in terms of its psychological and ethical boundaries. 'Persons' in the context of Buddhist psychology and ethics will have purposes of their own, and they are the sources of the values they generate; they are capable of taking decisions and accepting responsibility for their actions; and they will have rights and duties and are capable of being punished. In general, they are agents who can be rational and irrational but basically always responsible for their actions. Psychologically, it is of significance to say that persons have memories, thoughts, feelings and communicate with others. It is necessary to emphasise that what we find is a unity of functions – for example, walking, standing, perceiving, thinking, deciding, a proneness to get annoyed, etc. As the parts of a chariot work together, so do the body, feeling, consciousness and dispositions combine.[16]

Rune Johanson says that in this analogy there is a functional concept of personality:

> Here the functional unity of the personality is really what contemporary psychologists call personality. The car has clearly some sort of primitive personality, an individual constellation of parts. It is capable of functioning only when all the parts are there. None of the parts can be called 'car', not even all the parts together, if they are not combined in a very special way.... A personality is also not the body, not the perceptual function, not the feeling etc., but the proper combination of them.[17]

Conflict and Frustration

In the chapter on motivation the satisfaction of drives and needs was discussed. In the process of satisfying these needs, there is bound to be conflict and frustration, and the way that people respond to these situations leaves a mark on the nature of their personality. A mature personality would have flexible modes of adjustments. In this context the Buddha refers to three types of mentalities: one whose mind is like an open sore; one with a mind like lightning; and one with a mind like a diamond. The person with a mind like an 'open sore' is irascible and irritable and cannot withstand criticism and thus is bound to generate conflicts, hatred and resentment within him or her and often in others. The second person understands the doctrine of the nature of suffering and the four noble truths, and in the manner that a flash of lightning helps us to see objects in the darkness, his or her mind works like lightning, and it is very intuitive. One whose mind is like a diamond is liberated by the destruction of taints that may discolour the mind.[18] In another context the Buddha says that there are three types of person: first, one for whom when anger enters the mind, it becomes like a carving on a rock; in another like a footprint on the sand; and, yet in another, like a footprint in water. Such classifications indicate that the Buddha respected and understood the diversity in human character and was able, often, like a therapist with great skill, to offer advice that suited a particular person. When we use the concepts of the five aggregates and dependent origination, we are looking at an analysis which is 'impersonal', not the peculiarities of separate persons. Depending on the context these approaches are useful.

The satisfaction of basic derives and desires often generates conflicts and tensions, so it is important for a person to be able to adjust to such situations in a flexible way. The modes of adjustment of each person, depend partly on the personality type and, in such contexts, emotions play a crucial role. The management of emotions such as deep frustration, anger, impatience and unhealthy forms of reactivity and exaggerated anxiety would make adjustment difficult. The *Araṇa-vibhaṅga Sutta* presents a useful analysis of conflict and peace.[19] The term 'peace' has a specific meaning on the path to liberation, as the mastery of greed, hatred and delusion. However, at the level of the ordinary householder what is aimed at is a harmonious life (*dhamma-cariya, sama-cariya*). This is the concept of a well-adjusted and balanced person who can exercise restraint when necessary and does not take to excessive and illegitimate pleasures. According to the Buddha's analysis of the human predicament, stress (*dukkha*), tension and conflicts are part and parcel of the human situation. The householder who lives a righteous and balanced life does not come into conflict with either the moral order or the law. Basic Buddhist ethics of the five precepts, his advice to householders in the Sigālovāda Sutta and similar sermons provide the householder with resources for a balanced life. It is said in the *Dīgha Nikāya* that a person who is subject to strong craving and clings to the object of his or her desires with tenacity and avarice experiences in violent interpersonal relations, 'blows and wounds, strife, contradiction and retort, quarrelling, slander and lies'.[20] Thus, righteous householders are expected to achieve their aims by lawful means and without greed and longing.

There are three types of psychological conflicts faced by people in relation to their desires and wants: (i) between two pleasure-giving objects, equally attractive. For example, the proverbial donkey torn between two attractive bales of hay; (ii) the choice between two equally repulsive objects such as the man poised between the devil and the deep blue sea; and (iii) the most significant conflict is when the same object has both positive and negative valence. As the Buddha points out, pleasures are manifold and sweet (*kamā hi citrā madhurā*) but yet they cause much suffering (*bahu-dukkhā*) and much turbulence (*bahūpāyāsā*).

Fear plays an important role in our lives, ranging from mild cases of mental instability to standard issues in psychopathology. While fear is a normal part of our lives, problems arise with fears that are inappropriate. Anxiety is a kind of brooding fear involving what might happen. Sigmund Freud, who first highlighted the crucial role of anxiety in our lives, realised that initially he had overemphasised the importance of the sexual drive and came to focus on the 'ego as the seat of anxiety'. Freud first upheld that anxiety was the re-emergence of repressed libido, but he gradually shifted his position to emphasise the role of the ego in anxiety, which has some affinity to the Buddhist emphasis on ego-oriented desires (*bhava-taṇhā*). Three main types of anxiety, according to him, are objective anxiety, neurotic anxiety and moral anxiety. He also had a theory of 'separation anxiety' and the prototype of this separation is the separation from the mother. According to Buddhism, we have invested our energies in various objects of pleasure, wealth and power and when we cling to them (*upādāna*) there is also a submerged fear of losing them. *Bhava-rāgānusaya* – the subliminal ego-oriented drive – may be activated on the fringe of losing a dearly valued object. There are healthy types of anxieties in daily life such as getting to work on time or paying bills, which are necessary for survival. However, excessive attachments to objects of power, nourished by envy, jealousy and conceits, when these attractions do not make sense, is the root of suffering (*dukkha*). Freud also refers to what he calls 'objectless anxiety', which is quite interesting from a Buddhist perspective. Rollo May in his penetrating study, *The Meaning of Anxiety*,[21] refers to an insightful analysis of objectless anxiety by Goldstein in which, according to him, in this context the relationship between the self and objects breaks down. Existentialist philosophers and the Venerable Nanavira, influenced by existentialism, say that the basic psychological issue here is the *ambiguity in the self and world relationship*. In the Middle Length Sayings there is an analysis of anxiety (*paritassanā*) into subjective anxiety regarding the non-existent and an objective anxiety regarding the non-existent. When a person has lost something, such as gold, they grieve that something that belonged to them is no more, lament about it and fall into disillusionment. They could also think of something they were about to get, but missed due to some cause or other. This is referred to as anxiety about something objective. The eternalist who believes that the self will remain an everlasting entity hears the doctrine of the Buddha, the path leading to *nibbāna* and he becomes frightened and thinks, 'I will surely be annihilated, I will surely be destroyed, I will surely not be'.[22] This is referred to as anxiety regarding something that does not exist. While there are interesting points of intersection between the Freudian and Buddhist perspectives on anxiety, there are also deeper existential intersections between the Buddhist and existential perspectives. From a clinical and therapeutic standpoint, depending on clients and their needs, these different perspectives may be contextualised.

Conflicts and the Religious Life

In the way that householders have joy and grief, recluses also have movements of grief and joy, but at a higher level. There are 36 emotions, composed of six each of household, and renunciation joys; household and renunciation griefs; and household and renunciation equanimities.[23] What this analysis indicates is that the life of renunciation has its own types of conflicts, fears and anxieties and mindful attention need to be developed for the emergence of a healthy conscience (*hiri-ottappa*), which is distinctively different from restlessness and worry (*uddhacca-kukkucca*).

The Venerable Nyanaponika cites ways of converting negative emotions to positive transformations: this method has been discussed in Chapter 5 on 'emotions'. He says that we should not throw away our fears, anxieties and feelings of guilt, as with a little magic they could be converted into positive emotions of strength and balance. The Buddha used such counselling techniques, for instance, excessive use of energy may be counter-productive and create conflicts, and the right balance will avoid undue excitement or sluggishness. In the *Simile of the Lute*,[24] the Buddha gives advice to the Venerable Soṇa to follow his practice as a former musician: the strings in the lute should not be too loose or too tight, and Soṇa has to strike a balance, which is the balance between over-persistence and sluggishness (see Chapter 8). It is also said that the best way to keep calm and avoid any turbulence is to first use the strength of one's own conscience (*attādhipateyya*); if thoughts of sensuality and malice arise, a concern for what the world will think would act as a spur to vigilance (*lokādhipateyya*); if, however, one cannot be energetic and tends to be sluggish the respect for the dhamma should be an aid (*dhammādhipateyya*).

Social Dimensions of Conflicts

Today, we find it difficult to extricate ourselves from the tensions and conflicts in the society in which we live, and there is a great deal of current interest in conflict resolution, reconciliation and dialogue across different groups. There have been number of studies and articles that recommend different facets of mindfulness practice to ease tensions and work towards reconciliation. Deborah Bowman's article 'Dispelling the Enemy Image with Clear and Compassionate Speech' is an excellent study, which focuses on mindfulness of speech and imagery used for non-violent communication;[25] John A. McConnell's *A Mindful Meditation*[26] gives good advice on using Buddhist doctrinal resources for peaceful mediation; and my own article 'Ethics for the Rough Road: Exploring New Dimensions for Inter-faith Ethics', presented at a Buddhist–Christian dialogue on 'Sharing Values', explores the idea of developing Buddhist contemplative ethics for contemporary times with tension, conflict and even chaos.[27]

Defence mechanisms

'Defence mechanisms serve as inner controls to restrain unacceptable impulses from being expressed in uncontrolled ways. They help individuals avoid condemnation for breaking familial and social rules, as well as avoid experiencing anxiety, guilt, and shame from their desire to break rules.'[28] However, while some defence mechanisms may offer help, immature development of these devices in repetitive, stereotyped, automatic thought patterns used to cope with anxiety may not help an individual to adapt to challenging situations. Defence mechanisms also help to keep conflicts outside awareness, and unexamined psychological disturbances also can be damaging.

Sigmund Freud made a detailed analysis of defence mechanisms: repression, aggression, projection, regression, compensation, denial, isolation, rationalisation, reaction formation and sublimation, out of which only 'sublimation' be considered as a healthy response. An analysis of defence mechanisms in relation to anger, in the context of the Buddha's advice to monks, can be found in Chapter 18.

7
Mental Health and Sickness

In one sense everyone is subject to 'mental disease' except the *arahants*, who have destroyed the *āsavas* (influxes). It is also said diseases are of two kinds, mental and physical, and that even if one can handle the physical diseases, mental diseases persist till one attains perfection.[1] The Buddha speaking to an old man in the last stages of life, advises him: 'Wherefore householder, thus you should train yourself: 'Though my body is sick, my mind shall not be sick."[2] In this context, we see the average person dominated by craving and subject to the delusions of the ego.

There is a second perspective on mental health where we can talk of a well-adjusted and balanced life as well as living a righteous life (*sama-cariya, dhamma-cariya*). We can also speak of degrees of good mental health. The idea that the abnormal is not restricted to a closely labelled group of neurotics and psychotics and that the average person is beset by some sorts of anxiety and stress has even been accepted by Sigmund Freud in certain contexts. In fact, Freud said that he was merely trying to transform 'hysteria into common unhappiness'.[3] Anthony Storr said that the process of analysis for everyone may be a 'way of life than a form of treatment'.[4]

Mary Jahoda, in her work *Current Concepts of Positive Mental Health* observes: 'It is reasonable to assume that such conflicts are universal, we are all sick in different degrees. Actually the difference between anyone and a psychotic may lie in the way he handles his conflicts and in the appearance or lack of certain symptoms.'[5] She mentions six points around which one could outline a concept of positive mental health.[6] While using this framework and accepting its relevance, a more Buddhist perspective on these features is presented below:

Reality orientation: in the Western context, 'The normal individ-ual is fairly realistic in his appraisal of his own reactions and abilities and what is going on in the world around him.' It is the middle ground between running away from a situation and over-valuing one's skills. In Buddhism there is a more critical and deeper encounter with the changing nature of things (*anicca*), their basic unsatisfactoriness *(dukkha)* and moving out of deep seated egoism *(anatta)*.

Attitude towards the self: along with a deep reality orientation, it becomes natural to move out of the psychological grip of narcis-sism. As Erich Fromm observes:

> Well-being is possible to the extent to which one has overcome one's narcissism; to the degree to which one is open, responsive, sensitive, awake, empty.... Well-being means, finally to drop one's ego, to give up greed... to experience one's self in the act of being, not in having, preserving, coveting, using.[7]

Self-knowledge: after breaking the metaphysical and psychological frontiers of the ego with the practice of mindfulness, the mind would lose any form of rigidity, and clarity and luminosity does emerge. In the moment-to-moment flow of life, mindfulness prac-tice would help the individual to note, identify and label passing states of reactive anger, envy, comparison with others (conceits, *mana)* and yearning for things one does not possess.

Voluntary control and autonomy: as the mind becomes pliable and open it becomes easy to break through automatic, conditioned and compulsive behaviour.

Ability to form sensitive and satisfying relations with others: instead of developing relations based on greed, power, domination, depen-dence and power, there emerges productive relations of care, friendship, trust and compassion.

Body–mind integration: such integration may be seen in ordinary life or in highly developed tranquility and insight meditation. Chap-ter 9 on the body–mind relationship explores these issues in greater detail. Developing on this chapter, Chapter 8 presents a Buddhist concept of mental balance and describes the features of positive mental health.

The Negative Factors – Generators of Mental Illness

Now that some of the basic perspectives on mental health have been outlined, it is useful to pay attention to the negative factors, those generating mental disease or, in other words, those that are obstacles to the attainment of mental health. The Buddhist term for this is 'hindrance' (nīvaraṇa) and following are the five hindrances:

1. Sense desire (*kāma-cchanda*)
2. Ill-will *(byāpāda)*
3. Sloth and torpor (*thīna-middha*).
4. Restlessness and worry (*uddhacca-kukkucca*)
5. Sceptical doubt (*vicikicchā*).

These are called hindrances because they obstruct the development of the mind (*bhāvanā*). According to Buddhist teachings there are two forms of meditation (*bhāvanā*): tranquillity meditation (*samatha-bhāvanā*) and insight meditation (*vipassanā-bhāvanā*). Tranquillity meditation leads to the complete concentration of the mind in the meditative absorptions (*jhāna*). For achieving these absorptions the overcoming of the five hindrances is a preliminary condition.

The five hindrances can be explained as follows. Sensual desire is like the water in a pond being tinted by a variety of intricate colours so that one cannot see the image of one's own face in the pond; ill-will is like boiling water, indicating a turbulent mind; sloth and torpor are as if the pond is covered by moss and vegetation, too dense to break through; restlessness is like a pond that is wind-swept, as with an agitated mind; and, finally, doubt is like muddy water, an obscure and cloudy mind. Their emergence has first to be noticed and recognised, after which they can be overcome by the development of mindfulness. Strong desires generate strong attachments and anxieties, while ill-will can bring about strong antagonism, discontent and even depression; sloth and torpor means a mind that lacks zest, enthusiasm and energy and can succumb to weariness and boredom; and restlessness creates an agitated mind, swinging from greed to aversion and attachment to discontent. Doubt blocks directional movement and clarity of purpose. While these five can be considered as roadblocks to spiritual development and mental health, they also provide structurally the basic ground that creates different types of mental conflicts and pathology. One very crucial technique recommended by the Buddha is to maintain a balance among one's resources for good meditation as, for instance, faith, wisdom, mindfulness, energy and concentration. This concept of balance is discussed in detail in Chapter 8 on mental well-being: Chapters 7 and 8 should be read together to be understood fully.

There are different kinds of antidotes recommended by the Buddha for these hindrances, and they provide best advice for anyone wishing to integrate meditation practice and routine life. As recommendations for dealing with sense desires, they include sense restraint, meditation on impure objects for lustful personalities, moderation in eating, noble friendship (*kalyāṇa-mitta*) and engaging in suitable conversation and avoiding useless gossip. Ill-will can be handled by meditation on loving kindness and reflection on the doctrine of *kamma*, as indignation and anger at the universe, people or symbols will not help a person through difficult times, even if there is real injustice; and patience, forgiveness and resilience help people to convert in the words of Carl Jung, 'brass into gold'. Laziness and sluggishness may be overcome by simple dietary rules, changes of postures, open-air walking mindfully done and, also, the perception of light as a meditation exercise with a high degree of concentration. A stirring (*saṃvega*) by the tragic facets of death and suffering can break through sloth and torpor. Reflection on the noble qualities of the *Buddha*, *Dhamma* and *Saṅgha* also provides a way towards trust and confidence in our *saṃsāric* journey (the cycle of births and death). Doubt has to be overcome by right understanding and confidence and trust in the path advocated by the Buddha.

The final recommendation is to organise our lives according to mindful living and to practice meditation: the formal presentation of this is given in two sermons, the *Ānāpānasati Sutta* and the *Satipaṭṭhāna Sutta*. Reference to these sermons will be found in Chapters 13 and 14 on Buddhist counselling.

The place of mindfulness of feeling and the management of human emotions is central for issues in mental health and Chapter 5 on emotions will, in some way, supplement the discussion in this chapter. Chapter 8 will discuss positive conceptions of mental health, especially the recent positive psychology movement of Martin Seligman.

8
Mental Well-being

In Chapter 7 we looked at the Buddhist concept of mental health and sickness; this chapter attempts to look at the positive concepts of well-being in the light of the 'bridge building between Buddhism and western psychology' taking place in the contemporary setting. A movement has emerged in recent times pioneered by M. Seligman, former President of the American Psychological Association, described as the search for positive qualities for developing mental well-being and a critique of the exclusive focus on pathology, which was:

> Clinical psychology has focused primarily on the diagnosis and treatment of mental disease, and only recently has scientific attention turned to understanding and cultivating positive mental health. The Buddhist tradition, on the other hand, has focused for over 2,500 years on cultivating exceptional states of mental well-being as well as identifying and treating psychological problems.[1]

In an attempt to build bridges between Buddhism and Western psychology Wallace and Shapiro focus on four aspects of mental well-being. In Chapter 5, I have cited the importance of the *cognitive, motivational/conative* level (including both desires and volitional activity), the *affective* or the emotional level as well as a focus on the *attentional* level in meditative experience. I shall explore these dimensions in relation to the Buddhist ideal of well-being and mental balance. Lack of mental balance caused by craving, grasping and obsessions condition a great deal of human suffering, and it is man's innermost mind that we need to understand, and to some extent, the external social environment that contributes to human discontent. Compared with the time in which the Buddha lived, today, the world is dominated by materialistic values, hedonistic pleasures, consumerism and 'status anxiety', all of which make a major contribution to the generation of human discontent. The Buddha has presented an ethics and life-style for the householder and a more stringent one for the monks – something that may be described in modern terms as a 'sustainable life style'.[2]

Both the causes of mental imbalance and the presence of healthy well-being will be examined in this chapter in relation to the four dimensions in Buddhist psychology. An important Buddhist value in relation to all these dimensions is the Buddhist ideal of equanimity or equipoise, which is embodied in the Buddhist concept of *upekkhā*. The Buddha tells Venerable Soṇa that to be skilful in his practice he has to strike the right balance between generating excessive energy and sluggishness, as over-roused persistence leads to restlessness and overly slack practice leads to lassitude. Venerable Soṇa was in his early life a musician, and the Buddha says that in playing the lute the strings should not be either too tight nor too loose, and it is this musical analogy that the Buddha recommends to Soṇa as a monk. Basically, at different levels of Buddhist practice, of monk and householder, lack of balance may be at the root of the suffering found in routine secular life and the life of the sage or monk.

The idea of balance has to be first explored in relation to the conative side of behaviour, as intentions and volitional activity have a prior place: 'If one does not develop conative balance – a reality-based range of desires and aspirations oriented towards oneself and others' happiness – then there will be little or no incentive to try to balance one's attentional, cognitive and affective faculties.'[3] The Buddha has, in no uncertain terms, described the domination of the drive for the sensory-stimulus-based pleasures (*kāma-taṇhā*) in ordinary worldlings, as well as a strong egoistic orientation (*bhava-taṇhā*), thus grasping things that ultimately do not bring contentment and harmony in our lives. As will be demonstrated in Chapter 19 on addictions, people fixate on obsessive addictions that bring them only momentary pleasures discounting long-lasting rewards, and these people consequently develop an apathetic loss of motivation to free themselves from this predicament and make a move towards lasting well-being. It has become evident that many alcoholics, as well as gambling addicts, while knowing that the net result of their addictions will be disastrous to their mental and physical health, 'knowingly court disaster'.[4] They do not take charge of their lives and, apart from their motivational apathy, their cognitive skills are clouded by the spell of immediate pleasures. On the affective or emotional side, it has been found in clinical studies that, even if there is some temporary recovery, negative emotions of anger, frustration, guilt, anxiety tension, depression, boredom and apprehension induce relapse. Practising mindfulness exercises daily and gradually developing a good attentional/mindfulness stance could keep addicts away from the temptations of a stimulus (a nearby bar), but their state of mind is very weak. Educating addicts back to normality, as I have accomplished in a case study, calls for rejuvenation of the motivational, cognitive, affective and attentional skills in the client.[5] In a recent study of the psychological foundations of well-being and happiness, it has been observed: 'Human beings are powerfully driven by systems of desires which become attached to material possessions and social status. The gap between these desires and what the world can yield is an enduring source of frustration.'[6] As the Buddha observed: 'To wish for something and not get it is suffering '(*yam p' iccham na labhati tam pi dukkham*).[7]

Some desires that cannot be satisfied may be given up, but there are other desires which emerge with continuous pressure for satisfaction, and the attempt to satisfy hedonic desires without any restraint or moral qualm is bound to end up in boredom. Soren Kierkegaard, the Danish philosopher, in his philosophical novel, *Either/Or* depicts the life of a pure pleasure-lover without any ethical qualms and shows how he collapses into total dissonance and emptiness.[8] It is this life-style that the Buddha described as extremely profitless – as the way of sensuality (*kāma-sukhallikānuyoga*) in contrast to the other extreme, the way of extreme asceticism – and so he recommended a middle path. When the desires of people move away from the ideals of psychological flourishing and distress, it is described as a conative deficit.[9] When people become obsessed and fixate on such goals, it is described as 'hyperactivity', and when people desire things that are detrimental to their and others' well-being, it is described as a dysfunctional life-style. Thus the Buddhist path aims at conative balance by getting people to follow worthwhile goals as described in the eightfold noble path.

Today, artificial life-styles, fed by pretensions and false social values, are wrecking the well-being of families. As William James remarked: 'To give up pretensions is, as "blessed a relief" as to get them gratified. There is a strange lightness in the heart when one's nothingness is accepted on good faith'.[10] When one reflects on the transitory nature of hedonic pleasures and how these generate a basic dissonance, as the Buddha and Kierkegaard demonstrate, one sees the value of a refined form of contentment. In the words of Devall,[11] Buddhism advocates a life 'simple in means but rich in ends'. The harmful effects of conative deficits, hyperactivity, dysfunction and imbalance, as developed by Wallace and

Shapiro,may be applied to the cognitive, affective and attentional level. However, this analysis will not be explored in a detailed manner in this chapter but we will bring out some of the positive and negative aspects in relation to 'emotional balance'.

The cognitive level is related to our thinking and perception patterns as described in earlier chapters. In Chapter 5 on emotions, I mentioned the deep-rooted cognitive distortions or delusions basically emerging from our egocentric ways of viewing the world and other people. I also referred to the (*Vitakka-saṇṭhāna Sutta*) forms of unwholesome thought patterns that can be handled by skilful means. It is by the positive factors of developing the attentional factors, through the practice of regular mindfulness practice, that some clarity may be brought to refine the ways we discern the world. When mindfulness is sustained and voluntary attention continually focused on a familiar object without forgetfulness and distraction, then this method becomes a part of a regular routine and the grip of false cognitive distortions is loosened and a sense of refinement enters the way we see things, how we motivate to carry out or refrain from certain actions, and the way we feel and manage our emotions. The development of self-knowledge especially through what is described as 'meta-attention' is a central resource for developing our well-being and mental balance.

Emotions, Well-being and Emotional Intelligence

Emotions provide the finest clues to the causes of psychological unrest as well as well-being, because an emotion is made of thoughts, desires, intentions, physiological arousal and attentional factors. In my practice as a professional counsellor, I have developed a mindfulness-based emotion-focused therapy. A number of Buddhist discourses, including the *Bahu-vedanīya Sutta* and the *Cūḷa-vedalla Sutta*, stand out as a type of charter for exploring the nature of the affective dimension, of feelings and emotions. However, it is necessary to examine in detail how mindfulness practice may lead to a kind of 'intelligence' that generates tools for intelligent and constructive living. As mindfulness practice has been associated with a spiritual quest, it took some time for people to understand the role of mindfulness practice in generating what is now referred to as 'emotional intelligence'.

Living in today's world, where rationality and technology in the service of solving problems dominate, running throughout schools and university, there is hardly any time left for an encounter with emotions. The recent interest in emotional intelligence for professionals is an attempt to develop a class of emotionally intelligent professionals, but it comes too late in life. The public space for emotions is different from the personal space. Of course, education of the emotions provides a dimension to bring a human element into our social and economic issues. While Goleman's popular work, *Emotional Intelligence*[12] was in what may be called our public space, there emerged a kind of infectious interest in what he called EQ (Emotional Quotient, as opposed to IQ, Intelligence Quotient), but the issue about the role of mindfulness in emotional intelligence was not clearly explained by Goleman. A philosopher critic, E.M. Adams, was critical of the point, that *the mere awareness of feelings and impulses (and those of others) could make a person rational.*[13] He also remarked that intelligence is a cognitive matter involving comprehension and critical judgment; issues pertaining to the emotions need to be examined within an epistemological or educational framework rather than a therapeutic one. He also said that the tendency to bring about emotional transformation by a treatment or causal approach, rather than rational criticism or correction, is questionable.

I have written an article critically responding to all the questions raised by Adams in a chapter of a book: 'Ethics, Work and the Emotionally Intelligent Executive'[14] and Daniel Goleman was gracious enough not merely to respond positively to my article but also send me a book on leadership. Goleman, in defining his first component of EQ, says that 'My usage of self-awareness refers to a self-reflective, introspective attention to one's experience, sometimes called *mindfulness*'[15] but he does not develop this theme in detail. Adams did not understand how mindfulness practice enhances emotional sensibility. A decade of research in a new psychological discipline that builds bridges between Buddhist and Western psychology, research into mindfulness techniques in neurology, and an emerging group of mindfulness-based therapies, provide tangible answers to the questions raised by Adams.

1. Both in the work of the philosopher Ronald de Soysa and the neurologis Antonio Damasio,[16] the thesis unfolds that rather than emotions being sand in the machinery of action, they can actually promote rational behaviour in situations of indeterminacy. Writing about decision-making, Elster says:

> Their argument is not – or not only – that a person without emotions would make irrational decisions. They also claim...that in many

situations this person would make no decision at all or delay it for a long time, and that such abstention or procrastination could be irrational.[17]

Emotions provide a kind of 'salience' for controlling our beliefs and perception. While emotional flatness leads to indecisiveness, positive emotions can play a role in rational decision-making. The cognitive theories of emotions do provide a good focus for the rational criticism of emotions. However, an emotion is composed of feelings, desires, intentions, physiological arousal, and it is only a contemplative practice such as mindfulness that could penetrate all these facets of an emotion.

2. Adam's claim in rejecting a therapeutic approach to problems in favour of an 'educational approach' is flawed. Today, 'contemplative education' using mindfulness and related techniques has entered mainstream education in countries such as the USA. However, in the past, contemplative education has been an important ingredient of education in the East. A contemplative approach to living helps us to see the moment-to-moment flow of life with a sense of majesty and clinical sacredness. Today, in looking at ethics as a part of education, there is an attempt to diversify the methods of teaching beyond the use of logic and analytic techniques. The replacement of genuine moral reflection by procedures and protocols finally paralyses people's capacity for moral reflection. Moral life requires the personal facing of genuine moral difficulty, disorder and conflicts. In developing a moral sensibility and character, both reason and emotions have roles to play in education. In addition to critical analysis, the method of 'deep listening' helps to communicate different points of view in dialogues (political, moral and religious), and transform a listener's viewpoint, and thus this method is described as 'transformative dialogue'. Thus it is not a process of cementing any intellectual conviction but a transformation and perception of others.

3. Adams attempts to degrade the therapeutic approach – the attempt to bring about emotional transformation by a treatment or causal approach rather than rational criticism. In recent times emerging mindfulness-based therapies, which are examined in Chapter 13, provide a practical answer to Adams' doubts about the value of a therapeutic/contemplative approach for the transformation. I have discussed in detail, elsewhere, the value of contemplative education (see,

Chapter 11). There are many programmes devoted to the mindfulness path to human well-being and happiness: mindfulness-based stress reduction, dialectical behaviour therapy, acceptance and commitment therapy and mindfulness-based cognitive therapy. Cultivating emotional balance (CEB), developed by Ekman and Wallace was started as an educational venture and comes closer to the focus on emotions in this book, as well my own development of mindfulness-based emotion-focused therapy.[18,19] Training and practice, drawn from contemplative science, is also a core feature of CEB. Contemplative practice can lead to well-being through the alleviation of tensions and anxieties.

Martha Nusbaum says:

> They saw the philosopher as a compassionate physician whose arts could heal many pervasive types of suffering. They practice philosophy not as a detached intellectual technique dedicated to the display of cleverness but an immersed and worldly art of grappling with misery. They focused their attention, in consequence, on issues of daily and human significance – the fear of death, love and sexuality, anger and aggression – issues that are sometimes avoided as embarrassingly messy and personal by the more detached varieties of philosophy.[20]

What Nussbaum said of the Stoics and the Epicureans is also true of the Hindu, Buddhist, Chinese and Japanese sages. Zen Buddhism uses 'paradoxes' to stimulate the minds of those who have hard-line, and often dogmatic, beliefs, especially those who consider 'logic' as the tool for arriving at a 'truth'. It is a technique especially directed to those with conceits about their scholarship without any humility. Thus, in the context of the present chapter on emotional balance it has to be emphasised that emotional or affective balance has an integral relationship with cognitive balance, as well as conative balance and, most importantly, attentional balance. This revolution in balance and harmony offers a complete answer to Adams' doubts about emotions and the contemplative path.

According to the scheme devised by Wallace and Shapiro,[21] affective balance involves freedom from emotional vacillation, apathy and inappropriate emotions. In fact, as stated earlier by Ronald de Soysa, positive emotions avoid indeterminacy because they have a sense of salience and focus. Affective apathy refers to emotional deadness, and hyperactivity involves excessive elation and depression, hope and fear, infatuation and aversion.

Five Dimensions of Equanimity and Well-being in Buddhist Texts

The term 'equanimity'(*upekkhā*) is used in several contexts in the discourses of the Buddha, and it is necessary to understand a few of these that, in different ways, centre on the notion of balance and equipoise.

1. First, it is used as a neutral feeling different from pleasurable and painful feelings.

2. Secondly, it is used to mean even-mindedness in the face of success and loss, praise and blame and referred to as the eight vicissitudes of life: 'Loss and gain, disrepute and fame, blame and praise pain and pleasure are the eight vicissitudes of life.'[22].

3. Thirdly, there is the equanimity that emerges within the spectrum of meditative states, of which there are four emerging states of absorption described by the Pāli term *jhāna*. This state of equanimity is described as the equanimity of purity (*parisuddhi-upekkhā*). In the first three absorptions, even-mindedness is needed to balance four factors, initial investigation of the object (*vitakka*) which in this context is the breath and sustained observation, keeping the mind anchored (*vicāra*), pleasurable interest (*pīti*) and bliss (*sukha*). The culminating fourth state is a state of equanimity followed by the feeling of equanimity. Needless to say, the happiness and equanimity that emerges in these states of absorption are of a different level.

4. The fourth context in which the term equanimity is used is one of the most well-known practices – the practice of the four sublime states of loving kindness (*mettā*), compassion *(karuṇā)*, appreciative joy (*muditā*) and equanimity (*upekkhā*). As this sublime state of equanimity is a combination of even-mindedness and other mental factors, this background helps a person to treat friend and foe alike in a neutral way. Living at a time of tsunamis, bushfires, earthquakes and floods, we need some 'breaks' to free us from 'compassion panic'. Equanimity helps us to reflect that while we do sympathise with those suffering, this is a sign of the world order, and thus we should contexualise our kindness and compassion. Equanimity also has its own pitfalls, degenerating into blank indifference. Equanimity has to be a vigilant state of mind and backed with insightful understanding of the predicament of people suffering. Nyanaponika Thera says that equanimity is the crown and culmination of the other three sublime states.

5. Equanimity (*upekkhā*) is one of the seven factors of enlightenment and also the crowning factor with investigation (*dhamma-vicaya*), bodily and mental persistence (*viriya*), rapture (*pīti*), bodily and mental serenity (*passaddhi*), concentration (*samādhi*) and equanimity (*upekkhā*). When all six factors are working in harmony, this feature will be an important dimension of equanimity. The seven factors of enlightenment provide a central path for a meditator and, from my personal understanding, I feel that this path is, with regular practice, certainly within the reach of serious meditators. What you achieve depends on regular sustained practice with the guidance of a teacher.

Metaphors of Equanimity on Earth, Water, Fire and Wind

Just as when people throw what is clean or unclean on the earth – feces, urine, saliva, pus or blood – the earth is not horrified, humiliated or disgusted by it; in the same way, when you are developing meditation in tune with the earth, agreeable and disagreeable sensory impressions that have arisen will not stay in charge of your mind.

Just as when people wash what is clean or unclean in water – feces, urine, saliva, pus or blood – the water is not horrified, humiliated or disgusted by it,; in the same way, when you are developing meditation in tune with water, agreeable and disagreeable sensory impressions will not stay in charge of your mind.

Just as when fire burns what is clean or unclean – feces, urine, saliva, pus or blood – it is not horrified, humiliated or disgusted by it; in the same way, when you are developing meditation in tune with fire, agreeable and disagreeable sensory impressions will not stay in charge of your mind.

Just as when the wind blows what is clean or unclean – feces, urine, saliva pus,or blood – the wind is not horrified, humiliated or disgusted by it; in the same way, when you are developing meditation in tune with the wind, agreeable and disagreeable sensory impressions will not stay in charge of your mind.[23]

We shall conclude these different metaphors with a more general one, which is described as the metaphor of the acrobat that illuminates a way of resolving or balancing the dichotomy between working for one's own interest and that of others. A bamboo acrobat having erected a bamboo pole requests his assistant to climb the bamboo pole and stand on his shoulders and then tells his assistant, 'Now watch after me and I will look after you.' Then the assistant says, 'That is not enough – 'I will look after myself and you look after yourself.' The Buddha draws an important insight from this context, the best way to protect others is first to protect oneself, and when others protect themselves that also protects oneself.

Buddhism, medicine and Traditional Ayurveda: The Humoral Theory of Imbalance

The subject of imbalance has also been associated with the imbalance of the four humours in the early history of medicine, especially Greek medicine, and in the Ayurveda tradition in India, which later found a growing interest in Sri Lanka. In the Greek tradition, the four humours were identified as black bile, yellow bile, phlegm and blood, and they were linked to temperamental differences. There have been some interesting discussions of similarities between the Buddhist and the Ayurvedic perspectives on the imbalance of the humours: afflictions due to bile, phlegm and wind springing from conflict of humours in the context of a sermon by the Buddha, the Girimānanda Sutta. (Venerable Girimānanda was gravely ill and the Buddha requested Ānanda to communicate the contents of the Sutta.)

> The body is the source of much pain and many dangers; for all sorts of ailments arise in the body – and afflictions due to bile, due to phlegm, due to the wind, spring from conflict of humours, produced by change of climate, by unaccustomed activity, by violence, by kamma results; and heat, hunger, thirst, excrement and urine.[24]

An elaboration of a theme to develop a medicine inspired by Buddhism and Ayurveda is the subject of a book by Gunapala Dharmasiri.[25]

Neurology and Emotional Balance: 'Accelerator' and 'Brakes' Function of the Brain

I shall conclude this chapter by mentioning that, according to current research in neurology, the balance between emotion arousal and emotion regulation may be conceptualised as the relation between the subcortical limbic amygdala and the prefrontal cortex.[26] It is important to mention that following this observation, Daniel J. Siegel confirms that mindful awareness directly influences the 'non-reactivity' of consciousness' by altering the connection between the prefrontal cortex and the limbic zones.[27] Thus the prefrontal area is able both to assess the state of arousal and as well as modulate their firing. Here we see that the integrative prefrontal areas can coordinate and balance limbic firing so that life can have meaning and emotional richness, but not excessive firing, where life becomes chaotic, or too little, where life becomes dulled and depressing. In fact, in teaching meditation parallel concepts are addressed as excitement and dullness.[28] Siegel also says that that a further development would be the ability to pause before an action and consider the various options that are most important before we respond, which is 'response flexibility'. In conclusion, it may be said that experienced meditators develop the *ideal affective style*, the capacity to regulate negative emotions and resilience in maintaining high levels of positive affect and well-being in the face of adversity.

9
Mind–Body Relationship and Buddhist Contextualism

> Sound is not a thing that dwells inside the conch-shell and comes from time to time, but due to both, the conch shell and the man that blows it, sound comes to arise. Just so due to the presence of vitality, heat and consciousness, the body may execute acts of going, standing, sitting, and lying down, and the five sense organs and the mind may perform various functions.[1]

The Buddha denies the existence of any permanent entity, either physical or mental. He considers the human person as a psycho-physical complex. There is also no attempt to reduce the mental into the physical, or vice versa. The mind and body have a conditioned existence and they emerge within the dynamic continuum of a variety of relations. Basically, the Buddhist position is not dualistic or monistic (whether it is the materialistic or the idealistic type). Within this framework, the discourses of the Buddha make relative distinctions between the 'physical' and the 'mental', as when the Buddha refers to feelings which are mental or physical. The Buddha presents a contextual discourse regarding the mind and body relationship, discouraging any excessive entanglements in converting this into a metaphysical issue. In a deeper sense, the question of whether the mind is identical with the body or they are independent of each other is a question that the Buddha left aside, as an undetermined question.

We shall first deal with the metaphysical issue pertaining to the mind–body issue, then with the ethical facets of the issue, which has led to a fair amount of distortion of the Buddhist position, and finally present the insights of Buddhist experientialism.

Metaphysical Issues: 'Just as friends, two bundles of reeds were to stand, one supporting the other, even so consciousness is

93

dependent on name-and-form and name-and-form is dependent on consciousness... But friends if one of these bundles of reeds is drawn out, the other would fall down, and if the latter is drawn out the former one will fall down'.[2] Name-and-form have two important usages: name-and-form is a translation of the Pāli *nāma* and *rūpa*, and in the first context refers to the five aggregates of feeling, perception, dispositions, consciousness and the body. In the second context, which is relevant to the discussion that follows, name-and-form are the fourth link in the wheel of dependent origination. In this context, they arise together and cease together. Their relationship is *reciprocal*, they depend upon each other and emerge simultaneously and cease simultaneously. In general, the Buddha did not push questions like the body–mind issue towards ultimate answers but followed the call of a practical and pragmatic necessity. Out of the two questions, the second is important as it indicates how, through the aggregates of feeling, perception and dispositions, one becomes conscious of matter. In the context of dependent origination, matter, feeling, perception and dispositions may be rendered as name and matter (*nāma-rūpa*). And having any experience would involve name-and-matter as well as consciousness (*nāma-rūpa saha viññāṇa*). Matter may be considered as internal (*ajjhattika*) and external (*bāhira*).In our experience we cognise both, the internal in the form of 'this body of mine', and the external as 'the tree I see outside'. Thus, the most important relationships are made of the linkages of name-and-matter plus consciousness. They arise together and cease together. That is the central message of the context cited above, from the description of the dependent origination links. They are reciprocal, depend upon each other and they also emerge simultaneously. Name and matter are dependent on consciousness and consciousness is dependent on name and matter.

As we understand the point about reciprocity, dependence and simultaneous origin and cessation, it becomes easy to free ourselves from the traps of ontology like dualism and monism. This point is again emphasised in the anti-ontologising context of practicing meditation, where through absorbing experience we discern the phenomenal nature of experience and the 'designation' like nature of terms like feeling and the body. Thus, Buddhist pragmatism has a deeper contextual basis. When, for instance, we understand the synthetic nature of the perceptual process, we also see the use of terms as a linguistic device restricted to certain contexts.

The ethical issues arise due to two perspectives on the body which again need to be contextualised. In certain contexts, the Buddha had a focus on the consequences that befall a person with an excessive attachment to the body. In such contexts the body was symbolic of sensuality and deliverance is seen as getting out of the spell of the body. There are many metaphors tied to this perspective: there is a reference to the body as a wound, sore, and a fragile jar and so on. Meditation on disgust, death and sickness would focus on the fragility of the body. In other contexts, there is a different attitude: in condemning suicide, extreme asceticism was considered as a futile endeavour. The Buddha himself recognises the middle path he recommended without falling in the way pure sensuality and extreme asceticism. He also says that liberation is not achieved by matted hair, starvation, nakedness and living in a degrading environment. When the Buddha advocates restraint of body, speech and thought he also emphasises composure, erect physical posture, mindfulness of standing, sitting and walking. In dealing with asceticism, the Buddha had a more positive notion of the body. Balance and harmony of body and mind are often emphasised. Also, in insight meditation, the body plays a prominent role, especially in 'knowing the body through the experience of the body'.

The perspective of Buddhist experientialism through mindfulness practice also gives insight into the body–mind relationship. The Buddha says that in the final analysis, book learning (*sutamaya*) and intellectual knowledge (*cintāmaya*) have limited scope compared with experiential knowledge (*bhāvanāmaya*).

Buddhist Experientialism

The Buddhist practice of mindfulness has four divisions: body, feelings, thoughts and mental objects. In the context of meditation the body is unique, as mindfulness of the body is the starting point. This starts with a focus on breathing, and after systematic practice one may experience bodily rapture and the joy that comes with it. When you shift to feelings, one enters the area of the mind, and feelings are interesting as they may be linked to the body, mind or mind–body. As you move into the mindfulness of bodily postures like sitting, walking, and standing, and then extend this to the whole body, and practice these exercises in a systematic way, you could guess when you are in an angry mood by the way your lips move, closing your fist or the expression on your face. When you are calm and feel a sense of collectedness, breathing patterns are different. Thus, we enter a whole universe of body–mind discourse, which takes more specific forms in the experience of anger, grief or joy. The *Discourse on the Body*, in the *Middle Length Sayings*,[3] is a kind of charter for experientialism and the body–mind relationship. Current research on emotion studies presented in Chapter 5 helps the reader to see in greater detail the nature of body and mind in the experience of emotions.

Concluding Thoughts from East and West

Herbert Guenther renowned expert in Tibetan Buddhism says:

> What we call 'body' and 'mind' are mere abstractions from an identity of experience that cannot be reduced to the one or the other abstraction, nor can it be hypostatised into some sort of thing without falsifying its very nature.[4]

> Is it 'I' who draw the bow, or is it the bow that draws me into the state of highest tension? Do 'I' hit the goal, or does the goal hit me? Is it spiritual when it is seen by the eyes of the body, and corporeal when seen by the eyes of the spirit – or both or neither? Bow, arrow, goal and ego, all melt into one another, so that I can no longer separate them. And even the need to separate has gone. For as soon as I take the bow and shoot, everything becomes clear and straight forward and so ridiculously simple.[5]

John R. Searle says that the vocabulary that the West has inherited is based on the Cartesian dualistic tradition and describing the issue of mind and body in terms of apparent opposition, like mental verses physical, spirit versus matter, mentalism versus materialism.

> Consciousness is a mental, and therefore physical property, property of the brain in the sense in which liquidity is a property of molecules. The fact that a property is physical does not deny that it is mental.[6]

10
Towards a Holistic Psychology: Blending Thinking and Feeling

Hysterics behave as if anatomy did not exist

(Sigmund Freud)

I now proceed to urge the vital point of my whole theory, which is this: If we fancy some strong emotion and then try to abstract from our consciousness of it all the characteristics of bodily systems, we find we have nothing left behind, no 'mind-stuff' out of which the emotion could be constituted, and that a cold and neutral state of intellectual perception is all that remains

(William James)

Just as friends, two bundles of reed were to stand one supporting the other, even so consciousness is dependent on name and form (physical and mental phenomena) and name and form on consciousness. If friend, I were to pull towards me one of those sheaves of reed, the other would fall.

(Kindred Sayings, II, 114)

We examined the relationship between perception (*saññā*) and thinking (*vitakka*) in Chapter 3, in this chapter we are examining the very important relationship between thinking and feeling (*vedanā*). The release of a recent work, *Thinking About Feeling*[1] by Robert Solomon, is a significant landmark in the current philosophy of mind and emotion studies. Solomon was a pioneer in emotion studies and continued to write with freshness and vitality until his untimely death. A memorial volume to honour him, entitled *Passion, Death and Spirituality* (ed. K. Higgins and D. Sherman) was released by Springer in July 2012. In *Thinking About Feeling* he assembled together some of the finest contributions to emotion studies. This chapter, while working on the themes that emerge from this book on thinking and feeling, offers a Buddhist perspective on the central issues of *Thinking About Feeling* – the growing chasm among cognitive theories, with a focus on thoughts and appraisals, and the physiological arousal theories, with a focus on the body and feelings. John Deigh, who wrote the first chapter in the book, describes a basic conflict in emotion theories, and says that a major issue in emotion studies is to reconcile what may be described as the 'ideogenic' view of Freud with the 'somatogenic' view of James. He writes, 'James' ideas are the source of the view that one can fruitfully study emotions by studying the neurophysiological processes that occur with experience of them. He identified them with feelings.[2] Deigh also says, 'Though Freud often described emotions as flows of energy, his view of them as transmitters of meaning and purpose was nonetheless implicit in his notion of an unconscious mind and the way that he used this notion to make sense of his feelings, behaviour, and physiological maladies that seems otherwise inexplicable.[3]

In the previous chapter, we discerned one facet of the holistic outlook of Buddhist psychology by examining the mind–body relationship. Also closely related to the holistic outlook in Buddhist psychology is the relationship between thinking and feeling. In addition to working on the current trends in emotion studies in the West, my later professional work in counselling, described in detail in Part II of this book, brought me into contact with the use of multi-model therapies used in counselling, and these were able to cross the theoretical boundaries in emotion studies and blend physiologically oriented theories of emotions with cognitive therapies. Using mindfulness-based emotion-focused therapy (EFT), I was able to see these divergent approaches as merely contrasting perspectives, rather than conflicting theories. The discourses of the Buddha offer a 'holistic conception of emotions', in the same way that they offer a holistic perspective on the mind–body relationship discussed in Chapter 9. As much as this holistic perspective is of importance in emotion studies, it is of equal importance in EFT, as in counselling we deal with peoples real life problems.

Solomon himself, in discussing 'emotions, thoughts and feelings', shows a certain amount of flexibility, which perhaps helps us to reconcile the divergence in emotion theories:

> But what led me to an increasing concern about both the role of the body and the nature and role of bodily feelings in emotion was the suspicion that my judgment theory had been cut too thin, that in the pursuit of an alternative to the feeling theory I had too far

veered in the other direction. I am now coming to appreciate that accounting for the bodily feelings (not just sensations) in emotion is not a secondary concern and not independent of appreciating the essential role of the body in emotional experience.[4]

He also qualifies the above statement by saying that he is not referring to any concern with neurology but with basic phenomenological experience. I find this statement quite interesting. There has been some remarkable work on neurology and emotions, as in the work of Candace Pert,[5] to be referred to in the course of this book, and Richard Davidson's 'neuroplasticity thesis' validating the impact of meditation on developing positive emotions.[6] These discoveries certainly show the role of meditation in developing a healthy emotional outlook in a new light, but the Buddha himself did not refer to any neurological insights, and, of course, the science of neurology did not exist twenty-six centuries ago. The Buddha's focus was the phenomenology of experience, both within and outside meditation experience, in developing self-knowledge in daily life. Solomon also observes that short term emotions, such as fear, anger and disgust, involve characteristic bodily changes, and that these bodily changes can be felt and one could still make mistakes in identifying these symptoms with a particular emotion.[7] Here again, in meditation practice, breathing stands on the threshold between voluntary and involuntary function, and it offers a pathway to extend the scope of conscious control to the body and also discern how the mind interprets the bodily changes as fear or excitement. Focusing on the fundamental pulsations of the body during meditation is particularly fruitful.[8] While these bodily changes in emotional experience are important, Buddhism does not fully support William James, who holds that emotions are perceptions (conscious or unconscious) of patterned changes in the body.

The Emotion Concept in Buddhist Psychology

An emotion in the context of Buddhism is a construction, an interactive complex of a construct emerging within a causal network. The best way to understand the complex is to first look at the five aggregates that go to make up a person. As a meditator's mindfulness becomes sharper and clearer, the meditator learns to distinguish the five aggregates: matter or physical form (*rūpa*); feeling (*vedanā*), the affective tone of experience, painful, pleasant and neutral; perception (*saññā*), the factor responsible for noting, distinguishing and recognition; volition (*saṅkhāra*), the intentional facet of mental activity; and consciousness (*viññāna*), basic awareness operating through the senses. Thus, within the five aggregates we discern the three dimensions of the cognitive, affective and conative or volitional facets of human consciousness, as well as the body. It is necessary to understand the usage of the term feeling/*vedanā* in Buddhism, as this term refers to pleasant, painful and neutral feelings, which only get converted into an emotion with the additional factors of thoughts, appraisals and intentions. In short, the cognitive, affective (feelings) and the volitional (conative) dimensions go together to make up an emotion, along with physiological arousal: 'It should be made clear that, in Buddhist psychology, "feeling" (Pali: *vedanā*) is the bare sensation noted pleasant, unpleasant (painful) and neutral (indifferent). Hence it should not be confused with emotions, which, though arising from basic feeling, adds to it likes and dislikes of varying intensity, as well as other thought processes'.[9]

In more detail, it may be said that emotions emerge as a joint product of perceptions, feelings, desires, beliefs, appraisals and physiological arousal. Also, cultural and social filters have an impact on the experience of emotions.[10] It is the aggregate of volitional formations that bring out the key concept of a person's responsibility to the emotions. Buddhist Suttas (sermons) also focus on the role of the 'ego' in the experience of certain emotions, especially in what are described as emotions of self-assessment, like conceit, pride, shame, jealousy and feelings of humiliation, whereas humility and generosity are self-effacing emotions (see Chapter 20 of this book).

Emotions and Intentionality

A crucial role is played by the intentional/volitional dimension of emotions, as the distinction between skilful and non-skilful emotions rests on whether the action was a product of intention/motive (*cetanā*), choice, freewill and responsibility. Though Buddhism accepts that there is a subliminal layer (*anusaya*) to anger, lust and conceit, this concept does not negate responsibility. Anger may lie as a dormant tendency; lie at the level of conscious thought processes; display in the form of speech or action. Cultivation of mindfulness helps restraint at both the conscious and subliminal levels. At this point the concept of 'character' also becomes important.

Out of the philosophers who have written widely on emotions, Robert Solomon is emphatic that intentions and responsibility are central to emotions: 'I also want to contend that we are not merely passive victims of our emotions but quite active in cultivating and constituting them.

In other words, we cannot just use our emotions as excuses for our bad behaviour'.[11] He also argues that emotions are not only intelligent but also purposive, in a surprisingly robust sense. They are sometimes, perhaps even often, strategies for getting along in the world.[12] Like Robert Solomon, psychologist James Averill also accepts in very clear terms the links between emotions and responsibility. He says that the word *passion* has been used for approximately two thousand years, and as the derivation from Greek *pathos* and Latin *pati* (to suffer) conveys, emotions came to be associated with passivity.[13] In ordinary language we speak of being 'gripped' and 'torn' by emotion: 'drowned by sorrow', 'driven by anger', 'plagued by remorse' or 'struck by Cupid's arrow' are good examples of this passivity. Solomon quite rightly says that often the management of emotions is compared to 'taming and caging of the wild beast'.[14] Averill says that the experience of passivity is an illusion, and this can be seen by widening the area of self-awareness.

In focusing on the importance of choice and responsibility, Solomon does not want to introduce the metaphysical notion of the 'will'. In fact, one may translate the Pāli term *saṅkhāra* in certain contexts as character. Concepts like trying, attempting, weighing, deciding, making a commitment and more spontaneous and natural responses a person makes – all these and similar concepts provide the surroundings for charting out issues related to the nature of emotions and responsibility.

It is strange that William James brought out a point about volition in his references to 'judgment, character and will', which sounds odd in terms of a purely physiologically oriented theory of emotions: 'The faculty of voluntarily bringing back a wandering attention, over and over again, is the very root of judgment, character and will'.[15] Commenting on this statement, Kabat-Zinn says:

> William James obviously didn't know about the practice of mindfulness when he penned this passage. But I am sure he would have been delighted to have discovered that there was indeed an education for improving the faculty of voluntarily bringing back a wandering attention over and over again. For this is exactly what Buddhist practitioners have developed into a fine art over a millennium, based on the Buddha's original teaching, and this art is replete with practical instructions for bringing this kind of self-education about.[16]

Opting for a Componential Theory of Emotions

In my professional counselling I used a kind of 'componential theory' of emotions, working with specific facets or components of an emotion.

For instance, in dealing with accumulated anger, mindfulness practice may be directed to automatic thought patterns and appraisals, as is now popular with mindfulness-based cognitive therapy, or the attention of the client may be directed to the body, the calming of breathing patterns and alertness to physiological signals. To cite an example where intention and purposeful activity is important, in addictions there will be a strong focus on regaining the client's ability to make choices, recover an active interest in their life and direct the course of that life in a purposeful manner. I was able to give equal importance to the cognitive, physiological bodily factors, as well as the motivational and volitional factors. Appraisals became very crucial, as Albert Ellis, the pioneer of cognitive therapy, says, what matters is not the event but how a person interprets the event. Buddhism presents a holistic concept of emotions, and this is greatly facilitated by the mind–body relationship which we discussed in Chapter 9. Briefly, the Buddhist position accepts that there can be feedback mechanisms by which the body can affect the mind and the mind can affect the body. The Buddha discourages people from going into unending metaphysical wrangles on the mind–body problem and leaves it as an 'undetermined question' whether absolute answers are pursued. But on pragmatic, practical and experiential grounds, he accepts a reciprocal relationship between mind and body. In accepting some kind of reciprocal relationship, he avoided any kind of Cartesian dualism, monism or reductive theories like epiphenomenalism. The body–mind relationship is compared to two bundles of reeds, one supporting the other.[17]

It is of great interest to note that in the context of meditation, the Buddha adopts an 'anti-ontologising' perspective, and he considers the 'mind' and 'body' as designations. This approach is a phenomenological and experiential approach; it may be verified in the practical context of counselling which fosters deep listening without forging one's interpretations, and which Freud described as 'evenly suspended attention'. For instance, to relate this point to my work as a therapist, when you work with a componential view of emotions you have the freedom to select what facets of emotions work and what is relevant. I have found this flexibility and openness, without any theoretical thrust, a wonderful way to work through the client's problems.

In the area of counselling, the Buddha's advice about the danger of having fixed views is relevant and useful. Furthermore, the Buddha emphasised the danger of falling into the rut of strong attachments to fixed views, and for him, contextual, pragmatic and practical perspectives are necessary. 'Arguments for argument's sake' is criticised in the

Kalaha-vivāda Sutta,[18] where the Buddha says that clinging on to one's views and holding on to them at any cost, particularly when views are presented in pairs, one being true and the other false, is the root of contention that may be fierce and aggressive. This perspective brings an important point about philosophical disputes: the importance of contextuality, not theoretical finality; that instead of the alternatives black or white, there may be a grey area, with light and dark shades; certain issues may have many sides instead of two sides. The value of these perspectives may be seen in the therapeutic context, where there is 'deep listening' without forging interpretations.

A useful guide when dealing with emotions is the use of the fourfold mindfulness techniques of the *Satipaṭṭhāna* with four frames of reference: body, feeling, mind and mental qualities.[19] Emotions do not have clear boundaries, and qualities found in some of the more basic emotions like fear, anger, sadness, joy and disgust are somewhat different from the complex emotions of jealousy, envy, conceit and shame. Even in the case of fear, anger and sadness, in addition to their physiological patterns, thoughts help us to distinguish them from each other. It is possible to agree with James to a great extent that, in the case of the more basic emotions, physiology gives the 'emotional quality' of the emotion, but it is also possible to accept the thesis that thought components and appraisals best help us to understand the individuation of emotions. Even if in the future there are new discoveries on the physiology and neurology of emotions, cognitive factors like thought and appraisals will remain among the elements that comprise the concept of an emotion.

As a recent study has indicated, while the Jamesian view of emotions will always raise its head from time to time, it is only one side of the equation in emotion studies, and what is needed is critical integration. The following point has been highlighted: it is necessary to distinguish between an emotion as an episodic emotional disturbance and a long-standing emotional attitude. A person's judgment may be clouded not only by distress and agitation of the moment, as for instance in grief, but also long-term resentment and jealousies. In the Buddhist context, these dispositional traits are also important.

The second point is that there is no emotion prototype, as the conceptual complexities vary from one emotion to another, such as fear of physical harm, grief and anger, to others such as hope, remorse, compassion and pride. It may also be observed that a great many experimental studies on emotions have been on animals, and the distinction between humans and animals may be lost.[20] As Bennett and Hacker point out, some emotions have characteristic somatic accomplishments, some are emotional perturbations with behavioural modifications and yet some are expressive reactions like facial grimaces and others are voluntary and done with a purpose.

As Gerald Myer[21] and Robert Gordon[22] have pointed out, James appears to have been careless in formulating his theory, or he may have thought that the sound of paradox (we cry because we are sad) is more effective in communicating a very special perspective on emotions. There are few examples from routine life that fit James's theory: for instance 'the scared to death feeling' we have when we suddenly miss a step in a long winding staircase or an elevator with considerable height. But to move from the position that the emotional quality of our consciousness is caused by bodily feelings to the view that our emotions are caused by bodily feelings is a long road indeed.

Even Paul Griffiths, who has written a kind of paradigm on the domination of the physiological-oriented emotions and what he calls the 'affect program', accepts that there are higher cognitive emotions, like guilt, envy and jealousy, which are not governed by affect programmes.[23] In the Buddhist texts it is clearly stated that 'thoughts are translated into the sensations of the body'.[24]

Studies Towards a Holistic Concept of Emotions: A Recent Map on the Mind–Body Relationship

Candace Pert's book *Molecules of Emotion* has important implications for plotting the mind–body relation in emotions. She says, 'Emotions might actually be the link between mind and body'.[25] Pert, who started as a microbiologist, is credited with the discovery of the opiate receptor and several other peptide receptors in the brain and the rest of the body. She first began working on the receptors of psychoactive drugs like opium, heroine, codeine and demerol. She upholds that there is a chemical factor in the brain, almost like a keyhole, that receives all these opiates, and calls it the opiate receptor. She began measuring these receptors, which ultimately led to the discovery that the brain makes its own morphine, and that in the emergence of emotional states there is a release of chemicals called endorphins. Her astounding discovery was that endorphins, and other chemicals like them, are not just in the brain, but also in the immune system, the endocrine system and throughout the body. These molecules are involved in *psychosomatic communication*. She came out with the notion that, 'the body is a second brain'. According to Pert, this discovery has led to the understanding that chemicals act as informational substances – messenger molecules distributing information throughout the organism.[26] The neuropeptides and the receptors, the biochemicals of emotions, are messengers carrying information to link the major systems of the body into one unit, which we call body–mind. Emotions are cellular signals involved in the translation of information into physical reality, literally mind into matter: 'Emotions are at the nexus between matter and mind going back and forth between the two and influencing the two'.[27] The central point relevant to my analysis is that emotions become the bridge between the *physical* and the *mental*.

Pert has some interesting observations linking this picture of emotions and the mind–body relationship to issues of the health of the mind and body, with the role of meditation extending to the mental, emotional and even physical experience – the conversation going on at the autonomic or subliminal levels of the mind, where basic functions such as breathing, digestion, immunity, pain control and blood flow are carried out. Through meditation we enhance the effectiveness of the autonomic nervous system, where health and disease are determined minute by minute. Pert refers to the work on integrating mindfulness practice to deal with specific concerns like physical pain and the more psychologically oriented concerns of anxiety and depression, as found in the well-known work of Kabat-zinn.[28] Health is not just absence of disease, but a whole dimension of living in an unselfish way, a feeling of belonging, loving kindness and forgiveness. It is with such a lifestyle that we can rebuild body and mind.

Bill Moyers, in an interview with Pert, raised the following question: 'But is the anger mental or physical?' and Pert replied, 'It is both. That's what is interesting about emotions. They are the bridge between the mental and physical, or the physical and the mental, It's either way.'

Management of Emotions: The Domination of a Metaphor

In my opinion there are three important issues about emotions: the nature of emotions and emotion theories; the logic of emotion profiles like anger, fear, and grief; and issues about managing emotions. Philosophers have not been greatly immersed in the management of emotions, leaving it to therapists and, in a very limited way, to applied psychology. This chapter has already looked at the first issue and it was considered in greater detail in Chapter 5; the second issue is addressed in several chapters in this book, on anger, grief, sadness and pride. Solomon examined emotion profiles in his work, *True to Our Feelings*,[29] and made an important contribution to many emotion profiles, ranging from grief to humour. Solomon also deals with issues such as authenticity and integrity in relation to emotions, and in the Buddhist context such questions of authenticity, transparency, self-knowledge and deception are also important, especially in the context of the management of emotions. From an Asian/Buddhist point of view, questions regarding the management of emotions in the West appear to have come under what I call the 'domination of a metaphor'. Plato wrote on 'the bondage of passions' and saw reason as the charioteer and passions as the unruly horses. He was basically exploring a harmonious relation between reason and passion. Spinoza was fascinated by working out the geometry of passions – a ratiocentric model of emotions – working quite meticulously through the thought component of each emotion/passion. Hume turned the metaphor upside down and said 'Reason is and ought to be the slave of passions'. Jerome Neu, in his work *Emotion, Thought and Therapy*[30] and again in *A Tear is An Intellectual Thing*,[31] sees two paradigmatic conceptions of emotions in Hume and Spinoza, which also have implications for the management of emotions. Hume's focus is on 'feelings' and Spinoza's on 'thoughts'.

In my own studies on the management of emotions in Buddhism[32] I mention that apart from reason and feelings/passions, mindfulness is important, as in mindfulness practice we go beyond reason and passion. The replacement of cognitive therapy in counselling by mindfulness-based cognitive therapy vindicates my point. Though we can craft a neat cognitive explanation of an emotion, actual emotions are different: 'The mind relishes the way it is logical and controllable, the way it makes sense. It is so neat and clean and precise like mathematics – but the emotions are all over the place, aren't they? They are not precise, they are not neat and so they can easily get out of control'.[33] Also, mere rational conviction does not prevent us from being a victim to irrational passions. Mindfulness techniques are being used profusely, as a number of chapters of this book illustrate. In my own work on mindfulness-based emotion-focused therapy (EFT), the effectiveness of mindfulness therapy as well as the value of the attentional dimension in comparison with the cognitive, motivational and affective dimensions of our lives is quite evident. In discussing addictions and *akrasia* (weakness of will) Aristotle presented an important insight that there is a difference between 'knowing something' and 'bearing in mind' and it is mindfulness that captures one's attention.

Paul Ekman, in his book *Emotions Revealed*, presents a perspective much open to the practice of mindfulness during the different stages of the emergence and expression of a negative emotion like anger:

If we are to put a break on our emotional behaviour, if we are to change how we are feeling, we must be able to develop a different type of emotional consciousness. We must be able to take a step back—right while we are feeling the emotion—so we can question whether we want to go along with what our emotion is driving at us to do, or exercise a choice about how we will act on our emotion. This is being more than conscious of how we are feeling, it is another, more advanced, difficult to describe, form of consciousness. It is close to what the Buddhist thinkers call *mindfulness*.[34]

Ekman says that as the notion of *mindfulness* is linked to certain theories and a philosophy, he prefers to use the term 'attentiveness'. He says that this notion opens us towards a number of techniques for dealing with emotions. We can become aware of certain automatic appraisals, or what the cognitive therapist calls the autopilot of thinking patterns. Ekman also says that we can achieve 'impulse awareness' following the awareness of automatic appraisals. One can also develop attentiveness by becoming aware of certain causes of emotions and thus identify hot emotional triggers and take steps to weaken them. We can also, when more developed in this art, observe the emotional feelings and reactions of others. Ekman also says that this is a difficult art and needs gradual training.

Techniques of behaviour modification using mindfulness have been tested by therapists over the years. They include the focus on stimulus control; recognising the spark before the flame; before you start damage control; avoiding certain situations (as in addictions); de-conditioning; control of unwarranted intrusive cognitions; and modification of undesirable habits.[35]

In using the art of quiet listening to become aware of the emotional inroads in our mind, we develop diminishing reactivity to raw sensory events, avoid making automatic identifications with our reactions, develop openness, impartiality and flexibility and train our body and mind to 'wise seeing'. As we go along, our cognitive repertoire stabilises, and then moves into higher levels of understanding, and with a deep understanding of human emotions, there emerge 'transformative insights' – opening up a new window to grasp *epistemic shifts* in understanding human emotions. This book is dedicated to Robert Solomon, who spent a whole lifetime navigating through the field of human emotions in a lively, accessible and engaging manner.

11
Buddhism as Contemplative Philosophy, Psychology and Ethics

> The faculty of voluntarily bringing back a wandering attention, over and over again, is the very root of judgment, character and will. An education which should improve this faculty would be an education par excellence. But it is easier to define this ideal than to give practical instructions for bringing it about.[1]

Jon Kabat-Zinn observes that William James was not aware of the practice of mindfulness when he penned this passage but would have been delighted to discover that, in the practice of mindfulness, there was certainly an education for discovering that faculty of bringing back a wandering attention over and over again.[2]

The great contemplatives may be located across a wide spectrum, from those who have interiorised their outlook, such as the Christian desert fathers, the Himalayan yogis, the Sufi saints, Thomas Merton and the Buddhist forest monks, to those at the other end, where we find an emphasis on interconnectedness with the outside world, figures such as the present Dalai Lama, Hildegard of Bingen, Thich Naht Hanh, Gandhi and Martin Luther King.

Contemplative education in the classroom is considered as a kind of training for life rather than for a trade: 'When you are grounded in calmness and movement-to-movement awareness, you are most likely to be creative and to see new options, new solutions to problems. It will be easier to maintain your balance and sense of perspective in trying circumstances'.[3]

The Epistemological Outlook of Contemplative Education

Critical thinking is a useful tool as it helps us to delve into the coherence of thinking, of the validity of the sequence of ideas presented, as well

as the assumptions made in an argument. It also emphasises the importance of information and data on which we base our theories and the
deduction of inferences from them. Clarity of thinking and focus are
excellent virtues and philosophical skills to build our learning skills. In
fact the Buddha was also described as an analytical philosopher who
upheld rational analysis, an analyst[4] rather than a dogmatist. In fact,
he divides questions into four types: those which ought to be explained
categorically; those which ought to be replied with a counter question;
those which ought to be set aside (for example, if the flame of a candle
dwindles off, it is meaningless to ask, where it went); and those which
ought to be explained analytically.[5] He also said one should not accept
anything purely based on faith, on authority, on likes and dislikes, or
because the majority accepts it. These qualities of rationality are very
striking when set against the Buddha's presentation of a contemplative
tradition.

Today, those who encourage the development of contemplative education say that in addition to logical and analytical skills, we need to
develop the experiential, self-reflexive and contemplative dimensions
of learning. One teacher, discussing the value of contemplative education in the classroom, says that it includes knowing through silence,
beholding and witnessing the contents of our consciousness.[6] Practice of meditation can be integrated into a broad-based contemplative,
inward-looking, educational curriculum, blended with compassion and
empathy for others, qualities that cut across different groups (social,
religious or ethnic). Also, it must be mentioned that contemplative
education may be added to the school curriculum not as a substitute for the current rational-empirical perspective in schools, but as a
supplement. Contemplative techniques ranging from poetry to meditation may be so designed to quiet and shift the habitual chatter
of the mind, so that the mind develops skills of deepened awareness, concentration, self-knowledge and developing confidence and
trust within oneself. Also, the kind of questions that emerge within
contemplative studies curriculums are not essentially ones that have
quick answers, are information seeking or use computerised data.
Rather, these questions call for in-depth absorption, almost living the
questions.

In the context of Buddhism, understanding an issue like the 'nature
of the self' and the concept of the non-self (and all the basic issues
as such), involves different layers of understanding: there is what is
referred to as the material in the sermons of the Buddha, obtained by
reading the *Suttas* (sermons), which is a kind of book knowledge; this

can take a more reflective turn when a monk delivers a sermon based on the Sutta (*sutamaya-ñāṇa*); by analysing and discussion, which is a kind of intellectual level (*cintāmaya-ñāṇa*); the deepest is the experiential level (*bhāvanāmaya-ñāṇa*) through structured meditation practice under a teacher's guidance, carrying it into a deep reflective turn of mind in daily life, and seeing that one has the necessary self-knowledge to relate it to daily life and routine ethics. In different contexts, the Buddha adds a dimension of 'existential knowledge' and existential stirring – the hard knocks of life.[7] Understanding one's own vulnerability, having self-compassion and opening out, as practised in the four divine states of loving – kindness, compassion, altruistic joy and equanimity – is a dimension of meditative experience that is different from insight meditation, and this involves the transformation of the heart and emotions. This dimension is open to other religions and helps to cut across group barriers. This openness helps one to move through questions and convert them into a resource for transformation. The contemplative approach does not seek quick answers but encourages one to live through a question:

> Have patience with everything unresolved in your heart and try to love the questions themselves as if they were locked rooms or books written in a foreign language. Don't search for answers now because they would not be able to live them. And the point is to live everything. Live the questions now. Perhaps then, some day far in the future, you will gradually, even without noticing it, live your answer.[8]

One of the most important facets of contemplative knowledge is its self-reflexive quality: as Krishnamurti observes – listening to the operation of our own minds. He considers self-knowledge as the beginning of freedom. One who listens to one's own mind would open up to others as well. He also points out that if a person is weighed down by accumulated layers of learning, by facts and theories, these, surprisingly, may act as an impediment to one's own mind and that of others.[9]

Guy Claxton makes a distinction between what he calls the 'hare brain' and the 'tortoise mind'. Living in accelerated times, the mind seeks decisive, speedy and business-like ways of thinking, which he calls the hare-brain. To describe the tortoise mind, he picks up a metaphor from the Native American medicine cards, which gives a graphic description of the contemplative process: the turtle buries it thoughts, like its eggs, in the sand, and allows the sun to hatch its little ones. Like the tortoise laying eggs, we sit on our anger, impatience, anxiety, stress, tension and fear without destroying them – but contain them in their disorganised form and see them with the gifts of learning that calm and energise us.

The Psychological Frontiers of the Contemplative Perspective

It is at the psychological frontier that Buddhist resources for the contemplative approach would be seen most clearly, in the development of the mindfulness-based therapies which are examined in detail in Chapter 12.

Recently, psychotherapists, with their background in science and medicine, have begun to explore the possibilities of employing Buddhist techniques in a therapeutic context. I feel this is entirely consistent with the aim of overcoming suffering and improving the welfare of all sentient beings. Living experience of Buddhist meditation has given practitioners a profound knowledge of the workings and nature of the mind, an inner science to complement our understanding of the physical world.[10]

As I will discuss in Chapter 12, Mark Epstein has best integrated and written on the Buddhist contemplative tradition and the value of what he describes as 'bare attention'. Epstein feels that the Freudian technique of 'evenly suspended attention' and the bracketing of the critical faculty while listening to the clients, offers a marked resemblance to that of the Buddha, though there is no evidence that Freud was influenced by the Buddha. Apart from the different mindfulness-based therapeutic orientations described in the present book, there is the discipline of 'contemplative psychotherapy', which was introduced to the curriculum of the Naropa University. This was the first academic recognition of therapy in the contemplative tradition inspired by Buddhism, particularly Tibetan Buddhism. I had the great fortune of being a visiting scholar at the Naropa Institute (before it received university status) and learnt quite early in my academic life the potentiality of this discipline; they now have a faculty of contemplative studies and therapy. In many universities and institutes in the USA and UK, mindful-based therapies have been integrated into formal academic programmes and courses for training therapists. As this book as a whole has given a great deal of attention to the impact of Buddhist contemplative methods on psychology and counselling, I shall now devote the attention of the reader to the developing of a discipline which may be described as 'contemplative ethics', inspired by Buddhist teachings.

Exploring the Basis for a Buddhist Contemplative Ethics

Unlike the available interest in contemplative education, philosophy and therapy, a contemplative ethics is perhaps yet to be born. Having explored such possibilities during recent times, this analysis explores the great potentiality for developing a Buddhist contemplative ethics. My own writings on Buddhist ethics in the past have been influenced by Western models of ethics.[11] But now, while appreciating the content and the value of these articles, I am attempting to break new ground, especially as this analysis suits the chaos, conflicts and contradictions in the world around. Someone remarked that if the only tool you have is a hammer, the only problem that you see is hitting the nail on the wall! Contemplative ethics may respond to some of the new challenges.

Ethics is generally divided into meta-ethics and normative ethics. The term 'meta-ethics' indicates that we are not participating in the practice of ethics, but rather looking and reflecting on the very practice of ethics. It is like some who is a spectator at a soccer game (to whom the game is relatively new) rather than a player, understanding the rules of the game and how best it can be played. Normative ethics seeks directly to influence actions by passing judgments on right and wrong and good and bad. If one passes a judgment on the killing of an animal or lack of honesty in a trade, then one is making a normative judgment. In evaluating such actions, one may look at the intentions, the consequences, violation of accepted rules, infringement of rights, and so on, and theories have been built on the relative importance of such criteria used for judging actions.

A third dimension has emerged among teachers of ethics in the West who are attempting to broaden and diversify the methods of engaging in a dialogue across groups where there is a polarisation of views, conflict and the inability to listen to other points of view. Standard teaching of ethics would emphasise consistency of reasoning, validity in terms of facts and information, inferences which can be drawn from the ethical theory an individual upholds, such as the Aristotelian view, Utilitarian ethics or Kantian theories. The focus on proof and disproof, rather than on communication, dominates in the classroom, ability to criticise a tutorial, rather than the ability to understand what is communicated is valued. The increasing discussion of moral dilemmas, such as whether Peter should steal a drug to save his wife's life, has highlighted the importance of pedagogy in ethics. Imaginative encounters of moral situations, through narratives, stories, fiction and drama have been used in teaching ethics. In fact, existentialist ethics, where one may use a book like Soren Kierkegaard's *Either/Or* to look at alternative philosophies of life, have been used in class.[12]

Ethics For the Rough Road

The more narrowly we examine actual language, the sharper becomes the conflict between it and our requirement. (For the crystal purity of logic was, of course not a result of investigation: it was a requirement). The conflict becomes intolerable; the requirement is now in danger of becoming empty – we have now got on to slippery ice where there is no friction and so in a certain sense the conditions are ideal, but, also just because of that, we are unable to walk. We want to walk: so we need friction. Back to the rough ground![13]

The meaning of friction in the above statement may be interpreted as a reference to the uncertainties and chaos around our lives. But the philosophical worldview that pervaded the times of Wittgenstein, dominated by the rational-empirical model, which attempted to find neat answers to well formulated questions, had no space for ethical dilemmas, polarised and conflicting views on moral issues, chaos and uncertainty – all on the rough road of life. Ethics which are self-reflexive, experiential and contemplative are more suitable for the rough road. To deal with the apparent contradictions, paradoxes and the dialectical movement of things, a contemplative approach is helpful. In contexts of adversity, we need mindfulness and a reflective turn of mind, rather than a logical formulation for making choices, and it is such a perspective, as James remarked, that is 'the root of judgment, character and will'. This is not to deny the importance of rules and precepts, which are crucial for Buddhist ethics, but we also need a mind immersed in reflective concerns of morality and, most important, the moment-to-moment flow of morality.

Of the prominent philosophers in the West, Iris Murdoch remains the best exponent of a contemplative perspective on ethics, as she compares the moral journey to a person going on a pilgrimage. Murdoch says that, apart from the ethics that emerge when making a choice, what is important is the moral perspective that pervades continually, in the moment–moment flow of life: 'I would regard the daily, hourly, minutely) attempted purification of consciousness as the central and fundamental arena of morality'.[14] This is not to deny the value of moral principles, precepts and theoretical perspectives and criteria for evaluating good and bad actions in Buddhism – but we also need to look at their wellsprings in the deeper reflective/meditative base in Buddhist ethics. Bernard Williams says that we do not always face life armed with theories, but that reflective morality is equally important. Thus, morality involves a radical and deeper level of reflection, in addition to the clear daylight of decision making.

Joseph Goldstein, the well known meditation teacher, made the following observation in delivering the Wit Lectures at the Harvard Divinity School:

> The real awakening comes when we see that we can greatly reform our morals. It comes with training; it is not given. When we understand this – from whatever place we are starting, from whatever degree of commitment to non-harming – our moral sense can become increasingly refined. This is what makes the practice of morality so powerful.[15]

Goldstein says that for Buddhism morality is a practice and the very foundation of a spiritual life. One of the points he mentions about meditation is important today, when the commercialisation of meditation has uprooted the practice from the moral base which nourishes it. He points out that those who want great spiritual insight without actually grounding it in moral action are like people in a rowboat putting tremendous effort and exertion into rowing across a river while failing to untie the rope attaching the boat to the dock. Of the Western philosophers Aristotle comes closest to Buddhism; he considered virtue as the building of character, as it is a process of transformation and refinement. In Buddhism, unlike the dominant moral traditions in the West, morality is the basis of spirituality, where there is mutual enrichment of the two facets.

Spiritual Dimensions of Buddhist Contemplative Practice

At this point Buddhist perspectives on the contemplative dimension take a very different turn from other current philosophical, psychological and ethical systems. In the spiritual context, the Pali tem *anupassati* conveys the notion of contemplation: the term is derived from the verb 'to see', *passati*, and the emphatic prefix *anu*, meaning to repeatedly look at, closely observe or contemplate. The discourses of the Buddha also use the term contemplation to refer to a particular way of meditating, or to a standpoint: contemplating the 'body' as impermanent (*aniccānupassī*), and therefore something that does not give lasting satisfaction (*dukkhānupassī*), and as not-self (*anattānupassī*). These standpoints are in a sense even deeper than what happens in a good therapeutic transformation. In therapy, the not-self idea works by getting the client to drop identification with, for instance, grief, and look at it from a distance; get used to the notion of separation and loss, and the embracing of pain without reactivity. The spiritual transformation goes beyond a therapeutic transformation.

Part II
Pathways of Mindfulness-Based Counselling

12
Nature of Counselling and Theoretical Orientations in Psychotherapy

The actual contact between a counsellor and a person who is seeking help lies at the heart of what counselling is about. Although a counsellor may be able to use theory to make sense of the client's difficulties, and may have a range of techniques at his or her disposal for revealing and overcoming these difficulties, the fact remains that theory and technique are delivered through the presence and being of the counsellor as person: the person of the counsellor. An interest in the therapeutic relationship remains a common concern of all therapy practitioners and theorists. Even if different approaches to counselling make sense of the client–therapist relationship in different ways, they all agree that effective counselling depends on how this kind of relationship operates, what happens when it goes wrong and how to fix it.[1]

Even in short-term counselling, which may take a few hours, the counsellor will try to see problems from the perspective of the client, treat him with great respect and care, and maintain strict confidentiality regarding the proceedings. For instance, Carl Rogers laid down the principles of client-centred therapy with a focus on unconditional positive regard for the client, empathy and congruity (genuineness) as the central features in the relationship.[2] Clients having problems and in various states of emotional turmoil, anxiety and distress – experiencing stress at work, tensions in the family, bereavement and addictions – seek help from the counsellor. Counselling helps them to open up repressed thoughts and feelings and lay them bare as counselling progresses, thus developing self-awareness and allowing access to the inner self. Sometimes, counselling goes into the past and recalls traumatic experiences. The counsellor listens and helps the client to develop a conversation. Most counsellors do not offer direct advice, and such non-directive approaches help the client to make his or her own decisions. A fifty-minute session once a week is the standard arrangement for meeting, though I have used many variations of this in my professional practice. While a capacity for warmth and empathy are crucial, a therapist's own self-understanding of his strengths and weaknesses and his life history, and a sense of openness about the thoughts and feelings that emerge within his mind, are important. Mindfulness-based counselling, which I shall introduce as we proceed in this description of the counselling process, is based on fostering self-understanding and self-knowledge. In training for counselling, learning to be non-judgmental and accepting the client for what he or she is becomes crucial; adaptability and spontaneity, an ability for self-assessment, insightfulness and empathy help one to be a skilful counsellor.

Counselling and Psychotherapy

The word 'therapy' is derived from the Greek term '*therapia*', meaning healing. Psychotherapy is the healing of the mind by those who are trained and qualified practitioners. Psychotherapy and psychiatry are associated with a background in medicine, whereas counselling refers to non-medical contexts. Counselling is closer to normal life, and often can be extended to the development of educational issues, such as youth problems, families struck by natural disasters and accidents. Dealing with stress management, grief counselling, addictions, mild depression, issues at home and in the workplace are some of the concerns of a counsellor. The time devoted to training a psychotherapist or clinical psychologist is longer than that devoted to training a counsellor. Counsellors tend to use a theoretical orientation, and sometimes draw on several theories and their methods. The most dominant theories are: Freud's psychoanalysis/psychodynamic theory; behaviour therapy; cognitive therapy; person-centred therapy; existential therapy; and, more recently, emotion-focused therapy (EFT).

After a brief review of these dominant theoretical orientations, in the next chapter I shall first present, in a very clear way: (i) the nature of meditation and meditation practice; (ii) how the mindfulness concept is integrated into therapy; (iii) different types of mindfulness-based therapies, including my personal professional contribution in developing mindfulness-based EFT. I shall conclude by describing the Buddha in the role of both teacher and counsellor. The section that follows this background analysis will present the application of therapeutic orientations, and especially mindfulness-based EFT, to specific issues, with some case studies concerning a range of problems to which we apply the theory and methods of therapy: stress management; grief counselling; addictions; and managing specific selected emotions, and a concluding chapter on the Buddhist perspectives on the positive emotion of generosity.

Freud's Psychoanalysis (1856–1939)

Sigmund Freud is considered as the originator of the first therapeutic tradition in the West. He was first trained in medical science, with a focus on studying the brain. He gradually became interested in the relation between the mind and mental health issues. After studying a number of clients, first through hypnotism and then with a method he developed called 'free association' to engage in a conversation with the clients, he became more interested in the 'ideogenic' facets of mental illness, instead of the 'somatic' factors. He came up with the revolutionary thesis that 'hysterics behave as if anatomy did not exist'. This ideogenic background is very much rooted in what takes place below the threshold of normal consciousness. The pre-conscious consists of thoughts and memories which can be easily recalled, whereas the contents of the unconscious have been repressed; during the counselling sessions the therapist attempts to bring them to the awareness of the client. Sometimes there can be deeply buried experiences in the past, which Freud described as a 'dynamic trauma' – dynamic because, though repressed, it does have an impact on client's problems. Sometimes the client virtually 're-lives' these experiences. As the patient feels a sense of relief after this process, Freud used the term 'catharsis' to describe this experience, taking the term from Aristotle. For Aristotle, when people come to see drama, their own conflicts and tension and the emotions of shame, guilt and fear are often re-enacted on the stage, and when they leave the theatre there is some sense of relief.

Freud introduced two conceptual models to delineate the nature of mental personality: the conscious, pre-conscious and unconscious; and the id, ego and super-ego. The id represents archaic impulses and passions, which may turn out to be unruly, the ego restrains them, and the super ego is the voice of conscience and morality. The mind is also represented in terms of the interplay of dynamic instincts: the drive for sensual gratification, the drive towards egoistic and narcissistic pursuits and the drive towards both aggression and self-destruction. I have compared these drives to the Buddhist concepts of *kama-tanha, bhava-tanha* and *vibhava-tanha* in my work, *Buddhist and Freudian Psychology*.[3] Carl Jung (1875–1961) broke away from Freud and established the school of Analytical Therapy.[4]

Behaviourism and Therapy

In the 1960s the use of 'introspection' and Freudian psychology was challenged. J.B. Watson was one of the first behaviourists, but B.F. Skinner (1904–1990) was the most articulate exponent of behaviourism.[5] Contemporary behaviour therapy is, to a great extent, a blend of the classical conditioning theory of Ivan Pavlov, the operant conditioning theory of B.F. Skinner and the social learning theory of Albert Bandura.

With Albert Ellis and Aaron Beck we see an interesting merging of behaviour and cognitive therapy. The most important legacy of behaviour therapy is the set of methods of behaviour modification: focus on stimulus control, recognising the spark before the flame, avoiding certain situations, such as a bar for an alcohol addict, de-conditioning and modification of undesirable habits. According to Corey, behaviourism contributed to psychology in a number of ways: emphasising the importance of the scientific method in therapy; focusing on the client's present, rather than the past; making clients actively engage in specific action procedures; teaching specific skills of self-management; all often tailored to the specific needs of individual clients.[6]

The Rational Emotive Therapy of Albert Ellis

Ellis laid the foundation of what later came to be called the cognitive therapy of Aaron Beck, with Ellis's own system described as 'rational emotive therapy' (REBT). My personal interest in the contributions of Ellis arise from the fact that he was a pioneer in integrating the role of emotions into a therapeutic tradition. First introduced in 1955, Ellis's important thesis was that thinking and emoting are very closely related, and that both take the form of self-talk, or what is described as 'inner chatter' in our minds. This internal talk can generate and modify our unhealthy emotions, and also obstruct our long-term happiness. In the light of these issues, it is necessary to establish some sort of balance between our emotional outlook and the challenges of life. For instance, undue anxiety and groundless fears are often the result of irrational thinking. Anger may sometimes convey that there is some problem to be solved, but mere reactivity makes conditions worse. Negative emotions sometimes have a message. Rational beliefs are healthy, productive and consistent with social reality, and irrational beliefs are rigid, dogmatic and unhealthy. Beliefs emerge as preferential thinking linked to our 'demands' presented in words as 'must', 'should', and 'ought'. Ellis followed the Stoic philosophers in maintaining that what matters is *not the event but how one interprets* it. Ellis upheld that our emotions are linked to our beliefs, interpretations and appraisals and, thus, he offered a cognitive theory of emotions. In his therapy sessions, Ellis attempted to dispute unhealthy and self-defeating thoughts. We fall victim to self-defeating beliefs by a process of auto-suggestion and repetition, a feature referred to as the 'auto-pilot' in both cognitive therapy and mindfulness-based cognitive therapy. Mindfulness of thought patterns is crucial to Buddhist mindfulness practice.

The ABC theory a way of understanding or analysing emotions: A, activating event; B, belief; C, emotional and behavioural consequences. Emotional disturbances are fed by self-defeating beliefs: 'I cannot get a job', 'I am always a failure', 'The future looks empty'. D stands for disputing the beliefs and thus getting clients to change beliefs. The therapist tries to change these irrational beliefs and, unlike in psychodynamic theories, the focus is on the present rather than the past. Apart from disputing beliefs, the therapist gives a great deal of homework to the client, so that the client develops the necessary skills for dealing with the negative beliefs.

The System of Cognitive Therapy of Aaron Beck

Cognitive therapy (CT) emerged during the years 1960–1963. Beck rejected psychodynamic theories and, like Ellis, focused on the present, recognising and changing negative and maladaptive thoughts and beliefs. Beck expanded his therapy to include arbitrary inferences, selective abstractions, overgeneralisation, magnification and minimisation, personalisation (identifying an event as relating to them in an absolute way), polarised thinking, interpreting and categorising things in an all or nothing basis of black and white. But the REBT of Ellis and the CT of Beck have some differences. While REBT is directive and attempts to persuade the client, and often confronts the client, CT uses something like the Socratic dialogue form. Also, while REBT recognises the therapist as a teacher, CT emphasises the therapeutic relationship. Cognitive therapists train clients to be their own therapist. Beck became well-known for his contributions to developing a therapy for depression.

The Person-Centred Therapy of Carl Rogers (1902–87)

In 1951, Carl Rogers laid down the groundwork of what came to be described as person-centred therapy, where the therapeutic relationship takes central place. Genuine warmth, accurate empathy, non-judgmental acceptance and establishing trust with the client are very important strands of person-centred therapy. Rogers's system has been described as non-directive therapy, which encourages the client to explore what makes them unhappy and find self-direction and constructive personal change. It is the therapeutic relationship that is crucial, where the therapist does not force his way, but encourages the client to develop his growth potential. This is described as a humanistic approach to therapy, and also influenced other therapeutic traditions. As Rogers was opposed to the idea of elevating his therapy into an institutional school, it remains an approach to therapy, rather than a specific theory about therapy. He was also prepared to test his hypothesis through empirical/clinical tests. Rogers's thesis about 'unconditional positive regard, empathy and genuineness (congruity)' succinctly summarised his lasting contribution to therapy.

Existential Therapy: Victor Frankel (1905–1997); Rollo May (1909–94); Irwin Yalom

Existential therapy is to some extent different from the therapies so far presented, as it emerged first from a background of philosophy. The Danish philosopher Soren Kierkegaard (1813–55),[7] the German philosopher Martin Heidegger (1889–1976)[8] and the French philosopher Jean Paul Sartre (1905–80)[9] provide the philosophical background to existential therapy. The lineage of existential therapy runs through Victor Frankel,[10] Rollo May[11] and Irwin Yalom, and, of these, Yalom stands today as the most articulate existential therapist.

Gerald Corey sums up six components of existential therapy: the capacity for self-awareness; freedom and responsibility; striving for identity and relationship with others; the search for meaning; anxiety as a condition for living; awareness of death and meaning. Existentialism is an invitation for clients to recognise the ways in which they are not living fully authentic lives and to make choices that will lead to their becoming what they are capable of being. It also focuses on issues central to the human predicament and not limited to therapy, anxiety, guilt, loneliness, alienation and death. Existentialism helps the clients to define themselves, make choices when necessary and commit to authentic living – as against mechanical, automatic and deceptive lives, surrendering their sense of identity.

Strands of all these traditions may be found in the Buddha's attempt to diagnose the roots of human suffering and explore the way out – towards the life of renunciation or the balance and righteous life of a householder.

13
Mindfulness-Based Therapeutic Orientations

The Buddhist Concept of Mindfulness

The basic message of the Buddha has to be seen as a liberation quest from the wheel of suffering. Thus, his basic goal was not to offer 'a therapy for mental health' in the current use of the concept, although, as I discussed in the chapter on sickness and health, there are clear analogies to consider the Buddha as a physician of the mind and body and as a therapist. Yet, the dominant mindfulness therapies in the West today hardly offer a liberation quest in the sense of what the Buddha offered as the complete cessation of suffering and reaching sainthood (*arahant*). Secondly, the term 'mindfulness' is located in different mindfulness-based therapeutic orientations: according to the goal of their therapies. In my own life as a Buddhist and a therapist, the two dimensions have enriched each other, but this is something personal and one cannot adjudicate that there is only one way of blending the two.

There are also therapists who use mindfulness techniques for therapy but would, with some caution, leave the doctrinal facets of Buddhism out of their own perspective and that of the client. Also, Buddhists across the spectrum vary in their commitments to the moral life, practice of meditation and the highest ideal of final liberation. But it must be emphasised that mindfulness practice in Theravada Buddhism has its own location, which has differences with its location in current mindfulness-based therapies. In an article entitled 'Mindfulness: A Dialogue Between Buddhism and Clinical Psychology'[1] the Buddhist context is clarified: the training of the mind generates a robust sense of confidence in the path, which expresses in taking refuge in the Buddha, in his teachings and the community of monks. Out of this deep confidence in one's own training comes the practice of ethics, nurturing the wholesome and avoiding the unwholesome, and this training in blameless living results in freedom and lightness of mind. The most important initial practice is the restraint of the senses and mindfulness in everyday life. Deep watchfulness and practice of mindfulness brings a sense of inner contentment which can then be taken to the formal practice of mindfulness. Thus, it is necessary that certain therapists, including my personal practice, would combine the practice summarised above and yet function as a therapist; but a number of mindfulness-based therapists disassociate from any such commitment. A good example, to which we shall refer later, is acceptance and commitment therapy (ACT): 'Much of the understanding of and practice of mindfulness within clinical psychology arose from a dialogue with Buddhist traditions with the notable exception of ACT'.[2]

Mindfulness on the Liberation Path

The practice of mindfulness on the liberation path calls for greater effort and systematic understanding of the different phases of either tranquillity meditation or insight meditation than the techniques generally used in mindfulness-based therapies. Also, especially the insight meditation techniques are more complex but vibrant and generate greater energy than the tailor made methods of therapy, which have short term goals of getting back to normal functioning in routine life.

Mindfulness is a process of bringing one's mind to the present movement. When we try to bring our mind to the present movement, we observe its true nature – how it habitually wanders around, day dreams and fantasises. We are always preoccupied with the past and the future. The mind is rarely in the present.

With the focus on one object at a particular moment, we are able to see our mind wandering. The focus on the in-breath and out-breath may look quite superficial at the start, but gradually a refined and sustained process of mindfulness of breath emerges. Noting and observing the breath, one gradually finds a way of security from sensual desire, anger, sloth and torpor, doubts and restlessness and worry, which are considered as the five hindrances. Thus, perfected moral conduct is a prerequisite for further progress. The purification process looks more like a technical exercise, developing into a very refined process. The meditative focus that follows is more complex and is steered more towards liberation than are the normal mindfulness practices used in therapy.

In observing the totality of the in-breath and the out-breath, the yogi discerns gradually that the breath becomes shorter and subtler, and he has to maintain the continuous mindfulness that should be accurate, precise and vigilant, and then the yogi sees *the breath as the whole body*, and this is a kind of historic movement when the bodily dispositions (*kāya-saṅkhāra*) calm down. As one gradually discerns the shift to the calming down of the mind and mental dispositions (*citta-saṅkhāra*) one sees the margins between body (*rupa*) and mind (*nāma*). *This is a real traffic junction on the road to insight meditation.* With the qualifying comment that there are important differences between the practice of mindfulness in the heart of therapy and on the path to liberation, I shall give a breakdown of the different mindfulness-based therapeutic orientations.

Mindfulness in Therapy

As a useful description of the role of mindfulness in current therapies in the West, a short analysis of mindfulness awareness, regardless of where they are located in the practice continuum, is presented by Christopher K. Germer:

> It is non-conceptual – it is an awareness without absorption in our thought processes; present-centered, as it is always in the present movement; non-judgmental; intentional; participant observation; non-verbal; exploratory; liberating; freedom from conditioned suffering. These qualities would occur simultaneously in each movement of mindfulness.[3]

Neurologist Daniel J. Siegal presented five facets of mindfulness, based on a statistical study, as well their usefulness: non-reactivity to inner experience (for example, perceiving feelings and emotions without reacting to them); observing/noticing/attending/ to sensations, perceptions, thoughts and feelings (for example, remaining present with sensations and feelings even if they are unpleasant or painful); acting with awareness/not on automatic pilot, concentration/non-distraction/non-carelessness; describing/labelling with words; not-judging oneself and criticising for any negative emotions.[4] He also cites reflection or 'metacognition', second order awareness.

Mindfulness-Based Stress Reduction Program (MBSR)

Jon Kabat-Zinn is a pioneer in developing a practical guide to meditation, mindfulness and healing through his stress-reduction program. His work, *Full Catastrophe Living*, which focuses on using the wisdom of the body and mind to face stress, pain and illness, may be considered as a landmark in the development of mindfulness-based therapies.[5] In the second phase of his work, through his guidance, wisdom and support, he and his staff at the Centre for Mindfulness in Medicine, Healthcare and Society assisted in the emergence of mindfulness-based cognitive therapy. Attitudinal factors which constitute the major pillars of this program are as follows: non-judging, patience, a beginner's mind, trust, non-striving acceptance, seeing things as if they are in the present and letting go. They are all interconnected.

Non-judging: being an impartial witness of our own experience. We need to be aware that there is a constant stream of judging and reacting to inner and outer experience. The habit of judging and categorising locks us into mechanical reactions built on a hard crust. Thus, becoming aware of automatic judgments (made on 'auto-pilot') is important.

Patience: is a form of wisdom – accept the position that things will unfold in their own time, open to each movement, accepting it in its fullness.

Beginner's mind: a mind that is willing to see each step in meditation as if one is doing it for the first time!

Trust: in one's own intuitions.

Non-striving acceptance: we do not meditate to get something.

Seeing things as if they are in the present.

Let go.

He also adds commitment, intentionality and self-discipline. Kabat-Zinn's definition of mindfulness has been passed to many therapists using mindfulness techniques: 'The awareness that emerges through paying attention on purpose, in the present moment, and non-judgmentally to things as they are'.[6]

Mindfulness-Based Cognitive Therapy (MBCT)

Working alongside Segal, Williams and Teesdale, Kabat-Zinn inspired and assisted in the development of what is now recognised as mindfulness-based cognitive therapy; this was developed as a therapy specifically for depression.[7] This was followed by a more general work for a very-broad based readership, *The Mindful Way Through Depression*.[8] Compared with the early cognitive therapy of Beck and Ellis, MBCT attempts to change one's relationship to cognitions than change the cognitions. Also, instead of the disputation model, there was the attempt to have a present focus revelation of what was happening in the client's mind, without interpretation and projection. In fact, as Mark Epstein points out, this is what Freud described as 'evenly suspended attention' or the suspension of the critical faculty.[9] This was deep listening, very much different from the early cognitive therapy 'disputation model'. The use of the technique of de-centring is also important: the ability to 'step back' and observe one's thoughts or feelings in a less self-identified way. For instance, the anger that emerges in the mind is neither yours nor mine, neither good nor bad, but is an impersonal process. They use the term 'automatic pilot', the mind slipping into the habitual mechanical manner: if it is anger, for instance, 'he violated a promise', 'he should not have done it', 'I just do not understand why he did' and such ruminating thoughts will continue. The application of MBCT to depression is described as substituting the 'being' mood for the 'doing mood': it is a way of 'being with' the problem by letting go of the need to solve the problem instantly, and becoming aware of the tendency to avoid unpleasantness or being attached to pleasantness. Instead of the conceptual doing mode one becomes more present-centred. In spite of the variety of techniques they introduced, the core skill is 'stepping out' of the self-perpetuating rumination.

The basic premises of MBCT may be summarised as: the cultivation of awareness through mindfulness practice; an attitudinal framework characterised by non-striving, acceptance and a genuine interest in experience; an understanding of a central Buddhist theme, human vulnerability and suffering; rumination as a particular style of self-critical, self-focused, repetitive, negative thinking, experiential avoidance, an attempt to remain out of contact with direct experience of challenging thoughts, emotions and body sensation, focus on the present and being in touch with the world as well as the body; difference between the 'doing mode' and 'being mode'.

Buddhism and Behaviour Modification Theory: Padmal de Silva

Owing to the great impact of MBSR and MBCT, early contributions to Buddhism and behaviour modification theory have been neglected. This is important because behaviourism, as a psychological theory, preceded cognitive psychology. Padmal de Silva was an early exponent of integrating mindfulness practice to behavioural change, and along with a study of Buddhist texts he has cited a number of techniques, most of which he has used in his clinical practice, which I shall summarise. There are seven important features of behaviour modification: there is a strong emphasis on defining problems in terms of behaviour that can be measured; the treatment techniques are ways of altering an individual's current environment in order to help the individual to function more fully; their methods and rationale may be described with precision; the techniques are found applied in everyday life; these techniques are largely based on principles of learning, especially operant conditioning and respondent conditioning; the fact that a particular technique brought about a specific behavioural change can be demonstrated in a scientific way; emphasis on accountability for everyone involved in a behaviour modification programme.[10]

Padmal de Silva says, 'Examples of such behaviour change strategies found in early Buddhism are varied and numerous: Interestingly, some of these are not very different from the corresponding techniques used in modern behavioural psychotherapy'. He cites the following techniques: numerous instances of modelling, as a way of influencing and modifying the behaviour of others; examples of reciprocal inhibition as a fear reduction technique; modification of undesirable habits by multiple behavioural techniques; stimulus control as a way of dealing with undesirable behaviour; use of rewards as a way of inducing and encouraging desirable behaviour; control of unwanted cognitive intrusions; a graded stimulus approach for developing loving kindness, much like the hierarchical approach used in behaviour strategies; repeated exposure to disconfirmatory experience in dealing with false beliefs by the use of parables and analogies.[11] Padmal de Silva's untimely death was a great blow to the expectation that he would contribute to the future direction of mindfulness-based therapies.

Acceptance and Commitment Theory (ACT)

I wish to deal with ACT last for a number of complexities but also issues that raise important questions about some mindfulness-based therapies. As I mentioned earlier, ACT grew independently of Buddhism and there was some ambiguity in the relationship between ACT and Buddhism. In fact, Malcolm Huxter observes that some of the therapies using mindfulness techniques indicate a separation from the ethics and wisdom which are essential ingredients of traditional Buddhism, and, according to him, there are particular problems with ACT.[12] He emphasises the point that the dislodging of mindfulness from its Buddhist context may detract us from the depth and breadth of its clinical utility. He also cites that systems like ACT have as their model current scientific models which are materialistic and not sympathetic to the phenomenology of consciousness which is a form of subjective experience. In Chapter 1, I showed that recent developments in neurophenomenology and contemplative experience can combine with different scientific approaches to Buddhism. But in its own way, ACT has made a contribution to therapy and they also have a vibrant contact with those who follow their methods. I have also found some of their reflections on the universality of human suffering very 'Buddhistic', as well as the relevance of their thesis today: 'there are many forms of psychological disorders that do not constitute clinical disorders', as you may discern in Chapter 16, on sadness and depression.

To summarise what is important in ACT, their focus on what is described as 'experiential avoidance' is important and to counteract this problem, different mindfulness skills are recommended. ACT draws a clear distinction between 'pain' and 'suffering'. When we encounter a painful content within ourselves, we want to do what we always do, fix it up and sort it out so that we can get rid of it. But this process amplifies it and one gets more entangled in it. Acceptance is not a defeatist position; it is a way of tolerance which ultimately develops some wisdom and insight.

> Acceptance in the sense it is used here, is not nihilistic self-defeat; neither is it tolerating and putting up with your pain. It is very different than that. Those heavy, sad, dark forms of 'acceptance' are almost the exact opposite of the active, vital embrace of the moment that we mean.[13]

Dialectical Behaviour Therapy (DEBT)

DEBT was first developed by the American psychologist Marsha Linehan as a diagnosis for borderline personality disorder. She integrated some insights from Zen Buddhism as therapeutic tools. The term dialectical implicates the idea of mediating a middle path between two conflicting positions and polarised thinking, for example, between acceptance and change. Zen Buddhism is generally an ideal system as an ally to deal with apparent paradoxes and contradictions and thus this therapy is somewhat unique among therapies inspired by Buddhism. The key components of this therapy are emotion regulation, relationship skills, distress tolerance and mindfulness:

Mindfulness became crucial in learning and applying distress tolerance skills as a way to combat the destructive use of self-harm. Mindfulness was also an important skill that allowed clients to be with feelings rather than react to them. Mindfulness was a direct antidote to disassociation and was a powerful tool to deal with difficult memories. Also, mindfulness was a tool to examining and working through destructive thought processes, and a great deal of the skill for acceptance of what comes on the way.[14]

Psychodynamic Psychotherapy: Mark Epstein

Germer says that psychodynamic psychotherapists discovered the use of mindfulness in therapy before their behaviourist counterparts, since Freud's psychoanalysis shared common features with mindfulness practice.[15] Mark Epstein observes that, though there is no evidence that Freud was directly influenced by Buddhism, 'the resemblance of his attentional recommendations to those of the Buddha cannot be denied'.[16] The suspension of the critical faculty, the state of simple listening, of 'evenly suspended attention', of non-reactive, non-judgmental and open listening in Freud was highlighted by Epstein.[17]

In the neo-Freudian tradition, Erich Fromm stands out as a therapist who was inspired by Buddhism. First, in *Zen and Psychotherapy*, and later in a posthumous publication, *The Art of Listening*, he clearly accepts the importance of mindfulness as a therapeutic device, and he had some important correspondence with Ven. Nyanaponika, the German Buddhist monk living in Sri Lanka. On the level of theory, Epstein says that Buddhism has an answer to the issue of 'identity confusion', and on the level of therapy, he develops a mindfulness-based psychodynamic perspective. Epstein's *Thoughts Without a Thinker: Psychotherapy From a Buddhist Perspective* remains one of the seminal contributions to the interface between Buddhism and Western therapeutic orientations during recent times. He says, 'Bare attention is the technique that best defines the Buddhist approach to working with our minds and emotions. It is impartial, open, non-judgmental, interested, patient, fearless and impartial'.[18] Epstein focuses attention on the ability of a meditator to transform psychic disturbances into objects of meditation. He cites a Zen master, Suzuki Roshi, who says, 'When you pull the weeds and bury them near the plant, the weeds give nourishment. So you should be grateful to the weeds'. In the popular beaten path, Freud's work is always associated with buried traumatic unconscious, but Epstein says that Freud's work has a number of strands, ranging from the deeply buried unconscious to the ever present subliminal levels. He says that Freud went through three stages, the first is the cathartic view, when he used hypnotism for re-enacting and re-living traumatic incidents; the second was when he gave up hypnotism and used the method of 'free-association' to recall memories without inhibition; third is the stage where Freud moves from the pursuit of the forgotten past to the immediate present. Many interpreters and critics of Freud have missed the third stage embodied in the paper 'Remembering, Repeating and Working Through'.[19] This shift is so interesting that in the new edition of my work *Buddhist and Freudian Psychology*, I have recognised this change in describing the Buddhist perspective on the realm of the 'unconscious'.[20] I have moved out of the archaeological metaphor of digging up the past to a notion of 'subliminal activity', close to consciousness, and thus translate the Pali term *'anusaya'* as subliminal proclivities (see the section on the unconscious in Chapter 4). In cognitive therapy, for instance, the autopilot of repetitive thought patterns hover around threshold consciousness. Freud does use the dynamic trauma concept, which is one of the dimensions for looking at a deeper layer of the unconscious, but he also had the psychopathology of everyday life, which is closer to routine life, and this essay on remembering and working through brings a layer close to the Buddhist view of subliminal activity. As Epstein says, therapists at the time like Sandor Ferenzi and Otto Fenichel refused to accept this new strand in Freud; perhaps they did not understand the whole point of Freud's essay. I shall conclude this section with the words of Mark Epstein:

> What is ultimately therapeutic for many people is not so much the narrative construction of their past to explain their suffering, but the direct experience, in the therapist office, of the emotions, emotional thoughts, or physical remnants of emotional thoughts, or physical remnants of emotional thought with which they are stuck. These feelings peek out of the silences and manifest their presence when the room becomes quiet. Often in the form an angry neediness, a sullen hurt, or a hopeless rage, they are the evidence of the basic fault that has people repeating destructive behaviour without understanding why.[21]

Emotion-Focused Therapy (EFT) and Mindfulness-Based EFT

In my practice as a counsellor for six years, I have used a specific focus on emotions like anger, fear, sadness, grief, conceit and greed to get into the heart of issues presented by a client and the use of the techniques of mindfulness to explore the client's problems and the way out. This interest emerged many years back during my work as a philosopher looking at the logic of different emotion profiles. The links between philosophy of mind and counselling were a great resource, and this naturally extended to psychology and counselling. My earliest interest emerged when participating in a two year 'Emotions and Culture' professional training program run by the Culture Learning Institute of the East-West Center in Hawaii. This project was devoted to collecting emotion vocabularies in different cultures and emotion stories. There was a specific focus on Darwin's work, revived by Paul Ekman, on basic emotions.

As I gradually developed a therapy with a focus on emotions with mindfulness as a therapeutic method, I was impressed by the fact that EFT was more complex than cognitive therapy, which had a dominant focus on thought patterns, while also having a focus on bodily sensations. The profile of most of the prominent emotions include: a perception of a situation, evaluation and response, which are also fed by desires, intentions, initial feelings of pleasure/pain and the body. In addition, recent studies in neurology throw light on the complex facets of emotions. Thus, using this 'componential theory of emotions', any of the components like thoughts, interpretations, feelings, desires, physiological arousal, intentions, etc. can be used as a special focus in therapy. In fact, the charter for Buddhist mindfulness practice may be used exclusively on the body, feelings, desires or thought patterns. They also emerge as blends, like in jealousy and envy, and sometimes they emerge as clusters. They also often lay as subliminal propensities, of which greed, anger and conceit are very dominant. Greed involves attitudes to possess, accumulate, hoard and also results in addictions, while anger stands for a whole series of reactive responses. When a client develops refined mindfulness skills these subliminal propensities or 'sleeping passions' come within awareness, restraint in thought and physical action. A record of mindfulness-based EFT, as I practised for over five years, is found in a monograph I published, *An Introduction to Mindfulness-Based Counselling*.[22] In fact, the present book has several chapters on specific emotions.

Leslie Greenberg, the Canadian psychologist, is the world's foremost exponent of and pioneer in what he referred to as emotion-focused therapy (EFT). After attending his workshops in Sydney and studying his writings I was able to refine my version of EFT. I now present my work in the light of the pioneering studies of Greenberg, based on a paper presented at a conference at Mahidol University in Thailand: 'A Rationale for Developing Mindfulness-Based Emotion-Focused Therapy'.

A meditative approach is an alternative to avoidance: it involves paying attention to emotions in a particular way. A meditative process involves teaching clients the skills of describing their experiences to themselves in an objective manner as if they were an outside observer talking to another person.

Once people are able to distance themselves from the actual emotion, they will no longer feel overwhelmed by their anger, sadness, fear or shame. The meaning of their thoughts that kept adding fuel to their emotional fires will no longer absorb them.[23]

Prelude

While mindfulness-based cognitive therapy with a focus on 'thoughts' has entered the mainstream of Western therapeutic traditions, there is perhaps a need to spell out in detail my practice of mindfulness-based emotion-focused therapy. Within the context of Buddhist psychology, an emotion is more complex than thoughts: an emotion involves a blend of the cognitive (*saññā, citta*), the affective (*vedanā*) and volitional (*saṅkhāra*) facets, while a broader term motivational would include volitions/intentions and desires (*chanda, rāga*). To this we also add the physiological dimension of the body (*rūpa*). Interpretations and evaluative activity are closely linked to the cognitive aspect, though they may be separated. There has been an important confluence of the cognitive sciences and emotion studies, and it is accepted today that 'understanding emotion is central to understanding intelligent systems'. Leslie Greenberg is within the new revolution in emotion studies: emotional brain;[24] emotions and the biology of facial expressions (Paul Ekman); health and healing emotions, a work edited by Daniel Goleman;[25] the neuroplasticity of the brain;[26] theory of the body as a second brain[27] – all these developments indicate a veritable revolution in emotion studies. It is also necessary to mention that there other therapies making a limited use of emotions: behavioural theory using the concepts of de-conditioning and exposure; cognitive approaches see emotions as post-cognitive phenomena to be changed by rationally challenging beliefs.

As I have already indicated, there are a number of mindfulness-based therapies. There are some differences between the focus of Greenberg relating to couples and a number of theoretical devices, but in this analysis I am attempting to locate some similarities. Four important features stand out as similarities: emotions are related to issues of 'meaning', with a strong cognitive strand; emotions are motivators, directed towards goals with a conative/volitional strand; emotions have a strong affective component; managing emotions involves an attentional dimension – to transform and regulate emotional change. Some of the differences are obviously due to the ethical and spiritual features of Buddhism, whereas Greenberg stands on a more secular footing, though he is greatly inspired in his therapy to focus on the well-being of clients.

Principles of Emotional Change

1. In EFT the central mechanism of change is emotional processing and the emergent meaning making processes, and *awareness* of emotions is the basic principle. Once we are aware about what we feel, we reconnect with the needs signalled by the emotion, and are motivated to meet our needs. According to Greenberg, the therapist 'works with clients to help the client approach, tolerate and regulate, as well as accept the emotions'.[28] Acceptance of emotions, as opposed to avoidance, is an important step in emotional change.

2. Emotional *expression*: the client must also be in live contact with their emotions, and thus develop effective exposure to previously avoided feelings. While arousal and tolerance of emotions is necessary, optimal emotional processing involves the integration of cognition and affect.

3. Emotion regulation also involves getting 'some distance' from the specific emotion, whether it is shame, fear or powerlessness, whichever emotion is contextually important. Any attempt to regulate emotions by preventing themselves from feeling the disturbing emotions, withdrawing, avoiding, using distraction strategies or, the worst, transforming emotions to psychosomatic complaints – and even stimulus seeking diversions seeking to drown the unpleasant – are counter-productive techniques. At this point Greenberg observes:

> Important means of regulating emotion include regulating breathing and mindfulness – the non-judgmental observation and description of one's emotional states. Basic emotion regulation also include naming the emotion, describing the emotion in one's body, clarifying the emotion event that evoked the emotion, and understanding one's interpretation of the situation and actions prompted by the emotion.[29]

4. Reflection on emotional experience at a deep experiential level is recommended, as a way of consolidation.

5. Transformation of one emotion by another is the final method mentioned. He quotes Spinoza to illustrate this point: 'an emotion cannot be restrained nor removed unless by an opposed and stronger emotion'.[30]

Buddhist Perspective on Emotion Regulation

An emotion in the Buddhist context is an interactive complex or construction emerging from the five aggregates, thus blending the cognitive, motivational, affective and the physiological arousal factors. There is also a network following the causal patterns of dependent origination: sensory stimuli conditioning feeling, feeling conditioning craving and craving conditioning grasping. Also, the roots of greed, hatred and delusion feed negative emotions, and their opposites of generosity, compassion and wisdom nourish the positive emotions. In current counselling terminology, the negative roots would be addiction, reactivity and identity confusion. What I have described as the componential view of emotions help the therapist to use the four frames of reference in the *Satipaṭṭhāna*: body, feelings/sensations, thought patterns and phenomena. As an alternative, the therapist may use the causal psychodynamic patterns of sensory contact conditioning, and feeling conditioning craving and craving conditioning grasping. Subliminal activity is important, as if one does not use the 'breaks' for pleasant feelings, these tend to be aroused by the subliminal proclivity for lust (*rāgānusaya*). If one does not put the 'breaks' to painful feelings, subliminal proclivity for aversion and cognitive distortions (*diṭṭhānusaya*), also colour negative emotions (*paṭighānusaya*), is aroused. In terms of this many sided scheme, whether it be in routine life or in the context of therapy, the preventive approach rather than damage control is recommended.

Mindfulness practice should be directed to restraint (*saṃvara*), then abandoning once they have emerged (*pahāna*), developing positive skills which are new (*bhāvanā*) and stabilising once such skills have emerged (*anurakkhanā*). The Buddha used a number of metaphors to describe these methods: the watchfulness of a doorkeeper, instilling discipline like a horse trainer, the persistence of an army defending a fortress, exercising balance and the right pitch between laziness and excitement, compared to a well tuned musical instrument, like the lute and the balancing skills of an acrobat.

Similar to Greenberg's methods, remedying negative emotions by antidotes is recommended; for lust, unattractive and repulsive aspects of the body; for ill-will, looking at the good qualities of a person, patience, forgiveness, loving kindness and equanimity; for grief, respect, honour and gratitude to the lost person, and re-working the good qualities of the lost person in one's own life. Transforming instead of demonising is a classic Buddhist method, especially prominent in the Tibetan Buddhist tradition. Carl Jung likened this process to converting base metals to gold, calling it 'emotional alchemy'. The final method is to see the impermanence of the process of emotions like anger emerging, staying for a while and pass away.

The Body in Emotional Experience

> People need to attend to whether the emotional experience is felt in their bodies as hot or cold, a big ball or a small knot... Thus if you begin to notice and label the quality and location of your feelings as 'hot sensations in my chest', to notice its intensity as 'moderate' and its shape as a 'round ball', then the torrents will subside.[31]

> Bhikkhus, just various winds blow in the sky: winds from the east, winds from the west, winds from the north, winds from the south, dusty winds and dustless winds, cold winds and hot winds, mild winds and strong winds; so too various winds arise in the body: pleasant feeling arises, painful feeling arises, neither-painful-nor pleasurable feeling arises.[32]

While the cognitive theories of emotions came to the forefront of emotion study and therapy, partly due to the new revolution in the cognitive sciences, there has been a great revival of interest in body-based therapies, as well as the physiological facets of emotion studies. It was William James who first dramatised the body in emotions by saying, 'first we cry and then we feel sad, first we run and then we feel fear', and in spite of the limitations which I discussed earlier, there has been a revival of interest in what are called 'gut reactions' and 'embodied appraisals'.[33] James described the body as the mind's sounding board, allowing emotion signals to resonate as the sound of a guitar amplifies the sound of the strings. This means that through mindful awareness/suppression of some automatic bodily changes and consciously making others, we gain emotional control. The links between the body and emotions are recognised by both Greenberg and Buddhist mindfulness practice.

Cultivating Emotional Balance (CEB): Paul Ekman and Alan B. Wallace

I have already emphasised the importance of emotional balance. CEB is basically an education programme with some therapeutic components. Developed by one of the most renowned exponents on emotion studies, Paul Ekman, and a celebrated scholar of Tibetan Buddhism, Alan Wallace, the programme has been described as follows: 'The broad aim of CEB is to introduce large numbers of people to the well-being and fulfilments that can arise from grounded regulation and mind training skills'.[34] The curriculum is based on three basic skills: recognising emotional triggers, emotional behaviour and receptivity to the feelings of others. This programme upholds that the contemplative practice of meditation is a core element in their methodology, and this can lead to alleviation of psychological problems as well as the cultivation of prosocial behaviour, which is an ingredient in the education projects for groups. Developing self-awareness through contemplative practice and attentional skills is a technique central to the programme, with human flourishing and well-being as their educational goal.

14
Exploring the Content and Methodology of Buddhist Meditation

How What is Little Becomes Much

It has been observed that though the practice of mindfulness has entered the mainstream of Western psychology and therapy, and generated a lot of interest, the very practice of mindfulness (*sati*) has a very unassuming character.

> Mindfulness practice in fact has, if we may personify it, a rather unassuming character. Compared with it, mental factors such as devotion, energy, imagination, and intelligence, are certainly colourful personalities, making an immediate and strong impact on people and situations. Their conquests are sometimes rapid and vast, though often insecure. Mindfulness, on the other hand, is of an unobtrusive nature. Its virtue shines inwardly, and in ordinary life most of its merits are passed on to other mental factors which generally receive all the credit. One must know mindfulness well and cultivate its acquaintance before one can appreciate its value and its silent penetrative influence.[1]

It took the genius of the Buddha to perceive the power of the seemingly small – to explain how 'what is little becomes much'.

It must be emphasised that mindfulness is linked with a clear comprehension of the right purpose (*sampajañña*), activated during sitting practice, and this notion links mindfulness practice to the broader area of mindfulness of walking, stretching, bending, turning around, looking to one side and all other activities that make up ordinary life. If you commit to mindfulness practice in an intensive retreat then you set aside social relationships, conversation, writing and reading. Take care when having the midday meal and so on. As this chapter is written against the background of counselling and therapeutic issues, I do not wish to go further into locating mindfulness against the seven factors of enlightenment, but briefly mention that if you are pursuing a path beyond good mental health and mindfulness, practice on the liberation path would include: mindfulness, investigation, energy, rapture, tranquillity, concentration and equanimity. Sayadaw Pandita's *In this Very Life* is an excellent guide for those who wish to follow the 'liberation quest'.[2]

The Breath in Meditation

Because of the varieties of 'guides on meditation' available in the book market, I wish to restrict myself first to the preliminary scan of the bodily posture, depending on what sitting posture you adopt, or the use of a straight back chair or a meditation bench. The detailed steps of the 'body scan' are given later in this chapter. The second step is the 'noticing' of the in-breath and out-breath as they occur and then to the sensations of the breath, the most prominent touching point, tip of the nose or top of the lip. Thus, the two central foci would be: (i) the discriminative experience of the in-breath and out-breath; (ii) observe the prominent point at which stimulation occurs as the breath moves in and out. It is necessary to focus on the quality of the breath as it changes from a gross quality to a more refined one and is steady and calm, and then focus on the length of the breath. When the noting mind calms down, the air draft/breath becomes shorter and the distinction between the in-breath and out-breath becomes less apparent, this change, according my meditation Guru, is a healthy sign of improvement. As the prominence of the breath dwindles, the instruction is to see the breath as the whole body (*sabba-kāya*). 'The meditation will gather its own momentum and you will penetrate deeper in to the object of meditation. When your effort is balanced and your attention is precise and continuous, mindfulness will become strongly established and concentration will develop'. If you are more inclined towards serenity meditation, then Venerable Dhammajiva observes that the breath will settle down without any direction from the mind.

In insight meditation, instead of focusing our attention on the breath as 'breath' we change gears and experience it as the air draft, or the air element, which is also described as the 'striker element' (*ārammaṇa*); the base element (*dvāra*) is the point of touch – the tip of the nose or the top of the lip; we notice an experience of heat or coldness, a rubbing sensation and the expansion and contraction, and this is the ignition or fire element. The base element is the experience of 'solidity'. The 'water element' is always there at various points, like lips. The focus on the four elements provides one route for the practice of insight meditation, in understanding the impersonal nature of 'materiality' as ever changing in the form of vibrations. When meditation develops, occasionally the vibrations can be chaotic, but as one approaches the first *vipassanā jhāna* there is a relative balance and equilibrium within a dynamic, a kind of shifting setting. This requires greater skill as the object of meditation is in a changing setting. Our guru says that in this respect the focus in tranquillity meditation is like shooting an arrow at stationary deer and in insight meditation it is like firing at a moving deer. For the expert meditator, used to both forms of meditation, he can combine them in different ways. Also, one may follow up both forms of meditation by *mettā* meditation. Insight meditation needs heightened and discriminative observation. For both forms of meditation, in their first phase, 'concentration' and focus is necessary. Also, our guru says that personality factors are also important in selecting a particular form of meditation. But *mindfulness in daily life* is absolutely necessary for all forms of meditation. It is at this point that I find that my role as a meditator and therapist cross pathways – they are mutually enriching. But a therapist needs a great deal of flexibility, to understand the client's background and wisdom that fits the occasion (*upāya-kauśalya*), to 'discover' what elements of mindfulness practice would help the client. The Buddha himself varied his methods and sermons often when he understood the personalities of people who came for help and guidance. My point is that meditation is not merely a technology that a person picks up at a retreat and spends thirty minutes daily in practising it like a ritual, but along with understanding the techniques and practising it, this work should reverberate through your life – and then you will find meaning and fulfilment in your life. Gradually your practice reaches deeper levels, and equally you learn the art of balancing the different components of meditation, such as mindfulness, investigation, energy, joy, happiness and equanimity (see Chapter 8).

The Concept of 'Breath' in Meditation Practice

Breathing is the basis of life and common to all living beings. It is an activity that is performed automatically, without awareness. But it is also an activity that can be done deliberately. The most important point about breath is that we can regulate our breathing by observing the

breath in the quietness and the stillness of a meditation setting, and
it is possible to cultivate the flow of breath as a rhythmical and smooth
flow. It is the cultivation of our awareness focused on the breath and the
development of a quiet rhythmical pattern that form the basis of what
is referred to as tranquillity meditation (*samatha*).

Our normal breathing patterns change when we are in the grip of
stressful situations, when we experience excitement or anger. Mindfulness of breathing helps the quietening of both bodily and mental unrest
and helps us to take a 'step back' in anticipating a sudden change of
breathing patterns. If, for instance, we are late to office and while driving fast come to a traffic junction and just as we are about to cross the
junction the lights turn red: if we put a gradual brake to our body sensations and focus on the breath, we learn that there may be a sudden
rush of blood in stressful situations. The breath is a kind of emotional
thermometer, indicating the ups and downs of our moods and our emotional temperature. The most important point that has to be understood
is that the breath stands on the threshold between voluntary and involuntary bodily functions, and it offers a path to extend the scope of
the conscious control of the body. In formal meditation, as found in
the four fold frame of reference for meditation (*Satipaṭṭhāna*), as we
close our eyes we keep out any stimulation of the sense doors, and it
is the breath and the body sensations that come within our awareness,
then systematically, as we continue to practise, feelings and thoughts
become the focus of mindfulness. In formal meditation practice in the
first stage, the breath experience becomes the focus of attention. When
from the focus on the body, we shift our attention to feelings, it is a
more subtle and refined awareness, as we discern the reactivity of our
consciousness to pleasure giving, painful and neutral sensations. As we
saw in the chapter on emotions, feelings provide the springboard from
which emotions emerge with a mixture of thought elements. Then we
shift to the contemplation of the mind, the ethical quality of feelings,
which at a very early stage begin to take shape, and we get the advice
to keep off defilements as sense desires, ill-will, lethargy, restlessness
and sceptical doubt. Basically, the mindfulness practice starts with the
body, then feeling, followed by thought patterns and last the nature
of phenomena and the laws that govern the working of the body and
mind: *kāyānupassanā* (mindfulness of body); *vedanānupassanā* (mindfulness of feelings); *cittānupassanā* (mindfulness of thought patterns); and
dhammānupasanā (mindfulness of the nature of phenomena).

It is also necessary to mention that, unlike the functioning of the
breath, the operation of our sense faculties, seeing, smelling, hearing,

tasting and touching, are functions which we directly experience but the attention we pay to these functions is not done in a thoughtful manner: 'It is easy to eat without tasting, miss the fragrance of the moist earth after the rain, even touch others without knowing the feeling we are transmitting'.[3] In this manner we can be out of touch with our feelings and mindfulness can bring back a more sensitive encounter with the world of the senses.

The fact that our breath is controlled by the autonomic nervous system (ANS), except when it is under voluntary control (CNS), points to a very strategic relation between the respiratory system and the body's emotional and chemical activity. Groundbreaking research by Candace Pert indicates that the 'body is a second brain'. She says that chemicals act as messengers between the body and mind.[4] She emphasises the point that emotions are a real link between body and mind.

Basic Mindfulness Exercise on the Breath/Body

Start with three or four long breaths in and out. Be clearly aware of each breath in and out, and gradually shift your attention to inhale the breath sensation at the base of the skull (behind), and then let it flow down the spine. Then shift to the right leg (in front) and starting with the knee-joint let the breath flow down, and then the same with the left knee and leg. Then it needs to flow along the right elbow towards the finger tips and repeat the same with the left elbow. Now, move the breath to the base of the throat, slow down the speed and let the breath flow down in front of the body, past the lungs and the liver, all the way down to the bladder and colon. Repeat this exercise three times. Let all the breath sensations spread so that they connect and flow together. This background helps you to move towards the nostrils again with an energetic flow coming from the body. Feel the tremendous sense of silence around, and you begin with the silent present awareness of the breath, and as you continue with the flow of the in-breath and out-breath for a while, you will be able to build up a rhythm.

Opening Up to Sensations/Feelings

Each time you breathe in and out, try to maintain a sense of openness to anything that comes your way: sensations, feelings, thought patterns and the inner chatter of the mind. The ability to stay with your sensations/feelings is very important, and these may be physical or mental, stress, tensions and bodily pain. Mindfulness practice, when fully developed, works at different levels: sensory channels, body and breath, feelings/sensations, inner chatter of the mind/thoughts, desires and intentions that feed physical action. If there is denial and repression we bring about a type of denseness, a sluggish dullness (*thīna-middha*): it is one of the five hindrances which is compared to a layer of moss in water. At a more sophisticated level, there can be deception and disguise of the actual thought processes in the mind. Mindfulness practice helps a person to break through these repressive layers of the mind and expand the realm of self-knowledge and self-control.

Concluding Thoughts

There are precautions for those therapists who plan to use mindfulness techniques for therapy, and the following words of advice from a pioneer in the field sums up these fears:

> It becomes critically important that those persons coming to the field with professional interest and enthusiasm recognize qualities and characteristics of mindfulness as a meditative practice, with all that it implies, so that mindfulness is not simply seized upon as the next promising behavioural technique or exercise, de-contextualised, and plugged into a behavioural paradigm with the aim of deriving behavioural changes, or fixing what is broken.[5]

15
Stress Management and the Rhythms of Our Lives

In the context of the crucial issues in counselling, understanding the nature of stress and stress management provides a useful background for understanding more complex issues about fear and anxiety, loss of self-confidence and depression, sudden onrush of aggression/anger, responding to grief and taking to alcohol and drugs. The second reason why understanding stress is important is that stress is a necessary ingredient of normal routine life, but if you understand its logic you are in a position to avoid falling into more serious mental health concerns. Irwin Yalom made the following observation:

> The universality of stress is one of the major reasons that scholars encounter such difficulty when they attempt to define and describe normality: the difference between normality and pathology is quantitative and not qualitative.[1]

Good and Beitman, in a standard introduction to counselling, also follow Yalom's thinking: they say that stress is found in every corner of our lives, but these different types of pressures are not the problem, it is rather the way we respond or react to them. 'Stress is an unavoidable aspect of being alive. Hence, how people respond to stress determines, to a large extent, the impact of stress in their lives'.[2] Most of my clients were close to normal life and I often found that exploring stress levels and types of stress was very useful and an effective way of getting the clients to talk. Now, well-known Buddhist scholars like Thanissaro Thero translates the Buddhist concept *dukkha* (the first noble truth) as 'stress'.

This chapter introduces you to the first and most basic issue confronted by a counsellor when he meets the client in a therapeutic session. Stress is close to normal life, and for these reasons this is the first chapter that gives you an idea about the counselling process. This book covers specific counselling issues like addictions, grief counselling and depression, and more general concerns like stress and anger management, which are part and parcel of most counselling concerns. Especially for those readers who are new to counselling, stress is easy to understand as it is part and parcel of everyday life.

Dr Hans Selye, who first popularised the term 'stress' in the 1950s, opted to define it as a response and stressor to describe the stimulus. He emphasised the non-specificity of the stress response, saying that basically it is an adaptation to the pressure of experience – and how we adapt becomes crucial. He observed that it is not the potential stressor but how you perceive it and then handle it that it will lead to real stress. Sometimes, a minor event can make us overreact or a major emergency may be handled with calm and composure. In the area of mindfulness-based stress management, Jon Kabat-Zinn observes that:

> it stands to reason that by becoming conscious of our options in stressful situations and by being mindful of the relevance and effectiveness of our response in those situations, we may be able to exercise control over our experience of stress and influence whether or not it will lead to stress.[3]

What are the different types of stress? First, there are stresses of the daily hassles in life, like getting up as the alarm clock on the table rings, going to the office, and sometimes taking children to school on the same trip; getting stuck in a traffic jam; at home in the evening, the washing machine needs a check up, some bills have to be payed soon. There are environmental stressors such as physical cold in extreme winter, noise, the glare of the sun in summer; work stresses like a deadline for completing a project, the need to acquire new professional skills, even celebrating a well-earned promotion, lack of enjoyment with the new project that had just been thrust on you; domestic stresses in family relations; lifestyle stresses from diet, tobacco and alcohol.

Whatever the stress situation, a stressful reaction is a mental and physical reaction to an adverse situation that mobilises the body's emergency mechanisms like 'flight' or 'fight' and, if not, calm down and explore what has to be done. The term 'stress' is a metaphor from engineering referring to 'physical pressure' and, in general, a stress response is mediated by the autonomic nervous system (ANS), which has the function of moderating different bodily functions like heart beat, blood flow, digestion and sexual responses. The 'sympathetic' aspect of ANS tends to excite our body and the 'parasympathetic' aspect calms the body in relaxation or meditation. As ANS activity occurs without our conscious awareness, it is necessary that people receive some understanding of these mechanisms and regular mindfulness practice with some guidance helps one to be mindful of such processes. Sometimes, the stress reactions are a necessary part of our survival and they bring important messages, for instance, the need to attend to some urgent matter. All stress is not unhealthy, so long as you cultivate some awareness of these processes.

In general, stress management looks at four important areas, and mindfulness methods are effective at these different levels of stress management: (1) physiological level; (2) emotional level; (3) behavioural level; and (4) cognitive level.

1. Physiological level: the cardiovascular system, musculoskeletal system, nervous system and immune system. Symptoms are reactivity to alarms, bodily tensions, headaches, backaches and high blood pressure.
2. Emotional Level: stress responses – anger, irritation, annoyance, indignation, sadness–depression spectrum, worry, fear and anxiety.
3. Behavioural level: poor concentration, weak attention to work, inability to maintain interpersonal relations, fall in productive work and lack of flexibility.
4. Cognitive Level: weak self-confidence and lack of self-assurance, lack of enthusiasm and pessimism.

Moderate levels of stress are believed to give some exercise to the brain, so that all stress is not bad: 'no stress at all means that the brain does not get any exercise. A brain is not unlike a muscle, in that the cliché 'use it or lose it' applies. Moderate levels of stress keep our minds in condition, and help us to be sane. This 'good stress' promotes the neural growth of hormones that support learning'.[4] Paradoxically, some stress situations call for solutions to problems and thus, if well pursued, put an end to the earlier unattended load of stress. The following case study proves this point and is also a very good example for illustrating that an early attempt to 'nip the bud', without seeking the guidance of a counsellor, can be done at the family level with parents who have the correct temperament to handle such stress in children.

Case Study

Wilson is a 17-year-old student pursuing engineering studies at university. He is an only child and his parents are fond of him. There have been limitations in the family conversation regarding Wilson's links with friends, especially girls, though they did talk about t many other interesting things at dinner and tea. Wilson by nature is very shy and somewhat reserved in the company of girls. Wilson has taken a liking to Amy, who is in his class, and this feeling grows into infatuation without Wilson being aware of it. Amy may have had a slight suspicion about Wilson's soft feelings for her, but there was no frank conversation between them. With one more year to go for his finals, Wilson becomes a bit forgetful about his regular class assignments and tutorials. His mother found that the regular marketing Wilson did for the family was done in a very slipshod manner. He also stopped his part-time job at a restaurant. The parents gradually discover that the boy looks stressed, not merely in his conduct but in his facial expression. There were also bits of indecision in his routine things to be done for the day. Wilson's father, John, had a strange hunch that Wilson had fallen in love with one of the girls at school and, during an evening walk to the park, Wilson's father opened up a conversation in a playful mood.

John had a light-heartedness about him and was able to open issues in a very casual manner: he just told Wilson, 'Well Wilson, you will complete your finals this year, and after that are you going to do a treasure hunt, I mean find a nice girl?' First, Wilson's face turned red and was trying to go the way of denial, but after some very skilful cross-questions Wilson opened up like the cascades in a waterfall – he simply described what had been going through his mind in the last two months. Parents had some words of wisdom for Wilson, 'I am glad that your heart has opened towards someone. Now, go slow and see what sort of person Amy is and begin some conversation without any commitment, and there is no injunction that you have to do this in a week. Now your heart is warm, get back to your work and routine life with lot of joy and determination to get excellent results at the final examination and leave the field open – it may be Amy or someone else, the choice is entirely yours.' With this bit of magic from Wilson's father Wilson was back to his normal self.

This study is important as it shows how necessary it is to deal with young people with wisdom, calm and good humour, without imposing one's personality on them.

As a counsellor, I learnt some of these insights from my wife Kalyani, and we got used to treating our children like friends. She was a teacher and had a regular bag full of innocent jokes which cleared up the family atmosphere. Counselling and therapy do have their specialised territory, but there are occasions, like the case study of Wilson, if wisdom, understanding and good humour are developed in the family, where that would be the path to develop a 'therapeutic culture'.

Now I wish to take a more complex case of stress management but a type that is common today among young professionals attempting to settle down to a long term commitment to a job. This case study has been constructed from my experience with a number of clients who sought counselling and whose context for stress management was similar.

Ashok (30) and Amrita (26) are Asian migrants who have been in Queensland for over five years. They have two children, a son and a daughter. Ashok has a high-ranking executive post in a company and Amrita works in a department store. Everything goes exceptionally well for recent migrants Ashok and Amrita. Ashok's workplace is quite a distance from home, and he leaves home early, but also goes to the gym adjoining the workplace to keep fit. Ashok is back home by about 7pm and Amrita takes the children to school and picks them up again. There was some re-organisation of the company as it was venturing into a new field and most of the executives were advised to pick up new skills through training and workshops relevant for the planned changes in the company. There was no threat of redundancy, but there was a bit of fluidity and lack of clear direction in the workplace, which was a matter of concern and anxiety.

Ashok is a very reserved person at work and has a habit of quietly repressing the distress and anger that are part of the daily round of things. He also does not want to discuss his problems at home, except to say in a very casual sort of way that he has some workshops for training in a new field and an examination to follow. About a month before his exams, a close relative, Aunty Rita (who had looked after Amrita when she was small) came to spend a month with them. Ashok is normally a very cordial person and very open when he has Amrita's visitors. But on this occasion, it is certainly bad timing. By nature when Ashok has problems, he tries to be excessively nice to visitors and repress his distress. To add to these darkening clouds, there was a new recruit in Ashok's workplace, who appeared to be a favourite of his boss. During normal times, this sort of context would not have worried Ashok as he is not envious of others in the workplace doing well. When a good natured person like

Ashok is tolerating Rita's presence, the distress simmers within and he begins to have headaches. Fortunately, by this time it is time for Rita to leave, and it is not only a great consolation for Ashok but also provides some space to have a frank chat with his wife, and he discusses issues with Amrita in the most calm and gentle manner, without trying to find a scapegoat for his problems, and then ends up with a number of counselling sessions, first for Ashok and then jointly with Amrita. The counsellor is able to isolate the components of Ashok's problems and suggests certain mindfulness exercises with formal meditation in daily life. After about two weeks, Ashok discovers that he is not getting caught up in ruminating thought patterns about the future and is able to engage fully in the work in the office. The counsellor shows that Ashok was subjected to what in counselling is called 'experiential avoidance' and Ashok is amazed about the change in his thinking and feeling. Ashok has no problems in doing the new workshops and is well settled in the office without any anxieties, developing a great interest in learning new skills.

The counselling guidelines for stress related problems following the practice of counselling practice is basically focused on 'self-knowledge' without repression, denial and avoidance. The following guidelines have helped me in dealing with stress management in clients:

- Raising awareness without judgment, denial and reaction.
- Understanding the paradox that awareness and kind acceptance of the real malady within – which is painful – helps it to change.
- Developing mindfulness of ruminative thought patterns or 'the auto pilot' is a preliminary opening up, followed by mindfulness of bodily sensations and feelings.
- Develop a sense of aliveness of the body and the world around us.
- Develop a sense of connectedness with others at home. Entertaining close friends at home is a very fine dimension of developing connectedness to others. You may even entertain friends at the workplace.
- Ashok's world changed without any resort to alcohol or other diversions to suppress problems and he was able to spend more time with his children and wife, with an occasional vacation out.

Unwholesome Responses to Stress

Repression; denial; escape through diversions; hyperactivity and overworking; overeating; substance dependency: drugs, alcohol, cigarettes; self-harm; and suicidal thoughts.

Wholesome Responses

Sharing stress problems with family or friends is a form of counselling. Many schools, work places and counselling centres offer counselling services. With complex stress related issues, a professional counsellor is best. There are also projects like the one developed by Dr Craig Hassed for the Monash University Medical Faculty, a stress release programme using and incorporating mindfulness practice.[5] There are also projects focused on physical exercise, walking, recreation and music. For individuals, a diversified daily/weekly agenda is best. Friendship links, social work, regular visits to a library are other ways of spending time away from work.

In conclusion, it must be mentioned that the organisational face of the work environment, as well as its social face, has radically changed, and cohesive and lively relations with family and friends are great resources for living in a society undergoing rapid changes. There is empirical evidence that patient and less deliberative practices like mindfulness practice are effective when dealing with stress related problems, especially disorder and uncertainty around our lives.[6] Claxton has symbolised the world of speed, accuracy and target goals with the slow going, relaxed life, using silence and the meditative life with the alternative images of the 'hare brain' and the 'tortoise mind'. Chapter 11, on contemplative philosophy and psychology, examines these alternative paths in life, and provides a graphic background to locate mindfulness practice.

16

The Logic of Sadness and Its Near Allies: Depression, Melancholy and Boredom

Recently there has been an interesting dialogue about 'misrepresenting normal suffering as an illness' and turning sorrow into sickness.[1] In the context of suffering, to reflect on life and give meaning to it, and even embrace it, is the path of generating insight and discernment about life and death according to the Buddha, as he explained the first noble truth in his first sermon, 'Setting the Wheel in Motion'. The ground-breaking work, *The Loss of Sadness*, by Horowitz and Wakefield, says that there is a danger that normal sadness is being converted into a mental disorder:

> Sadness is an inherent part of the human condition, not a mental disorder. Thus to confront psychiatry's invalid definition of depressive disorder is also to consider a painful but an important part of our humanity that we have tended to shut aside in the modern medicalization of human problems. As science allows us to gain more control over our emotional states, we will inevitably confront the question of whether normal intense sadness has any redeeming features or should be banished from our lives. Such a momentous scientific and moral issue should not be spuriously resolved by using a semantic confusion in the DSM that mistakenly places states of intense sadness under the medical category of disorder. We can only adequately confront the complex and important concerns involved if we clearly differentiate normal sadness from mental disorder.[2]

Even among those who value the DSM (Diagnostic and Statistical Manual of Mental Disorder) criteria as an accepted benchmark for health professionals, there are dissident voices like that of Paul Biegler: 'Horowitz and Wakefield might ultimately be shown to be correct that

DSM "Overpathologizes" many people with quite legitimate sadness in the face of adversity'.[3] Thus, we may agree with Freud who observed that: 'Although grief involves grave departures from the normal attitude to life, it never occurs to us to regard it as a morbid condition and hand the mourner over to medical treatment. We rest assured that after a lapse of time it will be overcome, and we regard any interference with it as inadvisable and even harmful'.[4]

While the next chapter will present techniques of managing grief without medicalising those who experience grief and loss, this chapter has a conceptual framework for locating grief along with depression, melancholy and boredom. Grief is close to our normal life and it is important as it provides a context for reflection: 'It is as a result of the griever's focus on the whole of life of the diseased, that grieving tends to be a time for reflection. While commentators often note that grief is associated with social withdrawal or depression, they rarely discuss its reflective tone. But people in grief regularly experience a reflective time in thought about the diseased, about the meaning of life and death, about the passage of time'.[5] Horowitz and Wakefield also discuss the nature of grief as biologically based non-verbal expression, with the emphasis on its universality across cultures and its presence in non-human primates and infants prior to socialisation. Also, grief at the loss of a loved one, loss of meaningful relationships, loss of a job or of status, and chronic stress are different dimensions of grief. During recent times, natural disasters and war situations have brought a perilous kind of grief, which are discussed elsewhere in an examination of grief and sadness in 'panic cultures'.[6]

This chapter is basically focused on what may be called the 'lost art of sadness'. Freud, in examining the nature of mourning, differentiates it from melancholia and clearly rules out the claim that mourning is a medical disorder, thus affirming very early in the history of psychotherapy the claim by Horowitz and Wakefield (H and W) that 'sadness is an inherent part of the human condition, not a mental disorder'. It is necessary to emphasise that there are two strands in the Freudian concept of 'melancholy': one strand standing for 'depression' and the other strand, owing much to Robert Murton's work *Anatomy of Melancholy*,[7] describable as 'existential angst'. Burton described depression as of 'deep reach, excellent apprehension, judicious, wise and witty', and, thus, looking at the two faces of depression, one is a clinical disorder, the other a strand developed especially by the existential psychotherapist, Irwin D. Yalom, which is a more sophisticated revival of Burton's thought. Michael Ignatieff refers to this as a 'lost paradigm' and as a discourse to be understood rather than a pathology to be corrected.[8] Irwin D. Yalom's existential therapy is a more sophisticated revival of this perspective backed by a great deal of clinical data. In looking at issues of meaning and death, he integrates the voices of Dostoevsky, Tolstoy, Kafka and Camus. I explored the interface between Buddhism and existentialism as philosophy and therapy in *Explorers of Inner Space*.[9] Also, while the next chapter will deal with the Buddhist pathways for the management of grief, the concept of grief and loss and mourning are central to the focus on what is considered as the lost art of sadness.

Also, while sadness is a visible front of suffering, there is an unarticulated and unrecognised silent form of suffering described by the French term 'ennui' or the English 'boredom'. This experience may be called 'pedestrian depression' as different from clinical depression – emerging and getting submerged in the moment to moment flow of life – and it is a neglected emotion, which will be taken up later in this chapter. Buddhism and other Asian psychological traditions help to understand the issues about sadness, melancholy and boredom. But unfortunately the H and W study does not explore alternative, non-Western therapeutic traditions, as discussed in the next chapter on the management of grief and also in the chapter on mindfulness-based therapies.

My own personal therapeutic orientation, which I developed and used in my counselling practice for many years, may be described as *mindfulness-based emotion-focused therapy*. After I moved from direct counselling practice to counselling education, as a member of the Counsellors' & Psychotherapists' Association of Victoria (CAPAV), I have been able to formalise more clearly the integration of emotion studies to therapy. While gaining much from the work of the celebrated pioneer of emotion-focused therapy (EFT), Leslie Greenberg, in whose workshops in Sydney I participated, I have also integrated EFT to mindfulness practice and therapy. During very recent times, there has emerged a venture in practical education of grounded emotion regulation and training of mindfulness skills, which also has therapeutic value. Developed as cultivating Emotional Balance (CEB) by Paul Ekman, a pioneer psychologist of the study of emotions and facial expression, and the Buddhist philosopher Alan Wallace, it has a great deal of resonance with my concept of mindfulness-based, emotion-focused therapy.

In the context of the present chapter, Lewis Wolpert presented a very insightful analysis of the importance of emotion studies as central to understanding depression, and he says that 'depression is a disorder of emotions':

If we are to understand depression then we need to understand emotion, for depression, I believe is sadness that has become pathological... depression is a disorder of emotion.[10]

The Pervasiveness of Human Suffering

Three important emotions and their significance have been submerged by the overpowering pre-occupation with 'depression' as a clinical disorder: these emotions are sadness, melancholy as existential angst, and boredom. These emotions need to be understood with insight, and for that the mind has to be open and receptive. As the Venerable Sumedha says in discussing the four noble truths, Aññā Koṇḍañña was the first to be liberated after listening to the first sermon of the Buddha, and the pervading insight was that 'All that is subject to arising is subject to change'.[11] This is not a method of merely tranquilising the mind, which of course is a part of the practice; proper meditation is a commitment to wise investigation. This involves the mind being open to the subliminal tendencies for attachment/obsession, reactive aversion, sluggishness and boredom and the fine dividing line between being aroused by the tragic and getting drowned by it. What is operative is not a desire to 'get rid' of the unwholesome by their annihilation but to understand that cessation is the natural ending of something that has arisen. Such an experience is *nirodha* – cessation, emptiness and non-attachment. This is the Buddhist path towards *emotional maturity*, a concept that I greatly valued in my practice of counselling. Over the course of several sessions clients begin to see their anger, different patterns of aversion and reactivity, obsession and attachments, moments of dullness and depression. They look at them like a work of art and lose any embarrassment, shame and guilt in being subject to these states. When normal unhappiness and suffering is seen with detachment they do not get converted into forms of pseudo-suffering and neurosis. Emotional clarity, balance and maturity are the marks of a successful therapy. Sigmund Freud said these immortal words: 'I am merely trying to convert hysteria into common unhappiness'. Drury says:

> Freud showed real profundity when he stated that the aim of psychoanalysis was to replace neurotic unhappiness by normal unhappiness. A psychiatry based on a purely hedonistic ethics, a psychiatry that does not recognize that periods of anxiety and periods of melancholy

are necessary part of every human life, such a psychiatry will be no more than a superficial affair. Our task is not merely relieve but to interpret.[12]

Writing on the subject, the 'Danger of Words', Drury is critical of *some* of the current medicalisation of the word depression.

The pervasiveness of human suffering has been also voiced in some Western therapeutic traditions:

> Some mental health problems are pathological in the traditional sense. But short of giving nearly every citizen one or more syndromal labels, no amount of progress in the area of psychological disease will remove our need to explain and address the pervasiveness of human suffering.[13]

There are also many forms of psychological disorders that do not constitute clinical disorders, like for instance, loneliness, alienation, boredom, meaninglessness and low self-esteem. Normal people gain by counselling, despite their psychological problems being closer to normal life, and this was the case with most of my clients.[14] During the time of the Buddha, there was no clinical concept of abnormality, but he saw whole cultures driven by craving, addictions, self-indulgence and reactive behaviour ranging from anger to aggression.

Mourning and Melancholia

Freud's essay *Mourning and Melancholia* is a brilliant piece of writing, embedded with many insights, but as Jennifer Radden says, in spite of its brilliance there is a kind of opaqueness and ambiguity about it, and reading it demands the kind of skill that you need to apply when trying to figure out the complex meaning of a poem.[15] It is perhaps the earliest study in psychiatric literature that focuses on the importance of grief and sadness as distinct from clinical depression, though it must be mentioned that Carl Abraham's work in this area provided a useful background for Freud. Radden says that there is an interesting tension in Freud between on the one hand the belief that melancholic propensities are rare and pathological and, on the other, that they are common, and even a part of the human condition. The notion of considering melancholy as a part of the human condition is something that Freud owed to the tradition exemplified in Burton's *Anatomy of Melancholy).*[16] Radden also notes that melancholy was associated with genius, exalted moods and creative energy. The tendency to associate melancholy with the human condition is found in an important passage: 'all those situations of being wounded, hurt, neglected, out of favour, or disappointed, which can import opposite feelings of love and hate into their relationship or reinforce an existing ambivalence'.[17] As a way of resolving this tension, I have identified two strands in melancholia, one a positive facet of existential angst, and the other a negative one of pathological depression. In the H and W study, as has been noted, credit is given to Freud for clearly stating the position. H and W also note that grief is subject to a self-healing process and that a mourner will return to a normal psychological state.[18]

Depression and Boredom

Otto Fenichel described 'boredom' in an axiom: 'When we have to do what we do not want to do or not do what we want to do'. He considers boredom as characterised by an urge for activity, accompanied by an inhibition of that activity.

Erich Fromm, who during the latter part of his life maintained a deep and fascinating correspondence with the German monk in Sri Lanka, venerable Nyanaponika, offers some interesting insights on the relevance of Buddhism to what he calls '*la malaise du siècle*'. A state in which there are no symptoms except for feeling unhappy, strange and as if life has no meaning, no zest; a feeling of vague malaise.[19] He says that the misery which many people experience lies to a large extent not in the fact that they are sick, but rather in their separation from everything that is interesting or beautiful in life. Fromm says that they need an enlargement and intensification in life. He considers, 'boredom' as a sickness of our times. Linked to boredom is a feeling of isolation and lack of connections to others. Boredom emerges from the mechanical style of living we have today. Tibor Scitovsky, in his *Joyless Economy*, and Erich Fromm, in his *Have or to Be* and the *Art of Listening*, have highlighted this predicament. Scitovsky offers the idea that people should focus on 'activities pursued for their own sake'. This concept, referred to as the experience of 'flow', emerged from research related to work experience done by MIhaly Csikszentmihalyi. Interviewing and working on a wide array of people, including artists, mountain climbers, chess players, surgeons, writers and manual labourers, he found that the 'Sheer enjoyment of the act was the principle incentive'. The flow experience captures the moment–moment flow of life with quality and value and the paradigm experience is the practice of meditation.

Boredom is conditioned by value constraints, as Fenichel suggests, and also a theme developed by Calhoun that boredom implicates things one does without valuing them.[20] Thus, both on psychological grounds (Fenichel) and philosophical grounds (Calhoun), values play a part for the emergence of boredom; and according to Fromm lifestyles contribute to boredom in society. Goldstein, a well known meditation teacher, sees an attentional crisis at its roots:

> To realize that boredom does not come from the 'object' of our attention but rather from the 'quality' of our attention is truly a transforming insight. Fritz Perls, one of those who brought Gestalt therapy to America, said, 'Boredom is lack of attention'. Understanding this reality brings profound changes in our lives.[21]

As Mihaly Csikszentmihalyi confirms, the ability to be fully absorbed in what one does, music, art or cooking, is the key to both enjoyment and success in developing the skills. In the context of meditation, there is a deeper level of absorption, and Wallace makes a useful analysis of our attentional skills:

> An attentional deficit is characterised by the inability to focus on a chosen object. The mind becomes withdrawn and disengaged from its own internal processes. Attentional hyperactivity occurs when the mind is extensively aroused, resulting in compulsive distraction and fragmentation. And attention is dysfunctional when we focus on things in afflictive ways, not conducive to our own or others well-being.[22]

The Emotion Profile of Sadness and Working With Emotions

Bob Solomon says, 'But that trauma is not the whole of grief: The other side of grief, its precondition is love. Thus I want to argue that grief is not only bemoaning the loss. Grief is also a way of keeping the love alive'.[23] He also says that there is a commemoration factor in grief. People dedicate novels, name buildings, create fellowships and so on. It is important to note that, as Solomon says, grief is not an isolated emotion, it often comes as a constellation, and, as Kubler-Ross says, there is a whole enriching process going through denial, anger, distraction, guilt and sorrow. Thus, profound grief gets refined by going through such a process. Looking at the Maori rituals, he considers grief not as an interruption of life but as a continuation of the rhythms of life.

There have been a number of therapeutic approaches to managing emotions: 'Thus promoting emotional processing in *cognitive approaches*, arousal of fear by imaginative stimulation in *behavioural approaches*, emotional insight in *psychodynamic approaches*, increased depth of experience in *experiential approaches*, and communication of feeling in *interactional approaches* are all aspects of working with emotion that are seen as important within each perspective'.[24] All these approaches have made contributions to therapy, but in this chapter we are mainly concerned with emotion-focused therapy (EFT), as developed by its pioneer Leslie Greenberg, and my development of it as mindfulness-based emotion-focused therapy. Though my interest in emotion studies goes back many years, coming into contact with Greenberg's work in 2010 at a workshop in Sydney gave more confidence and direction to my emotion-based counselling. Independent of the therapeutic stream, there has been a revolution in emotion studies during recent times, as discussed in Chapter 5. In the development of emotion studies, there has been an integration of the affective, cognitive, motivational and attentional dimensions of emotions. A full-blown emotion has all these facets as well as the physiological dimension of emotions, which is central for the experience of emotions.

In working with emotions, using mindfulness practice as a resource, the charter for mindfulness practice is the *Satipaṭṭhāna Sutta* (The Foundations of Mindfulness) which embodies a fourfold guidance on the body, feelings, thought patterns and the nature of phenomena/mind–body relation;[25] and this basic structure is also found in the sermon *Ānāpāna Sutta* (Mindfulness of Breathing).[26] I found in my personal practice that when you take a paradigm emotion like anger, fear or sadness, and focus on the different components of the emotion, these different components in turn may be the focus of awareness and mindfulness: the body, feelings, perceptions, thoughts, thought patterns and the mind–body relationship. I have found this 'componential theory of emotions' useful in engaging with the client in a systematic way. In managing sadness, the first focus is the body, which is described as the 'felt sense': awareness of our body signals, of pressure and vibration, breathing, heartbeat, blood circulation and alertness to the body are important, while for the therapist facial expression gives significant clues. It is the breathing patterns which are central in mindfulness practice. While the five senses and the mind-door are the channels of information from the outer world, there is in Buddhism what is referred to as the 'sixth sense' that includes sensations in our limbs, our body's motions, the tension or relaxation of our internal set up including our organs, the lungs, heart and intestines, and the bodily aspects of our muscles, limbs and the face. We use the term *interoception* to describe this dimension, which in Pali is referred to as *anindriya-paṭibhattha-viññāna* – meaning non-sensory linkages of consciousness/independent of the five senses. In meditation all the sense doors are closed and *interoception* is possible. In insight meditation this focus is described as knowing the body through the body. Insight meditation develops as a focus on vibration patterns constituted by the four elements: air, solidity, water and fire. After the calming of the body, the focus is on 'feelings' and, as described in the chapter on emotions, the person who is skilful at being mindful of a painful feeling, an aversion or feeling miserable is able to 'apply the brakes' and not let it grow into anger or intense sadness; the focus on patterns of thoughts is crucial in cognitive therapy dealing with what they call the 'autopilot', breaking through automatic and repetitive thought patterns.

When we look at the emotion profile of sadness, in primary sadness there is the experience of parting and separation, loss, a feeling of being left out and difficulties of communication. Communication is crucial, as inhibition of a genuine need to communicate is damaging. The loss of a loved one, shattered hopes and loss of job, and being uprooted from safe and comfortable patterns of living, as we witness in the context of natural disasters, are some of the many causes for sadness. 'Secondary sadness' is more complex, with feelings of being hurt, damaged, wounded, ignored, unrecognised and rejected.[27] Especially in the context of an irrevocable loss, there is a emotional need for sympathy and sharing feeling with others. More creative people may take to music or use their literary skills. The most important therapeutic step is *acceptance*.

The goal in mindfulness therapy is to help the patient relate his emotional life, and all his experience, in a different way. It is not an attempt to eliminate sadness, worry or anxiety, but to help the patient to see things in a different light when they do arise. Thoughts and feelings are not in our control, but come and go on their own.[28]

Emotion-Focused Therapy

In Leslie Greenberg's emotion-focused therapy (EFT), awareness and acceptance is the starting point. The therapist 'Works with the client to help the client approach, tolerate and regulate, as well as accept their emotions'.[29]

Emotional expression: the client must also be in live contact with his emotions, and thus develop effective exposure to previously avoided feelings. While arousal and tolerance of emotion is necessary, optimum emotional processing involves the integration of cognition and affect.

Emotion regulation: when emotions such as sadness, shame, fear and powerlessness overwhelm people, there is a need to help people regulate their emotions by getting them some distance from them. Attempts to regulate feelings by preventing themselves from feeling the disturbing emotions, withdrawing, avoiding, using distraction strategies, transforming emotions by psychosomatic complaints or even seeking enjoyment to drown them out, are all counter-productive. In Buddhist practice, loosening the personal identification and seeking sadness as an interpersonal process that emerges, stays for a while and passes away is recommended.

In fact, at this point Greenberg integrates some aspects of mindfulness practice to EFT. Important methods of regulating emotions include regulating breathing and mindfulness – the non-judgmental observation and description of one's emotional states. Basic emotion regulation skills include naming the emotion, describing the emotion on one's body, clarifying the event that evoked the emotion and understanding one's interpretation of the situation and actions prompted by the emotion.[30] Naming and labelling are techniques used in Buddhist mindfulness practice. Reflection on emotional experience at the level of deep experience is recommended.

Transformation of one emotion by another is the final method Greenberg discusses, and he quotes Spinoza, 'an emotion cannot be restrained nor removed by another emotion unless by an opposed and stronger emotion'.[31]

Buddhist Pathways for Managing Negative Emotions

The method of restraint takes an initial preventative stand instead of damage control. The ability to 'step back' and make a mature choice is important, as choice takes an important role in managing emotions. Well-established mindfulness practice is helpful in many ways: if the emerging emotion is anger, the person will see it arising, and then let it quietly subside; he is able to anticipate that if the anger becomes more aggressive, the resulting impulsive behaviour would have damaging consequences; depending on the context, he could use resources like forgiveness and compassion towards the object of anger. This process, described as seeing the 'spark before the flame', is the pathway to using restraint. In a context like sensual desire, long term practice of restraint is the best method. Some of the specific techniques used for managing grief, along with a personal story, are the subject of the next chapter.

The method of remedying. The reference to Spinoza earlier in this chapter reminds one of the method of using antidotes. The four divine states of loving kindness, compassion, altruistic joy and equanimity are very effective, and a detailed analysis of them is found in the next chapter. The ability to embrace all parts of oneself without guilt and self-hurt, and the ability to connect with others, helps one to break away from any ego-centric predicament. In Buddhist cultures suffering and loss are seen as common concerns shared by others. The divine states also have a meditative dimension in addition to the socially engaging acts of charity. Buddhist equanimity brings a sense of realism and balance into our lives to get us through the hard knocks of life.

Transforming negative emotions instead of demonising them is a technique where anger/grief may be converted into patience, and each particular type of emotion has a different type of resource. Venerable Nyanaponika says not to throw away the negative emotions, as they can be transformed into something positive: 'If you throw away a thing it is gone. When you had something you have nothing. Your hands are empty, they have nothing to work on. Whereas almost all the things that you throw away, are capable of being worked over by a little magic into just the opposite of what they were'.[32]

Liberation from a negative emotion by insight. Here, one can use the componential theory of emotions, where emotions are seen as a construction out of bodily sensations, feelings and thought patterns, and if you take a hard look at them, gradually you see them emerging and passing away, and they appear empty and evaporate. Here the notion of impermanence is applied to these 'seemingly rock-like phenomena'.

Some of the methods cited in the next chapter, where grief and loss is a central concern, are also in certain contexts relevant to sadness and depression issues.

Buddhism and Depression: Anthropological Studies

H and W's study indicates that some anthropologists appear to deny the standing of depression as a universal category across cultures. The Sri Lankan anthropologist Gananath Obeyesekera claims that Sri Lankans view symptoms of hopelessness, meaninglessness and sorrow as a culturally conditioned philosophy of life and not an illness: 'How is the western diagnostic term "depression" expressed in a society whose predominant ideology of Buddhism states that life is suffering and sorrow, that the cause of suffering is attachment or craving, that there is a way (generally through meditation) of understanding and overcoming sorrow?'[33] H and W maintain that here Obeyesekere is clearly talking about normal sadness, and he does not discuss cases of chronic depression in this context, which might be described as a clinical disorder.[34] Catherine Lutz's celebrated study of the Ifaluk culture also contains similar observations on the genius of this culture in managing sadness through grief and loss. The term *'fago'* in this culture covers the emotions of compassion, love and sadness. 'Fago speaks of the sense that life is fragile, that connections to others are both precious and liable to severance through death and travel, that love may equal death'.[35] While accepting the great value of this study, H and W comment: 'Lutz provides an excellent description of normal sadness among the Ifaluk. Her critique ought to focus on the overexpansive definition of depressive disorders in Western psychiatry which might mistakenly classify these responses as dysfunctions.[36] While accepting the thesis of both, the universality of depressive disorders and also that there is an overexpansive definition of depression that attempts to absorb normal cases of sadness, it must be said that Lutz's groundbreaking study illuminates the power of cultural meaning systems to absorb what I call the lost art of sadness. The same may be true of Sri Lanka, though modernisation, social changes and natural disasters like tsunami have added new variables on the issues of suffering, sadness and depression.

One of the limitations of the H and W study is that, though they explore cross-cultural perspectives of depression and sadness, their focus on the management of depression is limited to Western therapies. The growth of mindfulness-based therapies in the West during recent times, owing greatly to the East, and especially to Buddhism, is important, as they bring a more psychological approach to understanding and managing depression. These therapies were examined in Chapter 13 and I do not wish to go into them in detail here, but merely mention that these therapies attempt to bring the consciousness of clients with depression closer to routine life. Segal *et al.*[37] provide a celebrated account of a mindfulness-based approach to depression. Their approach differed from the earlier cognitive therapy approach of Aaron Beck in not disputing and logically analysing negative thoughts but rather 'holding thoughts and feelings in awareness rather than trying to change them'. Beck did eventually integrate mindfulness techniques to his therapy. Thus, in relation to our main themes, restoring the 'lost art of sadness', mindfulness-based grief counselling and mindfulness-based counselling for depression bring a new dimension to our discussion of the H and W study. In addition to the work of Segal *et al.*,[38] which uses the objective scientific study format of verification, Morgan[39] used a more subjective and phenomenological approach. Thus, these approaches have generated new vistas for looking at depression, in addition to the dominant methods in medicine and psychiatry.

My own approach in mindfulness-based EFT is not to reify 'depression' as a 'thing' but to see it as an emotion constructed out of a number of components of perceptions of a situation, body sensations, feelings, thought patterns and intentions to act.[40] Also, this 'componential approach' helps us to distinguish sadness from (clinical) depression and follow the footsteps of Wolpert, who says in his book, *Malignant Sadness: The Anatomy of Depression*, that often depression is mishandled sadness or sadness become pathological.[41] Concluding the flow of argument so far, it may be said that the H and W study established the status of sadness as an autonomous emotion, or as what Paul Ekman refers to as a 'basic emotion'.

According to Ekman, depression too can be seen in terms of 'emotion blends':

> If sadness dominates depression, we speak of retarded depression; if agony is more prominent, it is an agitated depression. People who are depressed not only feel helpless to change their lives, they feel hopeless. They do not believe it will ever get better. In addition to sadness and agony, guilt and shame are strongly felt, for depressed people feel they are worthless...anger directed inward or out, and fear are often manifest.[42]

Boredom

Boredom has an emotion profile of its own, and if you understand boredom well, it is one dimension along which you may not merely manage sadness but find positive pathways to overcome it. As Cheshire Calhoun says, issues of value and meaning are important in understanding boredom, as value constraints play a crucial role in boredom.[43] Boredom may from another perspective be described as an attentional crisis.

Boredom as an Attentional Crisis

If you have an ability to be immersed in something that is exhilarating and beautiful in life, there is no room for the infiltration of boredom in your mind. Whatever the object, it is the subjective state of exhilaration that is within you that is important – it may be music, art, gardening, cooking or reading. One dimension along which one may manage sadness is to have an intense enlargement and intensification of interests in life. There have to be values and interests that energise one's life and dear ones that one has lost may be a great source of inspiration to pursue positive goals. Martin Seligman emphasised the value of positive emotions as an alternative to a preoccupation with pathology. His positive vision for the future may be summarised in his words:

> Patients need to be told that the drugs and therapies are temporary symptom relievers only, and they should expect recurrence when treatment stops. Hence, explicit successful practice in dealing with it and functioning well in spite of symptoms must be a serious part of therapy.

> Second, treatment should not end if suffering is relieved. Patients should learn the specific skills of positive psychology: how to have more positive emotions, more engagement, more meaning, more accomplishment, and better human relations. Unlike the skills of minimising misery, these skills are self-sustaining.[44]

Good attentional focus helps to develop positive emotions. In the area of education and psychology, Mihaly Csikszentmihalyi, who is an expert on the psychology of the flow experience, says that those who enjoy life and work have curiosity and interests in life, persistence and low self-centredness and are attracted by intrinsic rewards.[45]

To understand the boredom that comes with loss and grief, we need to look more closely at the nature of an attentional crisis, which is often a natural outcome but needs to be handled with a sense of balance. A useful study by Wallace and Shapiro on the many dimensional aspects of mental well-being (cognitive, volitional/conative, affective, attentional), which I referred to in Chapter 8, analyses three facets of an attentional crisis.

The Emotional Rhythms of Life

Robert C. Solomon inspired me to work on the logic of different emotion profiles in the area of the philosophy of mind. His untimely death was the context for a commemorative volume with a focus on his contribution to emotion studies.[46] I am thankful to the editors, Kathleen Higgins and David Sherman, and the series editor, Purushottama Bilimoria, for including a slightly different version of the present chapter especially focused on the different 'emotional rhythms of life' related to the emerging network of loss and grief, mourning and melancholy, depression and boredom. I have referred to a strange 'transition' that Solomon made in writing on laughter and humour following his reflections on grief, loss and the reflective temperament. Kübler-Ross, writing on *Death and Dying*, says that emotions emerge in a kind of network.[47] This rhythmical feature of our emotional life, which I would describe as the flow of an interconnected network of emotions (often lying at a subliminal level) emerges in the quiet, silent settings of counselling. My work in counselling gave a new dimension to the emotion profiles I saw through philosophical analysis. And mindfulness-based emotion-focused therapy opened for me the more enriching facets of the emotional rhythms of our life. The long chapter on emotions in this book is a product of the fact that the study of emotions has been a life-long hobby for me.

Emotional Integrity and Spirituality

Solomon's conception of emotional integrity adds yet another profound dimension for integrating emotions into counselling work:

> Emotional integrity is essential for the good life, fully embracing our being for others as well our need to live in accordance with our (and others' values).[48]

Following this trend of thought on emotional integrity, Solomon says that whatever the nature of different spiritual traditions is, the real valuable spiritual tradition integrates the whole discourse on the rhythms of our emotional lives as a central concern and brings thought, reflection and wisdom to their fold. It is in the spirit of these reflections of Solomon that I have devoted a great part of my life looking at the rhythms of our emotional lives within the fold of the Buddhist traditions. The Buddha told his son Rāhula to look at his mind in the way that one looks at a mirror: self-knowledge and self-understanding is the base for the kind of moral and psychological maturity that is necessary to move across the Buddhist path. Regular work in counselling opened up new pathways for enriching my interest in emotions and this book is greatly focused on emotion profiles: anger, fear, greed and addictions, conceit and pride, grief, sadness and depression and also of the emotions of loving kindness, compassion and generosity, fear, anxiety and jealousy.[49] Humour is an important facet of counselling and I have discussed this theme elsewhere.[50] It is thus appropriate to say that there is a sub-theme running through this book: the rhythms of our emotional lives.

17
Understanding and Managing Grief: When the Desert Begins to Bloom

The present chapter is a close ally of the previous chapter on the lost art of sadness, and though there may be overlapping issues, this chapter has a specific mission in narrating my own journey through grief, sadness and mild depression and a return to a vibrant, expansive and enriching emergence of a 'new sense of self' within me. The issues can easily be shared as there are both clients and therapist who have gone through a similar journey of loss, grief and an expansive sense of love and compassion. Also, going through a different dimension of a personal narrative, this chapter strengthens the claims of the last chapter.

> By being aware of grief rather than ignoring or denying it, and by working to understand what drives this pain, you can release yourself into the person you are and the person you want to be. In other words, with mindful-awareness of grief, you can move closer to the people in your life who matter most, and change habits or ideas that have been keeping you away from living fully. Full awareness, especially in grief, of your patterns of feelings, and behaviour can take you from living with misery and discontent to living with openness and passion.[1]

Kumar says that it is possible to channel the momentum of grief into a journey of self-awakening. Tolstoy says that grief can be seen as an extension of love, or what Buddhists refer to as loving kindness and compassion. In this chapter, we are looking at a new dimension of grief, grief in panic cultures, which are threatened by natural disasters and tense internal wars.

Grief counselling focuses on the ability to accept the loss and direct the pain into paths of emotional growth. This is a very positive path to understanding grief and loss. Reflecting on grief enlarges one's notion of love and deeper spiritual transformation, in terms of issues pertaining to the meaning of life. The transformative powers of grief over a loss to reach a deep reflective tone in life, added to by a wonderful resilience of the mind, are the result of the proper and mature management of grief.

In *The Lost Art of Compassion*,[2] Ladner says that in dealing with grief and love we need to move away from the exclusive focus on pathology that has dominated Western psychology for many years. Ladner refers to the words of Martin Seligman, a former President of the American Psychological Society: 'the exclusive focus on pathology that has dominated so much of our discipline results in the model of the human being lacking positive features that make life worth living'.[3] Ladner also observes that according to this disease model, we try to repair damage rather than aim at positive mental health. But a small, though veritable, revolution is taking place in the West today due to the impact of mindfulness-based therapies.

As already cited in the last chapter, the groundbreaking research of Catherine Lutz indicates that in certain cultures, such as that of the the Ifaluk, there is a durable and automatic link between the suffering of one person and their nurturing by others. In the context of my personal journey through grief and loss, the Sri Lankan Buddhist culture also has these qualities that help the grieving person to connect with others. Lutz says that on the surface, from a Western point of view, there is an apparent contradiction, seeing love as positive and sadness as negative, but at a deeper level, love as compassion is a kind of shock absorber, and we see signs of positive development of sadness into love as compassion. This is because in Eastern culture there is an automatic linkage between sadness and compassion.

The term *saṃvega* refers to the spiritual emotion that emerges in the context of grief backed by the four divine states of loving kindness, compassion, altruistic love and equanimity. Thus, coming to terms with grief in a Buddhist culture without repression and escape involves the attempt to understand, reflect and transform the experience as an insight into death and life.

Narrative

By using a personal narrative, I add a sense of authenticity and deep reflection into this chapter on grief counselling. As a study of emotions, which is one of the central dimensions of the present book, the focus on grief also includes a constellation of grief-related emotions: love, loving kindness and compassion. When you are unexpectedly struck by grief, as occurred in my life, there is an emerging chaos around you – a whole constellation of emotions: fear, anxiety, sadness, guilt, low self-worth, hopelessness, objectless-anger and a silent complaint – 'why has this happened to me?' Martha Nussbaum's book, *Upheavals of Thought*, is a voluminous study of human emotions written against the backdrop of her mother's death.[4] It contains an excellent contribution on the reflective dimensions of grief, searching for light, illumination and intelligence within the emotional chaos that is triggered by grief and sadness. My insights are drawn from the reflective, dedicatory and contemplative/meditative dimensions of looking at grief.

In February 1994 I visited Sri Lanka. Unexpectedly Kalla, my wife, fell sick in Colombo, at her sister's place, and we rushed her to the hospital. She was subject to a serious heart complaint and survived for only two days in the hospital. 10 February was Chinese New Year in Singapore, but here in Sri Lanka I was experiencing the most shattering tragedy of my life. If she had been fortunate to get to Australia before she fell sick there was the chance of a complete medical check up and things would have probably been different. She was exhausted by the last minute packing in Singapore, but being a person with a strong sense of will, she was able to muster all her energy to go through the anxieties of migrating to Australia.

As we had decided to settle down in Australia with our children, Kalla had been processing papers for immigration, cleaning our apartment in Singapore and packing personal belongings to be shipped out. The early part of our stay in Sri Lanka was very good. There was a touch of grace and charm in visiting old and familiar places, meeting relatives and friends. The visits to temples, reflection and prayer, a moment to calm down, and the stillness around, all this was a graceful way of preparing for the emotional storm and chaos to come.

My wife was only 56 years old when she died, but she had led a very productive life. She was a conscientious teacher, a good mother to our three boys and an ever-loving wife during the 32 years that we were married. At the ritual almsgiving for monks, the sermon by Piyadassi Thero was on the theme, 'A Life is not valued by the number of years of a person's life but its quality', a reflection that has stayed with me over the years. Next day, we performed another ritual of dipping ashes in the river, and as the ashes whirled round in circles and disappeared, the whole drama of attachment and impermanence ran through my mind.

I was able to go through the initial phase of the tragedy with some reflective calm, but when I spent a few days in Singapore before leaving for Australia, staying with close relatives, the sense of emptiness and aridity overpowered me. It is nearly 18 years now, since these reflections in Singapore, and of course now I have achieved some maturity and distance, with the passage of time. My positive shift from being a professional philosopher to a professional counsellor – offering free counselling for migrants for over five years – had a magical impact on me and opened up a new path to offer something in Kalla's name and memories.

Yet, I remember how the aridity and emptiness of life struck me 18 years ago in Singapore, which reminded me of a description of empty cigarette boxes floating in the river, the sound of coffee spoons – symptoms of superficial lives without meaning and purpose – some lines of poetry from T.S. Eliot which I learnt at school. But as I went deep into this mood, I felt that both Kalla and I had lived lives that had meaning and purpose.

Opening myself to this hovering feeling of emptiness, I discovered that there is a profound silence around, as the glimmering evening lights appeared – the contours of noise in the body and mind subsided – it appeared that the desert has its own therapeutic blooms and I was reminded of what the Gestalt therapist Fritz Perls said: 'sometimes the desert blooms'.

Very often, we try to master the day-to-day shallowness in our lives, the impact of routine monotony, but the more shattering feelings of absence and shallowness provide an opportunity for transformation, and a time for a spiritual re-awakening. Venerable Nyanamoli says that the experience of emptiness provides the back stairs for liberation.

Grief does not settle down with meditation practice for a few weeks. As Kumar says, grief comes in like a spiral rather than a linear process and the impact remained in a mild form for a while. And it was natural that there was an undercurrent of mild depression. Someone who was both a psychiatrist and a personal friend gradually helped me to come back to my normal self, engaging, active and compassionate – seeing a wonderful and exciting future ahead. I also had a very stimulating conversation with Ajahn Brahmavamsa, who told me in a semi-playful and semi-serious tone that 'depression is an interesting thing', look at it, learn from it – it is a wonderful thing, and you will get all your lost energies back. By now, I sought a change of environment and, with the assistance of my children Maneesh, Adeesh and Chandeesh, I moved into Lexington Gardens, a retirement village located in Springvale, a place with an invigorating air, clean green trees and flowering blossoms, and some wonderful friends. I have now lived here for nearly ten years and most of my recent work on Buddhist counselling emerged during this phase in my life. I have been grateful to the philosophers at Monash for giving me a place to read and write and to Constant Mews and Ian Mabbett for allowing me to teach the section on Buddhism in the 'Religious Quest' course for many years: there I was able to integrate a fresh path to teach Buddhism in the context of my personal encounters in life. More than anything, it was a context for self-expression. But a time came to move into fresh pastures, and with a very warm invitation from Patricia Sherwood (Director Sophia College of Counselling) to enrol for a Diploma in counselling with a course on 'Emotions' to teach, exciting new horizons emerged. She encouraged me to do the Advanced Diploma in Buddhist Psychotherapy and guided me all the way in my practical counselling training. I worked at the Springvale community centre mostly with migrants, offering them free-counselling, and most of them did very well and are now my friends. I initiated the 'Viveka Centre' for emotional healing and developed my personal technique of 'mindfulness-based EFT' (emotion-focused therapy). I also did a short counselling assignment for about three months at Lexington Gardens and edited their Newsletter for three years, giving it an orientation of my own. These were all wonderful changes and my experience with professional counselling opened up a new world for me Part of this book has been nourished by this invigorating experience. Above all, learning the craft of counselling added a great humanising dimension to my life and work.

Four Liberating Methods

1. Developing Insight and Understanding

Managing grief is more complex than managing anger, fear and stress. The reason is that most concerns, like the grief in my own personal narrative, are very natural and we do not label grief 'negative', in the way we would describe anger and the obsessions of greed. But excess grief is counter-productive as a way of managing the pain that comes with the loss of a loved one. When Kisā Gotami came to see the Buddha, requesting him to find a way of bringing her infant child back to life, he said that it could only be done if she could bring a mustard seed from a family that has not lost anyone dear to them, and walking round the village she discovered that this is part of the human predicament and this opened up to her a path for liberation. There are sudden reversals to the smooth flow of life, unexpected upheavals that disturb our safety zones, but these open us to the real world of change and uncertainty, what is referred to as the *'dhamma-niyāma'* – the nature of things. You do not have to destroy grief but transform it and bring it within the law of cessation – *something which emerges, stay for a while and pass away*. This was the transformative experience of Aññā Kondañña, the first monk to understand the law of cessation.

What did Kondañña know? What was his insight that the Buddha praised at the very end of the sermon? It was: 'All that is subject to arising is subject to ceasing'.[5]

2. The Four Sublime States (Brahma-vihāra)

The four sublime states are: loving kindness (*mettā*), compassion (*karuṇā*), altruistic joy (*muditā*) and equanimity (*upekkhā*). Loving kindness extends to all beings, as we are all wayfarers through the cycle of existence and are subject to the same law of suffering. What is special about compassion, as different from loving kindness, is that it is directly focused on the suffering of other beings, humans and animals. The Discourse on Loving Kindness (*Karaṇīya-metta Sutta*) expounded by the Buddha is a kind of charter for the practice of loving kindness. Practice of love has the power to transform people, as it is the best antidote for anger and envy and it transforms the people around you. Venerable Buddharakkhita, in his work *The Philosophy and Practice of Universal Love*, says that the *Metta Sutta* is a goldmine for therapeutic transformation.[6] Loving kindness is first directed towards oneself and then to those close to you, then to those not known to you and lastly to the people you do not like. Loving kindness towards oneself includes the ability to embrace all parts of oneself without guilt and self-hurt. Also, it generates the ability to connect with others and it is the best antidote to the illusion of 'separateness'. 'Through compassion (*karuṇā*), the fact of suffering remains vividly present to our mind, even at times when we are personally free from it. Compassion gives us the rich experience of suffering, thus strengthening to meet it prepared, when it does befall us'.[7]

Sympathetic joy (*muditā*) is the joy one gets by sharing the happiness of others, which is the opposite of envy. Such sympathetic joy indicates a sublime nobility of heart. Equanimity (*upekkhā*) is a perfect unshakable balance of mind rooted in insight. At a time when natural disasters and global warfare are destroying countless lives, some therapists who try to deal with victims of such disasters develop what is called 'compassion fatigue', and equanimity helps them to bring a sense of realism and acceptance to the suffering around. Chapter 8, which deals with dimensions of well-being, has a complete analysis of equanimity.

3. Dedication Through Gratitude (kataññū Katavedī)

In Buddhist cultures like Thailand and Sri Lanka gratitude (*kataññū Katavedī*) is a cultural value that pervades family relationships. This virtue is especially manifest in children's duties to parents, especially when the parents are old. Rituals after the death of parents and close relatives also display the dedicatory qualities. During the tsunami, for instance, many Sri Lankans living in foreign countries extended their gratitude by contributions to the tsunami fund. It is an emotion that blends with *mettā* (loving kindness).

4. Living a Good Life

The best security in times of suffering and crisis is the living of a good life; when there is a strong moral texture, other personal qualities of compassion and gratitude shine, and add a new sense of vibrancy to one's life. The practice of mindfulness and especially *mettā* meditation adds a new sense of trust and confidence that *mettā* is not a passing emotion but is rooted in one's character. As grief indicates our vulnerability to the vagaries of fate, fortune and change, it can be a transformative experience that brings one closer to the *dhamma*.

18
The Concept of Anger:
Psychodynamics and Management

How could we forget those ancient myths that stand at the beginning of all races, the myths about dragons that at the last moment are transformed into princesses? Perhaps all the dragons in our lives are princesses who are only waiting to see us act, just once, with beauty and courage. Perhaps everything that frightens us is, in its deepest essence, something helpless that wants our love.

So you mustn't be frightened...if a sadness rises in front of you, larger than you have ever seen; if an anxiety, like light and cloud-shadows moves over your hands and over everything you do. You must realize that something is happening to you, that life has not forgotten you, that it holds you in its hands and will not let you fall. Why do you want to shut out of your life any uneasiness, any misery, any depression, since after all you don't know what work these conditions are doing inside you?[1]

Most people live, whether physically, intellectually or morally, in a very restricted circle of their potential being. They make use of a very small portion of their possible consciousness...We all have reservoirs of life to draw upon, of which we do not dream.[2]

The Concept of Anger

All of us get angry – although some people might not believe this. Anger is an emotion that can occur when there is a threat to our self-esteem, our bodies, our properties, our ways of seeing the world or our desires. People differ in what makes them angry. Some people will perceive an event as threatening, while others see no threat in the same event. Our responses to anger differ greatly. Some people are able to use angry feelings as a way of solving problems rationally and effectively. Others turn their anger inward and engage in self-destructive behaviour. Other people strike out when they feel angry. And some refuse to acknowledge their anger – or they confuse it with other emotions such as vulnerability or fear.[3]

There may be multi-faceted reasons for getting angry, but if you reflect deeply you will discover that anger is a state of suffering (*dukkha*), and as a state of mind anger can affect our health and well-being. Recent discoveries in medicine and health indicate that anger, hostility, anxiety, repression and denial can affect the strength of the immune system and the robustness of the cardiovascular system, whereas calm, optimism, joy and loving kindness are beneficial to our well-being. At the ethical level, anger is defilement (*kilesa*) and is a roadblock to the path of liberation considered as one of the five hindrances, as ill-will (*vyāpāda*). At the social level, anger generates conflict, and when this state deteriorates there is confrontation and violence. According to the Buddhist analysis of the mind, anger has a subliminal base, or what may be called the sleeping passion of anger (*paṭighānusaya*), and this may emerge at the level of thoughts or physical activity. Practice of self-analysis and mindfulness of thought patterns may help a person to manage anger at the level of thoughts, and this awareness prevents it emerging in physical activity. Even a baby boy lying in a cot is attached to the body and has a proclivity to generate anger by sounds and physical expression. It is important to note that people often ignore the fact that the origin of violence is usually some form of anger.

The emotion profile of anger has to be grasped first, before we present the routes to anger management. Anger gets a new lease of life when it is justified on moral grounds. In fact, the philosopher Aristotle justified what he described as 'righteous indignation'. Aristotle, who wrote a fascinating piece on moral emotions and an insightful account of the 'golden mean', is considered as having a soft preference for what he described as 'righteous indignation', anger for the right reason, at the right time. I made a comprehensive study of the ethics of moral indignation in my V.F. Gunaratne Memorial Trust Lecture[4] and will here merely touch on the salient points relevant for the present chapter, when we get into the question of 'moral anger'.

The Emotion Profile of Anger

It is necessary to look into what may be described as the emotional profile of anger, before we get into the management of anger. Simple anger is a reaction we have when something obstructs our plans; for instance, we kick the ground in a mood of frustration. Anger proper is based on a belief that some offence has been committed to oneself and the desire to set the offence right, or even retaliate. Indignation is the anger over the violation of a moral principle that one cherishes, like not keeping up to a promise or violating the essential ingredient of a good friendship, or on a more objective scale, seeing an injustice done to an innocent person, whose cheap labour is exploited. There is a whole range of angry feelings, ranging from slight annoyance to rage: sulking is passive anger; exasperation is outliving one's patience. Revenge takes time for reflection and holding a grudge is long-standing resentment.

Hatred compared is a more enduring and intense feeling than anger. It is also a cumulative condition, and may go underground. When anger has a kind of subliminal existence it can take distorted forms like sarcasm and cynicism. Anger may take a superiority stance, feelings like disgust and contempt towards the hated person. Hatred is more dispositional and different from emotions which are merely episodic. Anger also becomes blended with other emotions like fear and suspicion. Envy and jealousy are blend emotions, but depend for their existence on anger. Malicious envy is unjustified hatred directed towards someone's good fortune, and also a wish that this good fortune disappears, even if one does not get the wealth or part of it. Admiration envy is a kind of innocent desire to emulate others. Jealousy is a blend emotion with a strong flavour of anger; there is also a fear of losing someone that a person cherishes, like one's girlfriend; shame, as one's self-interest is being challenged by a third party; sadness that a person may lose someone that is greatly cherished; ambivalence or a blend of love and anger towards one's girlfriend. We have already examined the nature of boredom, and anger can enter as a component into certain forms of boredom, like for instance, of a person in prison. Anger in its more simple form is a reactive attitude of aversion, and apart from boredom, it is often a component of depression and a quiet partner in the pathologies of greed.

There is a subtle form of anger which lies at the bottom of depressive moods, strangely enough, among affluent people, and this theme is the subject of a lively television drama by Alain de Botton, *Status Anxiety*: it is a kind of restlessness in the midst of plenty, and emerges specially in a society that overvalues external goods that generate envy and competition rather than compassion. He observes that 'it is a strange melancholy, often haunting inhabitants of democracies in the midst of abundance'.[5]

Moral Anger and Righteous Indignation

Aristotle expressed the view that one who was unable to express indignation at a wrong done is a coward, is stupid and displays a lack of moral sensitivity. But the problem is, as I have expressed elsewhere: 'It is ironic that the feeling of indignation has strong moral roots, the flavour of authenticity and warmth but it can be transformed into strange forms of violence'.[6] The context for indignation and how it is expressed is most crucial in seeing the complete case for and against righteous indignation. Indignation can take three forms: indignation over wrongs suffered by others; over wrongs we ourselves have suffered; and reflexive indignation over wrongs we ourselves have done. It can be directed to persons, acts and impersonal notions like nature or the world order. The feeling of indignation also runs through a complex circuit of hurt, resentment and anger, coloured by a sense of right and wrong, breaking of trust, conceptions of justice and so on. In the way that the sense of 'loss' is central to grief, and a sense of 'threat' is central to fear, the sense of 'injustice' is central to righteous indignation, and it is also linked to the importance of human agency, intentions and accountability. Thus, this emotion appears to be sitting on the fence between the most noble and ignoble, as it can degenerate into violence if fed by retaliation and resentment.

Unjust systems, as well as morally degenerate actions, have provided targets for diverse expressions of violence. As William Neblett observes, indignation can turn out to be purely negative without ushering in the transformation of the undesirable conditions.[7] It is also unhealthy if it is 'person-oriented', rather than 'act-oriented'. In the very bosom of non-violent demonstrations, the seeds of resentment and retaliation may exist at a subliminal level. A feeling of indignation needs to be presented in a mood of dialogue and realistic ways of bringing back good. In the study to which I refer above, I attempted a restoration of the valuable facets of indignation, 'so that we salvage its clear voice of protest at a wrong done from its potential anger and venom and resuscitate the notion of moral *responsibility*'.[8]

Anger and Its Psychodynamics

When the uninstructed worldling is being contacted by a painful feeling, he sorrows, grieves and laments; he weeps beating his breast and becomes distraught. He feels two feelings – a bodily one and a mental one. This experience is compared to a man hit by two darts. When he is touched by a painful feeling, he resists and an underlying tendency to resistance (*paṭighānusaya*) emerges in his mind. It is also said that such a person knows no other way out of this pain but an escape into sensual pleasures and thus ignited is the underlying tendency for pleasure (*rāgānusaya*).[9]

The motivational cycle is crucial for understanding the emergence of anger. Sensory contact conditions feeling, feeling conditions craving, craving conditions clinging. Pleasant feelings are fed by the subliminal proclivity for lust and painful feelings are fed by a subliminal proclivity for aversion. The motivational root of greed provides the base for attachments, hatred for the emotions of aversion and delusion for emotions with an ego-orientation. Following this psychodynamic analysis, it may be observed that anger, fear and sadness/depression are emotions of aversion; sensual passions and avarice, wealth and possessions emerge on the root of greed; while conceit, arrogance and vanity are rooted in an ego-orientation fed by delusion of the ego.

Anger Management

> Once an ill-favoured, ugly looking demon (*yakkha*) came to be seated on the throne of Sakka, the ruler of gods. Then the gods (thirty three of them) were annoyed, vexed and consumed with indignation at this very strange and unusual sight. Now in proportion as they became annoyed, vexed and indignant, that demon ever grew handsomer and more presentable and more attractive. The gods were disturbed and reported the incident to their ruler, and Sakka says 'Will this, then dear sir, be a demon who feeds on anger?'

> Then Sakka came to the demon, draping his robe over one shoulder, and kneeling over his right shoulder, and kneeling on his right knee, bent forth his clasped hands towards him, calling his own name thrice: 'I dear Sir am Sakka, the ruler of gods'.

> Now in proportion, as Sakka did this, the demon became more and more ill-favoured and ugly, till he vanished from the place. Sakka advises the gods that there is no place for wrath within him.[10]

Now that the concept of anger, the profile of anger and its psychodynamics have been described and analysed, we have a fertile background for exploring the Buddhist techniques for anger management. The above story exemplifies the insight that if you have the right attitude, with that attitude one can turn anger on its head and deal with anger with an assumed posture of humility – a complete transformation of the context and the evaporation of the solidity of anger. As the well-known meditation teacher Joseph Goldstein observes, often we are not aware exactly as to what emotion is present or whether it is wholesome or unwholesome. He mentions a number of steps to take us in the right direction:[11] as the emotions that appear in the mind have no clear boundaries and no definite sense of beginnings and endings, it is necessary to take care to recognise each emotion as it arises and to learn to distinguish subtle differences; secondly, as the negative emotions are unpleasant we tend not to acknowledge them, and clear recognition has to be followed by acceptance, as the emotions often do not appear as one emotion but as constellations; thirdly, the most difficult thing is to open ourselves to the whole range of emotions/feeling without any identification with them, but generate a distance to look at them. It is necessary to see a kind of paradox in this context, that a collection of negative emotions may provide the raw material for insight meditation. The important point is that first you need to take responsibility for your emotions and then disengage any mechanism of identification with them. Thus, both positive and negative emotions give a context to observe our own minds.

Venerable Nyanaponika, discussing the value of mindfulness, says: 'The greater part of man-made suffering in the world comes not from deliberate wickedness but from ignorance, heedlessness, thoughtlessness, rashness and lack of control. Very often a single moment of mindfulness or wise reflection would have prevented a far-reaching sequence of misery or guilt'.[12] Exercising the inner breaks of self-control and slowing helps us to free ourselves from our constant reactivity to unpleasant situations and experiences.

Meditation Techniques for Managing Anger

The term *samatha* refers to a state of mind which has been brought to a rest and is focused on breathing and limited to that activity without allowing it to wander. As one practises this type of meditation and becomes skilful, he is able to reach the first stage of absorption, described in Pāli as *samādhi*, and then move into more advanced stages. It is a state of calm and clarity. In insight meditation, while the initial stage is common to 'tranquillity meditation' (*samatha*), the meditator begins to see the breath as a air draft and focuses on the rubbing sensations and gradually discerns the vibration patterns in terms of the four elements of air, solidity, liquidity and fire (hot sensations and temperature), which prepares the ground for gaining insight (*vipassanā*). The insight meditator uses his concentration as a tool to deal with the encountering of illusory constructs that prevent him from seeing reality. With the insight meditator, he gradually moves away from thoughts of 'me' and 'mine' and sees anger merely as an experience that emerges, stays for a while and ceases or passes away. Thus, when the meditator creates a 'distance' between himself and the passing emotional state of anger, it helps him see the emotional state face to face, without concealment, obsession, rationalisation or various ways of avoidance and escape. As Ven. Nyanaponika points out, there is a twilight world of frustrated desires, suppressed resentments, vacillations, ambivalences – all drawing nourishment from the subliminal tendencies described by the Pali term *anusaya*. Three of the seven *anusayas* are linked to negative emotions of anger/hatred (*paṭigha*), lust and greed (*raga*), conceit and arrogance, inferiority (*māna*). It is insight meditation, when well developed, that helps the meditator to break through these subliminal tendencies. While anger and lust are mastered at an early stage on the path of liberation, conceit remains until the final stage of perfection.

During regular meditation sittings, if disturbing thoughts and feelings intrude, the method of naming and identifying negative feelings and emotions is a useful technique. We can also make them 'objects of meditation'. The *Satipatthana*, the fourfold method for developing mindfulness, offers a number of entry points for dealing with anger: body and the breath (*kāya*); painful/ pleasurable/ neutral feelings (*vedanā*); thought patterns with their links to desires (*citta*); phenomena (*dhammā*).

Body and Breath in Anger

Breathing is controlled by the autonomic nervous system and so does not come within average consciousness, unless we turn to the awareness of the breath as a special technique. The central nervous system functions when we receive and process messages and make conscious choices. When we become stressed, or experience sudden anger, breathing patterns change. Evolution or our biological heritage has developed ways to manage what are described as 'emergency reactions' of flight (for fear) and fight (for anger), which may convey important messages. When such alarm bells ring, Joseph Ledoux, the neuroscientist, says that the emotional brain hijacks the rational brain. According to him, in impulsive reactions the part of the brain called the *amygdala* is active and begins to respond before the *neocortex* processes the information and makes a rational response.

The practice of mindfulness, observing the breath in quiet moments of meditation, helps the breathing patterns to get habituated into a rhythmical, quiet and steady flow, a pattern that is both healthy and wholesome. Thus, instead of attempting damage control after the impulsive actions have been done, it is better to take preventive steps by cultivating mindfulness first. As Paul Ekman, one of the foremost exponents of emotion study (who came to influenced by Buddhism), observes: it is harder to be attentive and mindful when one is angry, but if we have cultivated mindfulness, it is possible to step back, and then exercise a choice as to how one should respond; for instance one may try to understand the person who provoked you and excuse him.[13] For Buddhist ethics and psychology, mindful intentions are important. Along with the clarity that comes with the practice of mindfulness, openness, acceptance, forgiveness and compassion generate a new sense of space to the mind.

Feelings

We examined the nature of feelings in relation to emotions in Chapter 5 and so I will be brief in saying that pleasurable, painful and neutral feelings have, in a germinal form, what may develop into an emotion, as they also feed on the subliminal proclivities for anger, lust and conceit. For those who wish to explore in detail and research the *Sutta* material on feelings, three important sermons need to be read: *Bahu-vedeniya Sutta, Culla-vedalla Sutta* and *Salāyatana-vibhaṇga Sutta.*[14] Thoughts play a crucial role in dealing with negative emotions. It is said that the monk should develop mindfulness so that he would know a mind with lust (*raga*) and a mind without lust (*vītarāga*); know a mind with hate (*dosa*) and without hate (*adosa*); know a mind with delusion (*moha*) and without delusion (*amoha*). The *vitakka-saṇthāna Sutta* (pathways of thought) to which I alluded in earlier chapters, is considered as the Buddhist charter for cognitive therapy: look at a different object to anger (forgiveness, live and let live, understanding); look at the perilous consequences of anger; ignore the thoughts; if all these methods fail, control with forceful effort. Mindfulness-based cognitive therapy has a whole system for dealing with the auto-pilot of repetitive thoughts, and anger is a good example. In the final section of the *Satipaṭṭhāna,* dealing broadly with the nature of phenomena (*dhammā*), the important point is to make anger an object of contemplation, looking at the arising and passing away of anger, seeing that it is a delusional construct and attempting to loosen one's identity with anger and see that anger is a form of suffering. Thus, you focus on the doctrines of impermanence (*anicca*), non-self (*anatta*) and suffering (*dukkha*): this perspective sums up the deeper approach to convert anger into an object of meditation.

Anger and Defence Mechanisms

The concept of 'defence mechanisms' is Freudian. Both the layman and the recluse are advised to look at their mind as they would look at a mirror, thus developing clear self-knowledge. However, people often push their conflicts and desires to a subliminal/unconscious level, and it has been described as a mechanism used to handle frustrations by pushing them into unconscious levels. Impulses related to lust, anger and conceits may be related to these mechanisms. Though there is no systematic analysis of such mechanisms, there is a canonical reference related to anger oriented defence mechanisms.

It is fascinating to find that 26 centuries ago, the Buddha's advice to the monks on anger management covers the basic defence mechanisms:[15]

1. Repression: when monks reprove a fellow monk for committing an offence, the reproved monk pleads forgetfulness, 'I don't remember'.
2. Aggression: when monks reprove a fellow monk for committing an offence, the reproved monk gets angry and says, 'what right have you to talk, you stupid fool?'.
3. Projection: when monks reprove a fellow monk for committing an offence, the reproved monk says, 'It is you who committed the offence'.
4. Regression: when monks reprove a fellow monk for committing an offence, the reproved monk evades the question and reverts to childlike disorganised behaviour.
5. Compensation: when monks reprove a fellow monk for committing an offence, the reproved monk tries to drown the talk and talks with lot of gesticulation at the assembly.
6. Isolation: when monks reprove a fellow monk for committing an offence, the reproved monk tries to disregard it and isolates from the problem.

7. Denial: when monks reprove a fellow monk for committing an offence, the reproved monk says that he is not guilty and not concerned about it.

8. Physical isolation: when monks reprove a fellow monk for an offence, the reproved monk says that they need not worry about him at all and gives up being a monk.

19
Addictions, Self-Control and the Puzzles Regarding Voluntary Self-Destruction

Gene Heyman's book, *Addiction: a Disorder of Choice*, offers fresh and fertile thinking on the nature of addictions as well a thesis on self-destructive behaviour.[1] Liz Sheean, in an editorial review of the book, highlights the following quote from Heyman's work: 'The varieties of voluntary human destructiveness are at the heart of many, if not most, literary accounts of the human condition'.[2] Heyman says that, contrary to the common view that addicts display compulsive and involuntary behaviour, they are making choices when they take to addiction, and they can also make a choice to move away from addiction. Against this background I wish to present my own perspective of counselling for addictions in the light of my training in Buddhist psychotherapy and especially mindfulness-based counselling.

A Buddhist Perspective on Self-Control and Addictions

Self-control is the virtue of living according to one's values, in so far as one has the capacity to do so by exercising courage and persistence, supplemented by wise understanding, motivation and mindfulness. Lack of self-control is described as weakness of will. Such weakness may be occasional or habitual, is sometimes limited to specific vices and comes within different degrees of control and awareness. The real puzzle is, 'why do people knowingly court self-defeating forms of behaviour?' The irresistibility of addictions is seen in the areas of gambling, smoking, drug and alcoholic addiction and irresponsible sexual behaviour. Uncontrollable anger, though not a form of addiction, also comes within the domain moral weakness and weakness of will. The focus of the present chapter is the general nature of moral weakness and addictions, with special reference to alcoholic addiction.

This section explores Buddhist therapeutic resources in managing addictions at the cognitive, motivational, affective and attentional levels. I then follow up this section by describing my attempts to develop a therapeutic methodology in relation to clients. A detailed case study on which these reflections are based is found in my monograph, *An Introduction to Mindfulness-Based Counselling*, a work partly used for helping clients.[3] A modified study is found at the end of this chapter. Case studies used in this work are depicted as vignettes, smudging their historical location and using different names or constructed characters.

A very important point related to my counselling practice needs to be mentioned. I had many clients who were not Buddhists, and in such contexts I used mindfulness-based cognitive, behavioural, psychodynamic and EFT techniques without any doctrinal factors obstructing the consultation. The client-centred approach of Carl Rogers was also useful. In fact, just to cite an example, I had a client, Anna, who was a strong Catholic with mild depression caused by social status concerns. In spite of the fact that she had a wonderful home, a husband who was doing well and resources for a simple and contented life, she had a disturbed mind activated by 'status anxiety' when relatives visited. I made her understand that the close relatives would like to see the old Anna for what 'she is' and there was no need to decorate the house with expensive carpets and find the most fashionable dress. Anna was completely transformed and lived happily with the husband for the rest of their lives. The auto-pilot thought patterns were drained off by showing that contentment and enjoyable leisure and work contained the key to her recovery, using mindfulness techniques independent of any doctrinal residue was very effective and productive. She recovered, and thanked me for strengthening her faith in her own religion – contentment cuts across all groups and faiths. The key to transforming one of my clients, who was an addict as indicated later in the chapter, is the simple philosophy of contentment, peace and the simple joys of life – that kept the bottle away. This resource, which I used with many clients, was summarised as a sub-theme in my monograph on counselling: 'the magic of the ordinary and the elegance of small things' (see the case study at the end of the chapter).[4]

Theoretical Issues: The Nature of Alcohol and Drug Addiction

Self-control is the virtue of living according to one's values, in so far as one has the capacity to do so by exercising courage, persistence or simple discipline. Lack of self-control often takes the form of *weakness of will* in which we judge that we ought to do something, have the power to do so, but fail to do so; when the judgment is specifically moral, it is moral weakness.[5]

Michael Stocker observes that people in moods of apathy, tiredness and even despair see all the good to be won but lack interest, desire and strength.[6] This sort of weakness may occur either in a dramatic form, where one realises that very soon one will get into a very miserable state, or in a more humdrum, occasional or habitual manner. It may be regional, for example a student's failure to stick to a regular timetable for studies, even though he exhibits no such laxity in other areas of life, like keeping to promises or not falling a victim to irresponsible sexual behaviour, gambling or alcohol addiction. To have self-control in all regions of life would be a remarkable accomplishment. Also, self-control may be a matter of degree, rather than an all or nothing situation. Issues centred on self-control may be examined within a discourse which is purely psychological and therapeutic. In general, the moral dimensions are significant for Buddhism, though in the meditation setting, depending on context, one may bracket moral considerations: 'My anger is neither good nor bad, neither mine nor yours, as it is an impersonal process which emerges, stays for a while and passes away'. Yet, if you shift contexts, the last of the five precepts upholds that one should refrain from taking alcohol. In my practice I have often used mindfulness-based cognitive therapy blended with some focus on emotions (EFT). Not merely for addictions, but for other ailments too, where necessary, I have been cautious and, depending on the context, at times I have avoided moral and spiritual issues, especially with non-Buddhists.

The Greek philosophers who discussed the issues pertaining to self-control used the Greek term *akrasia* to refer to weakness of will and *encratia* for self-control. Aristotle, who presents a comprehensive study of *akrasia* in his work on ethics, says that weakness of will in relation to greed and lust has to be condemned, but the incontinence of losing one's temper is different, as anger is a common frailty. It is very important to note that according to Aristotle the vicious man who has bad moral principles is hard to educate, compared with the incontinent man who has good moral principles but fails to live up to them. In fact, it has been observed that *akrasia* is the price that virtue pays to vice. Socrates presented the time honoured puzzle and paradox that those who have genuine moral knowledge are bound to produce good conduct, which is contained in the axiom 'virtue is knowledge'. This appears as a paradox as there are many instances where people have the requisite knowledge about moral rules but give in to temptation. Another critical point is that it has been observed that in this axiom there is an illegitimate passage from 'is' to 'ought': the knowledge that a person has about moral rules is descriptive of his state of knowledge but there is no normative logic that such a person should stick to the rules.

The issues around the irresistibility of addictions have been the subject of the behavioural sciences and psychological research, as, for instance, found in the writings of Jon Elster, George Ainslie, Alfred Mele and Stanton Peele. In consuming drugs, alcohol and cigarettes and engaging in compulsive gambling, people knowingly choose to do things that they will regret. It is necessary to understand the logic and psychology of such behaviour patterns – forms of *self-defeating* behaviour: why do people knowingly court disaster? Socrates thought that to know what is morally right is to do it. Aristotle deviated from Socrates and thought that the 'self-controlled' person can master the passions to which weak people fall victim. Thus, Aristotle emphasises the motivational factors in addiction, in addition to the cognitive factors. From the experience of my own counselling practice, using 'mindfulness techniques', there is a clear limitation in the thinking of both Socrates and Aristotle as they identified self-control with the rational faculty, whereas Buddhism has the additional focus on 'attentional factors' (mindfulness). Mindfulness techniques have been used over the years to manage addictions by Allan Marlatt[7] and Bien and Bien (2002)[8], with great success. Also, according to Mele, Aristotle's analysis, though looking at the motivational factors, is predominantly a focus on the rational faculty.

Mele's observations also point out that the Greek philosopher's emphasis of the rational faculty has limitations in understanding addictions:

> I follow Aristotle in understanding self-control and *akrasia* as two sides of the same coin. However, I distance myself from him on a metaphysical matter. Aristotle identifies the *self* of self-control with the agent's 'reason' (faculty). I identify it holistically with the person, broadly conceived. An agent's desires and emotions that run counter to her best judgments are rarely plausible seen as alien forces (Mele, 1996, 100).[9]

Buddhism, in its own way, has a holistic focus on cognitive, motivational, affective and attentional factors in managing addictions. The most important starting point is the knowledge that a person is free to make decisions before he takes to addictions and even to come out of it, in spite of the fact that the mind is constrained by the spell of addiction. The practice of mindfulness, qualities of commitment and persistence in the face of adversity and ardency, along with presence of mind and the purposive nature of the goal oriented activity – these are qualities of the mind that help a person to move out of the vicious circle of addiction. Free will is an important pre-condition, as intention and intentional agency are central in Buddhist ethics and moral psychology. It is only an action emerging from an intention that becomes the subject of moral evaluation as wholesome or unwholesome. Thus, Gene Heyman's thesis that addiction is not a disease but a disorder of choice is central to Buddhist therapy for addictions.

Peter Harvey offers a useful way of classifying actions in relation to responsibility, accountability and intentions (*cetanā*):

1. An action done without intending to do it, like accidentally treading on an ant without any thoughts of harming would not incur blameworthiness and bad *karmic* results.
2. A type of action which is performed by an agent who knows it to be evil, but does it while he is not impassioned and not in full control of himself, that is if the person is 'agitated and out of mind' (*visaññā*), it may be a lesser evil.
3. An evil action carried out when one is not clear about the object affected by the action is moderately blameworthy.
4. An action done with full intention, fully knowing what one is doing and knowing that the action is evil is the most obvious of wrong actions, especially if it is premeditated.
5. An evil action where one intends to do the act, fully knowing what one is doing it (as in 4) but not recognising that one is doing wrong is seen as the worst of all actions.

This useful classification helps us to get an overview of the place of intention/volition and different types of knowledge and ignorance that play a role in developing a concept of moral weakness or weakness of will. Now, if one looks at the fifth category, we may cite the difference between an instance where one does not know one is harming someone, and the more spiritually blatant position – *one does not realise or bring to one's mind* that harming a sentient being is wrong. Also, one may know that it is wrong to harm a sentient being, but yet do it. There are many variations of the lack of mindfulness. Aristotle, for instance, says that we may deliberate to refrain from addictions but suddenly give in, which he called 'last-ditch *akrasia*'; we can also, without having carefully deliberated, 'rush in' to doing something, which Aristotle called 'impetuous *akrasia*'.

Apart from rational deliberation, emotions play a significant role in both addictions and moving away from addictions: anger, impatience, guilt and lust feed incontinence, whereas self-compassion, caring for others, patience, persistence and self-knowledge strengthen a strong will towards incontinence and clear and mindful perception of situations. Sometimes in our conversation we use phrases like 'driven by anger', 'struck by temptation' and 'plagued by guilt and remorse' that give a passive picture of a person and, thus, as Averill observes, help a person to abjure responsibility.[10] The chapter on emotions in this book, which in a sense is a part of the Buddhist moral psychology, illuminates the role of emotions in decision-making. I have discussed the issues about responsibility and weakness of will in detail, as there has been a clear misunderstanding of the Buddhist position in the context of managing incontinence by Western scholars, such as George Ainslie. In his book, *Breakdown of Will*, Ainslie makes the following remarks about Buddhism and understanding moral weakness:

> Buddhism for instance, concerns itself with emancipation from 'the bond of worldly passions' and describes five strategies of purification, essentially: having clear ideas, avoiding sensual desires by mind control, restricting objects to their natural, 'endurance', and watching out for temptation in advance. However, the ways that nonwestern religions enumerate causes of and solutions to self-defeating behaviours seem a jumble from any operational viewpoint trying to maximise a good.[11]

Ainslie took this reference to Buddhism from the book *Teachings of the Buddha*, by B.D. Kyokai.[12] There are a number of critical points to be made regarding Ainslie's reference to Buddhism. First, the reference he has taken from Kyokai's book is not accurate, and if one reads the sermon called 'Discourse on All the Influxes' (*āsava*) in the *Middle Length Sayings*, these methods refer not merely to worldly passions (*kāmāsava*), but also to attachment to becoming (*bhavāsava*) and attachment to wrong views. It is said that these influxes may be got rid of by the following methods: by vision, by control, by use, by endurance, by avoidance, by elimination and by development. While the purpose of these methods goes well beyond dealing with self-defeating behaviour, it is unlikely that Ainslie understands the complete context of the methods. Regarding Ainslie's claim that Buddhist techniques have no operational value: as I will illustrate in the analysis that follows, mindfulness-based techniques have entered the mainstream of therapies, including addiction management. For instance, the work of Bien and Bien is a product of extensive clinical activity run for several decades.[13] Also, in my work as a professional counsellor, I have used mindfulness techniques for the management of addictions.[14] Stanton Peele, commenting on Bien and Bien's book, says:

> Mindful Recovery combines two hitherto unrelated worlds – that of modern cognitive therapy and Buddhist reflection. The connection makes incredible sense, since Buddhism is not a religion in the traditional sense so much as a method for directing one's thoughts and experiences. By centering oneself in one's here-and-now, lived experience, addicts can avoid the infantilism, the regrets, the efforts to seek unrewarding results that are the basis for self-destructive behaviours.[15]

Today mindfulness is offered not merely for mental health concerns but for enlightened living in a more positive way, a positive psychology.

The third point I wish to convey is that in spite of his misunderstanding of Buddhist contributions to addiction studies, Ainslie has made an important contribution. In fact, one of his claims is that the person who falls prey to addictions in spite of a commitment to self-control, *becomes prey to a momentary pleasure close at hand, and ignores the long term suffering.* But human beings need not be at the mercy of temporary rewards. They may act in the pursuit of a long-term contentment. This insight is in line with the Buddha's insistence that we should not get enamoured by the spell of temporary passing pleasures.

The Harm Reduction Model for Alcohol Addiction

As a person practising counselling, I sometimes get sandwiched between the two goals of complete abstinence and ideal moderation. Allan Marlatt, with whom I had some useful correspondence, presents what he calls the 'harm reduction model', the pragmatic and humane way of converting alcoholics to moderation, when that is the only effective alternative method to use. Also, there is a possibility that moderation can be used as a halfway towards complete abstinence, where the client wishes to move towards that goal and is confident of sticking to it.[16]

Marlatt realised that enforcing immediate abstinence often deters substance users from adhering to treatment and through great compassion he attempted to get the client to move towards reduction of alcohol rather than complete abstinence, according to challenging contexts. Though he was greatly attracted by Buddhist philosophy and mindfulness techniques, and though Buddhism upheld abstinence in one of the main ethical precepts, this pragmatic approach brought good results, and something that contextually a Buddhist would admire. Marlatt was trail-blazing in this new road to addiction therapy and research, and a deep sense of empathy and compassion is embedded in this harm reduction model. In fact, Bien and Bien, who present a Buddhist model par excellence in their therapy for addictions, and thus would in general move towards abstinence when possible, also appreciate this half-way ideal of moderation.

From a Buddhist perspective, a multiplicity of factors have a bearing on the phenomenon of the weakness of will. And there is a real need for educating victims of incontinence back to stable personalities with rigour and ardency in their lives. Mere conviction about why alcoholic or gambling addiction is bad is not enough, unless these beliefs are fed by strong motivational roots and such motivational roots may strengthen the beliefs or judgments about addictions. As John Atkinson, the psychologist, points out: 'The magnitude of response and the persistence of behaviour are functions of the strength of motivation to perform the act relative to the strength of motivation to perform competing acts'.[17] Mele takes the stand that good judgments offer 'no motivational magic' when we act intentionally to do what we are strongly motivated to do. Perceived proximity to prospects for desire–satisfaction also plays an important role in temptations, and the Buddha thus asked people to avoid certain places and people. In active normal life, one's attentional stance is important, and the practice of mindfulness in daily life is the best safeguard to the kinds of temptations confronting people. As Mele says, we need to be aware if there is a misalignment between the assessment of desired objects and the motivational strength of desires. This approach would diffuse the Socratic paradox that 'virtue is knowledge'. There is, of course, one qualification to this analysis: Buddhism accepts a higher level of wisdom beyond the normal secular life and the very heights of spiritual perfection, which analytically rules out wrongdoing. But we are not examining here the lives of perfect saints (*arahat*) but the lives of ordinary people, and even on the road to perfection there is a spectrum of knowledge and goodness. Higher knowledge as compared with ordinary layers of knowledge or conventional knowledge has a high epistemic standing.

Prevention of Alcohol Addiction

Ronald A. Ruden says in his work *Craving Brain*, 'Buddha's clever solution was not to fight the craving response once it occurred, but instead to prevent the pattern recognition process before it began'.[18] The Buddha emphasised that prevention is better than damage control – to see the spark before the flame. This stand implies the practice of restraint and the avoidance of certain places and even people. Ruden also recommends the combining of *biobalance* and mindfulness practice. Elster also cites craving as a significant causal factor for addictions: 'The hedonic and non-hedonic effects jointly influence the state of craving, which is the central explanatory variable in the behavioural study of addictions and its consequences'.[19]

Freud and Buddhism On Self-Destructive Behaviour

The Buddha explained three forms of human craving: craving for sensual pleasures (*kāma-taṇhā*), craving for egoistic pursuits (*bhava-taṇhā*) and craving for aggression and destruction of unpleasant objects, situations, people and one's own self in suicide (*vibhava-taṇhā*), which has its roots in aversion/anger (*dosa*). In *Buddhist and Freudian Psychology* I compared these three cravings with parallels in Freud, the drive for sensual pleasures, the ego-instinct and the death instinct.[20] While all these craving patterns have some relation to addictions, the death instinct/*vibhava-taṇhā* parallel help us to understand certain forms of self-destructive behaviour. Freud's concept of death instinct, as presented in his work *Beyond the Pleasure Principle*,[21] is full of rich material and a number of components were identified by J.C. Flugal.[22] This work cites six possible strands in the apparently baffling concept of the death instinct. By the year 1915, Freud came to realise that the element of hate, later to be called the aggressive instinct was separate from sexuality, but later he was baffled that there was an instinct that threatened the ego's natural self-love:

> So immense is the ego's self-love, which we have come to recognize as the primal state from which instinctual life proceeds, and so vast is the amount of narcissistic libido, which we see liberated in the fear

that emerges as a threat to life, that we cannot conceive how the ego can consent to its own destruction.[23]

Out of the different strands of the death instinct, hatred, destruction of unpleasant objects and what is called the 'repetition compulsion' are relevant to understanding addictions. Some of the addicts who succumb to relapses move in a vicious circle of self-hate and guilt, and thus develop a disposition to drown the unpleasant array of feelings with another drink – this is an instance of repetition compulsion, trying to master the unpleasant repetitive thought patterns. There is a kind of demonic compulsion. In terms of a metaphor used by the Buddha, it is like a man scratching to get rid of an itching skin problem. Edwin Schneidman, the expert on suicide studies, says that in attempted suicide, there is a kind of ambivalence to destroy the body and yet a cry for help. There is a similar kind of drift in addicts – to consume or not to consume. Aristotle, for instance, says that when a person's mind is caught up in alcohol or drug arousal, it is as if he both knows and does not know the consequence of his behaviour.

Cue dependence is, according to Elster, a well-documented mechanism: 'By the mechanism of conditioned learning, addicts may experience euphoria or craving at the mere sight of an environment associated with consumption'.[24] The importance of such 'cue dependence', acting as a trigger for craving, is quite crucial for the Buddhist analysis and figures as an important factor in addictions.

Though Aristotle did not consider the *akrasia* of anger to be as important as the *akrasia* of greed, my own personal experience with clients indicates that, at times, there is a great deal of reactive anger that feeds alcohol addiction, and especially relapses. Once you remove the anger component, especially with spouse and children, there is a relaxed accommodation of the ups and downs of the addictive dispositions. Often a few sessions with the addict and spouse help to clear the ground. Repetitive, compulsive behaviour that emerges due to frustrations in the workplace or home are triggered by accumulated subliminal anger. Boredom and lack of absorbing interest in life, being forced to do work one does not enjoy, not getting the kind of job that one wishes to have, working round the clock, lack of a diversified agenda in routine life – these factors all provide a fertile ground for the emergence of the addict to alcohol, drugs, smoking and gambling. A great deal of anger and depression pervades their life.

In the final analysis, especially from a Buddhist perspective, the individual's ability to make decisions and have free choice is important.

Stanton Peele feels that the highly medicalised view of drug addiction appears to view addiction as the result of specific biological mechanisms that lock the body into an invariant pattern of behaviour.[25] Of course, when there is radical change in the biochemistry due to constant alcohol usage, techniques such as detoxification become necessary, but Peele's general claim could be accepted. It is necessary to recover the sense of control, commitment, persistence and direction that an individual may contribute, not merely on the preventive side but as real signposts on the road to recovery and well-being. This, in brief, is also the message of Gene Heyman's claim that addiction is not a disease but a disorder of choice.

Social Dimensions of *Akrasia* (Weakness of Will)

While the individual is important, society does play a key role in moving potential addicts towards the path of healthy living and addicts on the road to healthy recovery. Amelie Rorty, while presenting a very good analysis of the socio-pathology and politics of *akrasia*, makes the following observations:

1. The structure of the *akrasia* of anger differs from that of desire, but the explanation of its obduracy and entrenchment is similar.
2. Both the *akrasia* of anger and the *akrasia* of greed are typically dispositional rather than episodic; and both express conflicts among entrenched habits.
3. Because a good deal of *akrasia* is sustained and reinforced by socio-political and economic arrangements, patterns *of akrasia* are often a common form of social pathology.
4. The most effective form of reform of *akrasia* lies in the reform of its epidemiological sources – its socio-political and economic origins – rather than the attempt to correct the immediate beliefs or desires that prompt individual cases. There is a diagnosis of the social roots of *akrasia*.

During the time of the Buddha, this kind of socio-pathology of addictions did not exist in the way it is found today, though where necessary he looked at certain social patterns that fed on human greed. While accepting the very useful analysis of Amelie Rorty, there is of course no substitute for personal counselling and the kind of group work done today for addicts. A morally vibrant social consciousness is certainly needed today and also critical assessment of the kind of advertising and commercial interests trading on alcoholic addiction, drug addiction and subtle forms of gambling.

The Place of the Body in Addictions

The most significant and valuable criticism of alcohol and drug addictions comes from the current findings of health science. Christine Caldwell, a body-centred psychotherapist, describes the call of the body for good health in a very graphic way:

> We threaten our lives when we introduce large amounts of toxins into our bodies. We damage our lives when we practice addictions that cause long-term illness or break the fabric of our families and societies. We limit our lives when we fail to grow, when we keep ourselves sedated or distracted, when we fail to contribute to others. We promote life when we commit to our happiness and the happiness of others. Moving from life-threatening to life-promoting actions is a tremendous step.[26]

Buddhist Resources for Managing Addiction to Alcohol

Now that the theoretical and some of the therapeutic issues concerning *akrasia* in general and in particular drug addiction have been examined and discussed, I shall present the resources I used in my practice as a professional counsellor:

1. Clients with addictions can recover to the extent that they decide to take charge of their lives. Taking responsibility for one's own life is the starting point.
2. It is necessary that the clients accept that an addiction is hurting them and wish to overcome it. They must also realise that this addiction causes pain and suffering. In cognitive therapy, the therapist attempts to change the way that the addict perceives his situation of incessant temptation, by looking at the thought patterns, which is described as the auto-pilot. The Buddha's celebrated sermon *Vitakka-saṇṭhāna Sutta* (Pathways of Thought) is a resource I use for mindful awareness.
3. Once the cognitive framework of the addict changes for the better, motivational strength is crucial. The clients need to feel enough efficacy and confidence that they can manage their time during the

period of withdrawal from alcohol and the therapist has to find ways and means of developing the client's motivational strength; the family and close friends also need to play a useful role in this context. The secret of this level lies in taking small and effective steps, and one may say the devil is in the details.

4. Mindfulness and the attentional stance. The clients are given simple exercises in mindfulness practice which have to be developed to break through the stimulus–response mechanism in addictive behaviour. If they find alternative ways of spending their leisure, away from the hustle and buzz of a hectic workday, and enjoy the stillness of an evening at the temple or home, it becomes possible to break through that emptiness that comes to addicts in the evenings. Music, gardening and enjoying long walks help them to generate energy and improve their mindset. If an addict cannot find absorbing and interesting ways of spending their leisure, especially in the evening after work, the demon of boredom invades them: 'When you stop taking the drug of your choice, there is a hole in your life where the drug used to be. Suddenly you are left with empty hours that you don't know what to do with'.[27]

5. As the accelerated speed of our times, working with computers, statistics and programs for speed and accuracy dominate our lives today, people get baffled when they encounter uncertainty, sudden setbacks in the workplace, ambiguity and even some kind of chaos. Guy Claxton says that people who are accustomed to the tempo of the hare's brain need to slowdown and get used to the tortoise's mind.[28] Today, in addition to having a personality geared to speed and accuracy, we need to have resources to slow down and listen to one's own mind and body.

6. A solution to this kind of predicament has been offered by Csikszt-mihalyi in a learning model of complete absorption and joy called the 'flow' – a state in which people are so absorbed that nothing else matters.[29] Working with artists, mountain climbers, athletes, musicians and other people in diverse vocations, it was found that the people who got completely absorbed in what they did had no holes to fill with cheap entertainment or alcohol.

7. There is also what I have called the 'magic of the ordinary and the elegance of small things',[30] drawn from the inspiring essay by Thich Nat Nahn, 'Eating a Mandarin' – enjoying simple things like making and having a cup of tea. One has to develop a great deal of self-compassion and enjoy a wonderful recovery of well-being based

on the simple things in life. The philosophy of contentment is a great therapeutic resource. Self-compassion has to be supplemented by developing a sense of connectedness and healing relationships with others close to you, as loneliness is also a kind of demon that invades addicts.

These are the significant signposts on the path of recovery from addiction to positive well-being.

Case Study: 'The Magic of the Ordinary'

Anthony is neither a gambler or a smoker, nor is he an alcoholic. He is very devoted to his family. However, he enjoys life on the higher social levels, attached to status, and is very generous with his wealth. Unfortunately he has some conflicts with his boss and is transferred to another branch of the company, which is somewhat poor in terms of both status and income. The work atmosphere is not very pleasant and he begins to drink more than he usually would. Without his knowledge he starts slipping into addiction, and people at home, especially his wife, are becoming restless. Her reaction to his behaviour makes things worse. One day he is driving after drinks and he nearly has a car crash.

Fortunately, Anthony attends counselling, assisted by one of the social workers in their town. Counselling makes him aware of the dangers of falling into addiction; Anthony is feeling tired and depressed but is not doing anything about it. The counsellor gets in touch with Anthony's wife and asks her to be kind, to make something special for tea when he comes home and to get the children talking to him. Gradually Anthony listens to the counsellor. Anthony does have a relapse but emerges from it and the counsellor conveys to him that complete abstinence is not the target, but to be a controlled drinker: he does not have to hide the bottle in the house, but when he feels better it is okay to have a drink, but he must follow a conscious limit at parties. More than everything the counsellor works out a diversified agenda, with gardening, cooking and evening walks, lots of music and once a month a holiday out. The counsellor helps him to get a new job which is excellent, has a positive atmosphere and very bright prospects, and he is selected for special training.

He is good at practising mindfulness in daily life and doing things which are creative and absorbing. He makes Vesak lanterns in the temple and is fully present and enjoys what he does. I tell him that he has at last discovered what I call the *magic of the ordinary*: instead of look-ing for the bottle in the fridge, he has begun to enjoy cheesecake and coffee, which his wife prepared. I also tell him that according to the celebrated Buddhist thinker Thich Nhat Hanh the person who is happy and contended will completely enjoy a simple thing like 'eating a mandarin'!

20
Pride and Conceit: Emotions of Self-Assessment

Robert Solomon, who wrote the first comprehensive, well-known study of emotions during recent times, maintains that a central feature of emotions is that they are 'self-involved'.[1] He also says that in many emotions the judgment of the self is implicit or in the shadows, implying that the self casts a shadow on emotions like admiration, anger and envy. 'Anger, which always involves a judgment that one's self has been offended or violated, may nonetheless focus its fervor strictly towards the other person. Resentment, although clearly self-involved and based upon a personal stance of defensiveness, protects its self with a projected armour of objectivity'.[2] He says that in every case the self is an essential pole of emotional judgment. Solomon even seems to suggest that the nature of emotions will remain incomprehensible without a theory of the self.[3] But ultimately, the self in emotions is a point of reference implying subjectivity. Even today, in examining the problematic relationship between emotions and the self, there is a kind of unwillingness to probe deeply into the question of the *reality of the self*, as well as the *moral criticism of the emotions*.

To cite another study, where there is reference to the self in an extremely rich and interesting analysis of jealousy, Leila Tov-Ruach makes the following observation: jealousy is an emotion that perceives a danger to the self at its centre and all the varieties of jealousy depend on a 'contextually determined state of the person's ego'.[4] But having presented a very stimulating analysis of jealousy in relation to the self, there is a reluctance to take this analysis further and examine the status of the 'self' concept: 'whether the sense of the unity of the self and protection it evokes is an illusion, is a question we must leave for another occasion'.[5]

Another very important contribution to emotion studies is Gabrieli Taylor's work, *Pride, Shame and Guilt: Emotions of Self-Assessment.*[6] This work is important as the relationship between the self and emotions holds a central place in her analysis. She discerns a difference between a person experiencing, on the one hand, anger and fear, and on the other hand, pride, shame and guilt. For instance, the experience of fear by Peter may be explained by the reason that Peter believes that 'snakes are poisonous', which is a kind of causal explanation which may not apply to Fred because he has some bad childhood experience that explains his fear. But reference to pride and shame are more integrally bound up with a person's sense of the 'self': this is so because the person experiencing such an emotion does not just see the situation in evaluative terms' (the snake will harm me), he also assimilates what he values or disvalues into a structure of his achievements or failures, as so viewed by him. His evaluation of the situation, in the case of pride, may change his evaluation of his achievements or failures, and may alter his view of himself. Though this difference between emotions like anger/fear and that of pride and shame may not always be so clear, the agent's view of himself colours the emotions of self-assessment.

While the analysis of the different emotions of self-assessment is a useful contribution, and the conception of the self is quite central to this analysis, the very concept of the 'self' does not receive any critical analysis. Taylor says, as a passing remark, that there is no unchanging object of consciousness, which may be referred to as 'self' but that the concept of a moral agent requires a degree of connectedness between states of consciousness.[7] But here again, apart from these classificatory passing comments, the issue is not integrated into the main texture of the work. Especially as the Humean notion of pride is one of the main concerns of this study, a more focused discussion of the issues pertaining to the reality of the self and the consequent implications for emotions would have been rewarding. And since Hume did consider the self a 'fiction', the discussion of pride deserves more sustained examination. The Buddhist point of view is that a false sense of the self is the foci of many negative emotions and the liberation from this deception is a path to generate and developing positive emotions. Taylor's analysis is concerned with the reflexive nature of certain emotions like pride, shame and guilt and beliefs related to the emergence of these emotions but the issue about the reality of the self which is a Humean concern is not pursued, in the way that it is pursued in Buddhism or Hume. But, to be fair, it must be said that she comes to the margins of this problem – in saying that there is no unchanging object called the self but that the notion of a moral agent requires that there need to be connexions to states of consciousness. Her comments on reflective self-evaluation, the need for some coherence in a person's actions and reflections as a moral agent are certainly consistent with a Buddhist perspective. But there is a need to mention that the Buddhist notion of 'higher ethics' warns the authentic traveller on the liberation path to be careful of 'conceits' that emerge like 'I am more pure than others'. This continuous self-criticism is important as conceits remain till the last stages of perfection. In fact, Taylor does raise questions about Hume's claim that excessive pride is vicious and examines the claims for it, like a person's pride being disproportionate, badly grounded and excessive. She also says that excessive pride being vicious may be due to an 'undue degree of self-preoccupation'. While these comments take us up to a point in looking at the logic of the emotions of self-assessment, and due credit is given to Taylor for opening up this neglected territory in emotion studies, we need to go to Buddhism, Hume and a study by Terrence Penelhum to go more deeply into the relationship between the unreality of the 'self' and negative emotions.

In the philosophy of mind and psychology there are potential objections to using strong generalities like the self/ego as a conceptual tool to keep our study of emotion taxonomies tidy. But it has to be said that emotions can be understood at various levels of generality, and these levels of generality need not be isolated from each other. In fact, if one follows the Sartrean perspective, one could say that emotions involve a whole mode of orientation toward the world. While it may be futile to search for absolute patterns of order or some fixed foci for classifying emotions, there are some recurring residual strains in some emotions, casting a longer shadow and pointing toward a relatively larger and unifying focus. In understanding emotions, we move in two directions, we look for some specific conditions linked to different emotion profiles, as well as the larger frames for obtaining an integral perspective. Also, different kinds of emotions profiles have different logical features, as for instance, pride, shame and guilt having a relation to self-assessment. The ego-emotion relationship has been an important concern of philosophical orientations both in the West and the East, in ancient as well as modern times.

Terence Penelhum's paper 'Self-Identity and Self-Regard' raises certain significant issues about the idea of the self in our emotional lives.[8] He says that he is raising the question in relation to Humean exegesis, and he is also interested in the more general implications of the issue – 'the role that the idea of the self plays in our thinking about some of the areas of the emotional life that Hume considers'.[9] Towards the end of the paper he remarks, 'There is an interesting historical contrast to Hume's procedure, one which would have surprised Hume if he had been aware of it... Buddha is said to have argued that the Hindu view of the self as identical with the cosmic soul is false, somewhat as Hume rejects substantial analyses of the self'.[10]

Thus, Penelhum presents us with some significant issues: what place does the self have in our emotional lives? If the self is a fiction, as Hume says, does it have any role in our emotional lives? Finally, if there are parallels between Buddhism and Hume, how does Buddhism deal with this problem? Penelhum also feels that Hume's attempt to link up the emotion of pride to the sense of the self creates a problem, as there is a great deal of ambiguity in the use of words like *pride* and *humility*:

> Pride is often discussed in theological contexts as though it included all forms of inordinate self-concern or self-absorption, not only those that involve a high estimate of oneself. One very common form of such self-absorption is obsession with one's own inadequacies, so that one can find oneself speaking of some apparent forms of humility as examples of pride in this sense.[11]

Apart from these critical comments on pride and its link to the Humean notion of the self, Penelhum also points out a kind of tension (if not an inconsistency) between the analysis of the self of thought and imagination in Book 1 and the self and passions in Book 11. Thus, there are three points that emerge in the discussion: the issue about pride and humility, the self and passions and the parallelism between Hume and Buddhism. While appreciating the fact that Penelhum has focused interest on some key issues, I shall attempt a critical response to these comments. What is valuable in his analysis is that he puts his hand into the central issue – if, as Hume says, the self is a fiction (as laid out in Book 1 of the *Treatise*), then are we to say that passions are fictions, and are we deluded when pride and humility emerge within us?

The Humean Position on Self and Pride

David Hume is associated with the celebrated view that what is called the 'self' is but a bundle of perceptions. Hume basically associated the self with the 'mind' and the mind, for him, is a theatre where you can see emerging and passing photographic impressions. Yet, Hume was perplexed that people had some habits that were paradoxical: the habit of talking about people as single and unitary beings, though they are constantly subject to change. In the words of Hume, 'what then gives us so great a propension to ascribe an identity to these successive perceptions, and to suppose ourselves possessed of an invariable and uninterrupted existence through the whole course of our lives'.[12] Here Hume rejects the metaphysical view that accepts the self with perfect identity and simplicity. But Hume feels that the spell of the illusion is so strong among men that the only remedy is 'carelessness and inattention'. This is the general outlook of Book 1 of *A Treatise of Human Nature*, whereas in Book 2, there is a slight change of focus. The first book deals with the notion of the self in terms of thought and imagination but the second book in terms of emotions.[13] In the words of Hume: 'We must distinguish betwixt personal identity, as it regards our thought and imagination, and as it regards our passions or the concern we take in ourselves'.[14]

In the second book, Hume makes an analysis of the passions, of which the most important are *pride* and *humility* as they are related to our idea of the self. Hume divides what he calls 'perceptions of the mind' into impressions and ideas and the impressions admit another division into original and secondary. Original impressions, or impressions of sensation, arise from 'the constitution of the body' or 'from the application of ideas to external objects'. 'Secondary or reflective impressions' proceed from original ones. Either immediately or by the interposition of ideas: (1) Of the first kind are impressions of the senses, and all bodily pains and pleasures; (2) of the second kind are the passions and other emotions resembling them. He says bodily pains and pleasures can be a cause for certain types of passions, for instance, when a fit of gout produces pain. But his focus is on the reflective impressions, which are again divided into calm and violent passions. The former are those with an aesthetic flavour, such as the raptures of poetry or music (beauty in action, composition and external object). The passions proper are those of love and hatred, grief and joy, pride and humility. Of these, pride and humility are central concerns in the Humean analysis of the passions. Also, the study of passions provides a new and stimulating entry to the notion of the fictional self. As Amelie Rorty remarks, 'the passions provide the distinctive elements that compose the fictional idea of the self' (Rorty, 1990, 257).[15]

It would be useful to look at the emotion of pride in greater detail. Hume makes these comments about pride and humility: 'The passions of PRIDE and HUMILITY being simple and uniform impressions, 'tis impossible we can ever, by a multitude of words, give a just definition of them...the utmost we can pretend to do is a description of them'.[16] Thus, in an attempt to describe the emotions, he says that though pride and humility appear as contraries, they have the *same object*, and the object is the self. We get elated by pride and dejected by humility. When self does not enter into consideration, there is no pride or humility. There is also the cause of pride; if a man is vain about a beautiful house that belongs to him or he has built, here the *object* of the passion is the self and the *cause* is the beautiful house. The cause itself has two aspects: the quality that operates upon the passion (beauty) and the subject in which the quality inheres (house). These qualities generate pleasure and pain and the subject on which these qualities are placed (house) is related to the self. The initial pleasure about the beautiful house is independent of pride. A minimum condition for the experience of pride is that the beautiful house is considered as 'mine'. The self features in the analysis as the object of pride, that towards which pride is directed. Thus, it may be summed up in this manner: 'So pride on this account can be summed up as consisting of a self-directed pleasure based on a distinctive pleasure derived from something that is also mine'. Regarding the difference between 'joy' and 'pride' he says we may have joy but yet not make the transition to pride. Hume lays down specific features about pride and vain glory: the connection between the self and the agreeable object is close; it involves a comparison with others rather than the intrinsic worth of the object; the object of pride must be relatively enduring; we feel more proud when we appear to others as beautiful or virtuous; lastly, custom and opinion also have an impact on the direction of passions.

The Critical Examination of the Humean Position

> Hume's project does not require that he shows the strict identity of a person's motivational structure. All that the common sense idea of the self requires is that such changes form a continuous narrative.[17]

Rorty's interpretation appears plausible and offers a satisfactory answer to Penelhum's fear about an inconsistency between Hume's Books 1 and 2.[18] Rorty, in fact, notices in an additional note that: 'It is not surprising that Derek Parfit saw Hume as a predecessor who defended a theory of personal continuity, rather than strict personal identity with the characterisation of that person's interest and motives'.[19] Steven Collins's *Selfless Persons* provides an excellent study of the parallels among Hume, Buddhism and Parfit.[20]

In Book 2, Hume describes how the idea of self is derived from passions. Pride and humility are passions par excellence, bound to the idea of self, though it is a fiction: 'It should not therefore be surprising that the passions provide the distinctive elements that compose the fictional idea of the self as distinguishable from a reorganization of impressions and ideas that compose external objects'.[21] Hume would, of course, allow causes other than passions to generate the irresistible notion of the fictional self, but in this analysis we are looking at Hume on passions and the self.

Apart from issues pertaining to the fictional nature of self in Books 1 and 2, the issue about the moral criticism of emotions has been raised by Penelhum. The question of whether pride and humility are to be considered morally evil or bad is a hard question to answer in the light of the Humean scheme, as at times Hume considered pride as morally neutral, and yet at times makes a distinction between pride and conceit. This is an issue that highlights significant differences in our discussion of Buddhism and Hume. Buddhism makes a clear distinction between positive and negative emotions, as well as emphasising the fact that negative emotions are fed by the attachment to a notion of a permanent ego. This attachment between the negative emotions and the fictional notion of the self is a central facet of Buddhist moral psychology.

How do we decide about the soundness of a specific emotion? We can say that a person' pride is excessive, that his achievements are not as he imagined them to be; may be due to a wrong appraisal of the facts, for example high assessment of wealth and a low estimate of scholarship; we can question the reality of the supposed achievement; we can also say that the *supposed connections between the self and the emotions do not exist*. Penelhum feels that the last claim is the most important. According to him, this can emerge on three grounds: it may be said that the affluence of my children is a mater about which my pride is possible, but not that of my neighbour, and it ought not lead to pride; if my report is based on a false report of my son's success, then again the connection does not exist; if the very notion of the self generates pride then it rests on a false supposition of personal identity. Penelhum says, 'This would not preclude pride and humility from occurring, but it would make them ineluctably groundless, for they would pre-suppose that the object of the high or low that the subject made incorporated stretches of personal history that it could not incorporate'.[22]

A Buddhist Perspective on the 'Self' and Pride

Penelhum sees the Buddhist position as an interesting contrast to Hume's and says that Hume would have been surprised if he heard of it. He sees some parallels between Hume's rejection of the substantialist view of the self and the Buddhist analysis of the metaphysical conceptions of the self current in India at the time. But when Penelhum says that the Buddha went beyond the rejection of the eternalist conception of the self to the 'denial of the conventional belief in the persistent identity of the individual',[23] he does not take into consideration the Buddhist meaningful but cautious use of the 'person' concept, a use that is aware of its conceptual pitfalls. It is true, as he says, that whereas Hume advocated carelessness and inattention as the only panacea for the spell of the illusion of the self, the Buddha advocates another path for the eradication of the illusion.

But the Buddha also uses a meaningful and cautious logic and vocabulary to talk about the emotions, as well as a critical view of 'personal continuity' rather than strict identity. While not accepting the substantialist concept of the self based on permanence and pleasure, what the Buddha accepted left room for the meaningful use of a concept of 'qualified continuity'. In rejecting the existence of a permanent soul, the Buddha is not rejecting the critical use of a continued person, as an agent of moral action, one capable of generating values and having purposes of his own, having memories and thoughts and capable of emotional expression. It is basically a psychophysical process in flux, but maintains a relative individuality within a cosmic scheme. Though there is no substratum, one serial process may be distinguished from the other. The doctrine of no-self does not mean that a person is just protoplasm, without any sense of direction. It must be emphasised that within the contemplative practice in Buddhism, the dissolution of the ego does not imply a diminution of one's co-ordinating powers. *Somewhere within the narrow ridge between the paths of chaos and nihilism and the traps of identity illusions, one has to penetrate through a razor's edge, a realm of interim and critical identities, dissolving as we cross them, transcending them as we cut across their inner dialectic.*[24] There is obviously some tension between the 'illusionist' and the 'integrative' perspectives on identity, but one needs a refined contemplative practice, reflection and what in Buddhism is described as '*yonisomanasikara*', aided by the relevant conceptual clarification to walk through these tensions.

Another important point is that what is described as a 'false' sense of the self has some kind of 'phenomenological reality' or, in Hume's terminology, 'persistence and power'. It is also very important to remember that what is called *sakkāya-diṭṭhi*, the spell of the wrong views associated with the notion of a self, will be eliminated at the first stage of liberation but its manifestation as conceit (*māna*) will remain until the final stage of perfection. Of course, as one proceeds on the path one becomes proud of one's refined development rather than any secular possessions or attainments. The 'I' conceit in *māna* is more subtle than the belief in a 'false self'.

Regarding positive emotions, Derek Parfit has shown that this non-self perspective does open up the horizons for compassion as, according to him, there is a homology between earlier and later 'selves' constituted by ones sense of continuity and the 'selves' of other people. In the words of Steven Collins, 'the rationale for action which acceptance of Buddhism furnishes provides neither for simple self-interest nor for self-denying altruism. The attitude to all "individuals" past and future selves, past, future or contemporary others is the same loving kindness, compassion, sympathetic joy and equanimity'.[25] There is a touch of paradox here – the stronger the realisation of the fictional self, the more robust and vibrant are the positive emotions of compassion, and Buddha's compassion was described as *'mahā-karuṇā'* as it was boundless. This would be a way of offering an answer to Penelhum's question: how can positive passions emerge on a fictional self?

Pride, Conceit and Humility in Buddhism

Penelhum says that in theological contexts, the term pride is used to cover all cases of self-concern or self-absorption, not only those that involve a high estimate of oneself, and that it is even used as a blanket term to cover sensuality. On the contrary, the Buddha defines terms like pride and humility with care and respects the context of their application. What is conceived as a negative emotion in Buddhism is conveyed by the Pali term *mana*. I shall consistently render this term as 'conceit' rather than the more popular word 'pride', which in English usage and also in cross-cultural usage has a more healthy meaning. In fact, in a research project I did for the East–West Culture Learning Institute in Hawaii, on 'Emotion Taxonomy in Sri Lanka', in the data on Sinhalese usage, the emotion cluster on pride was as follows: pride (*abhimāna*), conceited (*ahaṅkāra*), arrogance (*mahantatvaya*), inferiority complex (*hīna-māna*). Pride in this context is what you may feel about the achievements of your own country; the other terms have a negative connotation.[26]

As the Humean analysis of pride is not consistently anchored on a moral point of view, and also as Hume slips from usage of pride as vicious to a more neutral form, the strong moral/psychological flavour in the Buddhist reference to conceit may be noted. Second, the Buddha does not use the term conceit (*mana*) as a blanket term to cover all kinds of self-concern. Its specific features in terms of its origin, nature, persistence and possible extinction will be shown in the analysis that follows. The Buddha has shown that the basic egocentricity of man finds expression in three forms: as craving, as a wrong conception of the self and as conceit. Thus Penelhum's reference to the loose usage of pride as a blanket term may not apply to Buddhism. Thirdly, humility is considered a virtue in Buddhism, and is clearly distinguished from inferiority complex (*hīna-māna*). *Mana* (conceit) is metaphorically described as 'flaunting a flag', implying a desire to advertise oneself.[27] Etymologically the term is derived from *māneti* (to honour) or *mināti* (to measure), giving us the connotation of conceiving false notions.[28]

There is in man what is called 'the bias towards egocentricity' (rooted in a wrong belief of an abiding entity) that manifests at various levels: linguistic, intellectual, emotional, ethical and so on. The acquisitive and possessive personality structure, according to the recurring analysis of the Buddha's sermons, is threefold: in craving (*taṇhā*), conceit (*māna*) and false views (*diṭṭhi*). Craving is expressed in the linguistic form, 'This is mine', conceit manifests in the form, 'This I am', and false views in the form, 'This is myself'. It is very important that self-conceit (*māna*) is distinguished from ego belief (*sakkāya-diṭṭhi*) which implies a definite view regarding the assumption of an ego. This is the first of the ten fetters, and disappears when one becomes a stream winner, whereas conceit, which is the eighth fetter, can vary from a crude feeling of conceit to a more subtle feeling of distinctiveness that prevails until the attainment of *arahatship*. Thus, the *I-sense* is more subtle than the *self-view*. This detailed analysis indicates that *māna* as conceit is not used as a blanket term to cover all forms of self-concern.

Self-conceit takes three forms: it can take the form of a feeling of superiority, with the thought 'I am superior to others' (*seyya-māna*); it can be a conceit based on the feeling of superiority, with the thought that 'I am equal to others' (*sadisa-māna*); and it can be conceit based on the feeling of inferiority, with the thought 'I am inferior to the other' (*hīna-māna*). It is very important to be aware that these conceits may lie at a subliminal and dormant level (*mānānusaya*), to be aroused by certain situations. Superiority and inferiority feelings are the dual manifestations of the same root, an inflated sense of vanity (*māna-mada*). Buddhism considers these forms of conceit as unwholesome. An important distinction to be made in the light of the Buddhist analysis is that though inferiority feelings are unwholesome, humility is a great virtue. It is not based on a sense of inadequacy; on the contrary, it is based on self-confidence and the insight that one should not be over-powered by one's achievement.

There are many contexts in Buddhist social ethics where due humility is praised. It is also necessary to notice that Hume has a negative valuation of humility:

> Accordingly we find, that a beautiful house, belonging to ourselves, produces pride; and that the same house, still belonging to ourselves, produces humility, when by any accident its beauty is changed into deformity, and thereby the sensation of pleasure, which corresponded to pride, is transformed into pain, which is related to humility.[29]

Tachibana, reflecting on the place of humility in Buddhist ethics, observes:

> Buddhism as a religion of self-control and contentment will naturally regard humility highly. This is another important Buddhist virtue. When a monk is spoken of as walking, turning his eyes to the ground and being fully possessed of decent deportment, it is not merely his outward appearance, but also his mental condition, that is in view. The outward appearance is merely a visible manifestation of the inner psychology; and decent deportment implies a humble restrained mind.[30]

The Buddha also placed humility at the very centre of the family ethic, in the celebrated *Sigālovāda Sutta*. It is a charming ethics for family relations, where respect, reverence, tender concern, compassion, gratitude and humility are blended in the most refined way. The Buddha also emphasises that even in the higher reaches of spiritual attainment there should not be any conceit based on a comparison with the achievement of other monks. In fact, Venerable Sāriputta says that in the attainment of the second *jhāna*, he was free from the thought, 'It is I who am attaining the second *jhāna*'. It is maintained that the leaning to I-making and mine-making was rooted out from him.

Humility in Contemporary Philosophy of Mind

The Buddhist perspective on humility I have formulated above has some resonance in current reflections in the West. Norvin Richards, discussing the virtues of humility, says that the important point is not to deny the meritorious actions of a person but to deny that meritorious people are capable of humility.[31] He refers to Gabrieli Taylor's analysis, and says that this view has to be corrected. Taylor says 'The man who accepts his lowly position as what is due to him is the man who has humility or the humble man'.[32] Richards says that Taylor's analysis precludes the humility of a person in a high position (achieved through hard work). 'Such a restriction is especially unappealing however, in that normally we not only allow that those who rise can be humble but we find them especially admirable when they are'.[33]

Emotions, Humility and the Self

Though the discussion on pride and self by Hume has been a very rewarding venture, Hume does not consistently use his analysis for a viable moral criticism of emotions, and in this respect, Spinoza, in his study of emotions, provides a more holistic way of looking at the moral standing of emotions. As interpreted by Stuart Hampshire, Spinoza's position is as follows: 'The passions and negative emotions of men rest, intellectually, upon an error of egocentricity and of short-sightedness. One sees the universe as revolving around oneself and one's own interest as central in it'.[34] During recent times, Iris Murdoch has maintained that self-centredness interferes with obtaining moral objectivity, and she has a very insightful understanding of humility:

> Humility is a rare virtue and an unfashionable one and one which is hard to discern. Only rarely does one meet somebody in whom it positively shines, in whom one apprehends with amazement the absence of the avaricious tentacles of the self.... The humble man because he sees himself as nothing, can see other things as they are.[35]

The issue of moral objectivity in relation to the distortions of self-centredness and fantasy has also been discussed by John Kekes, who agrees with the general standpoint of Murdoch, although he does not completely follow Murdoch's notion of 'unselfing'. Kekes says that Murdoch's notion of accepting our own nothingness may not leave room for vigorous moral action. Kekes, of course, qualifies his comments by saying that 'unselfing' may be just a metaphor and perhaps what Murdoch means by unselfing is the 'process of getting into the habit of not allowing selfishness to distort what we see'.[36] He also says that before we can heed the call to unselfing, we need to build a 'robust self' or strong self. Of course, what the Buddhist says may at first sight looks a bit paradoxical – the more penetrating our insight into the doctrine of non-self (*anatta*) becomes, the more vibrant the self-transcending emotions are.

Some Contemporary Thinking

You have to be somebody before you become nobody – Jack Engler

This issue about first developing a 'robust self' before we embark on unselfish activity has emerged recently in relation to therapy. Engler says that psychotherapy may be seen as a prelude to spiritual work, as he feels that Western students who 'jumped into meditation with little preparation sometimes experienced emotional distress'.[37] This question has to be contextualised: for some people, psychotherapy may be seen as a useful prelude to spiritual work; others, like those who do practical counselling, find that there is a two way interaction, therapeutic insights enhancing meditation and meditation work enhancing therapeutic insight. Epstein says that his own development as a therapist is as follows: 'Meditation helped me to come to grips with various narcissistic issues before I had any real therapy, helping me to become somebody'. A balanced view on this issue may be to say that a prerequisite level of personality organisation is useful for meditation/therapy. But, if you look at the inroads of conceit on the Buddhist path to liberation, (which has been a central concern of this chapter) Mark Epstein's comments fit well with the context under discussion in this chapter:

> Just as this narcissistic residue reverberates throughout the life circle, affecting goals, aspirations and interpersonal relationships, so it can be seen to reverberate throughout the meditative path, where psychic structures derived from this infantile experience must be, at various times, gratified, confronted or abandoned.[38]

Epstein also says that the Buddhist ideal of perfection (*arahat*), representing the fruition of meditative practice, provides a means by which the narcissistic remnants that inevitably persist are seized and re-directed. I think it is necessary to contextualise the many-sided aspects of this debate.

A second criticism of the Buddhist position is as follows: Engler says that a defensive pursuit of the ideal of self-lessness leads to a 'fear of individuation', and thus prevents the individual from taking responsibility and being assertive and competent. At the doctrinal level, there need not be a problem about 'individuation' (*atta-bhāva*), which gets drowned out due to the spell of the *anatta* doctrine. The psychological wholeness and coherence of each person, as distinct from the state of being, may vary. The idea of not-self does not deny that each person has an individual character. The Buddha respected this point in prescribing certain forms of meditation that suit the individual.

As my meditation teacher, Venerable Uda Eriyagama Dhammajiva, says, the recommended meditation exercises were 'not obtainable over the counter' but depended on the prescription of the Buddha. In looking at the five hindrances, the Buddha realised that the domination of each of these varies from person to person, and he even presented an analysis of personalities located in the different roots of greed, hatred and delusion. There is also a great variety in those who attain perfection. The great diversity and variety of the Buddha's sermons emphasises the contextuality of people with different kinds of temperament and perspectives. In fact, to give one example, the Buddha says that in some people anger remains like a carving on a rock, on some anger remains like a footprint on sand and yet in others it is like a footprint in water. Defilements like anger and reactivity, greed and acquisitiveness, as well as positive qualities of non-reactivity, equipoise, generosity and emotional balance vary in different people, and understanding the origins and routes of the negativities, as well as their gradual weakening and cessation, is one of the deepest strands of insight meditation practice.

Avoidance of responsibility and accountability is a third problem area cited by Engler. He says that the goal of freeing oneself from egocentric desires may result in the avoidance of anxiety producing situations, which in turn leads to the avoidance of taking responsibility and taking charge of one's life. In doctrinal Buddhism, freedom, karmic correlation and 'serial individuality' give meaning and direction to the notion of responsibility, and the focus on mindfulness in daily life is important. In my own practice of mindfulness-based counselling, and especially in dealing with issues like addiction, in making the client 'take-charge of his or her life', the concept of responsibility is being conveyed to the client as the way to move forward. There is a great deal of misunderstanding on this issue and Rubin, for instance, says, 'in throwing out the bath water of egocentricity, Buddhism eliminates the baby of human agency'.[39] Rubin has missed the distinction between the 'conventional self', which helps to locate the notion of agency, and the self in a more ultimate sense, accepting the full implications of the *anatta* doctrine. There are a number of other issues in relation to Engler's critical views, which I have discussed elsewhere,[40] but here I have restricted my discussion to the Buddhist analysis of the self.

21
The Culture of 'Generosity' and the Ethics of Altruism

In this chapter we develop the Buddhist philosophy of 'giving' (*dāna*) and generosity (*cāga*) and discuss how actions are evaluated in terms of motivation, nature of gifts, contexts of generosity, the impact on personalities and culture. We use Erich Fromm's distinction between the 'having mode', dominated by greed, power, acquisitiveness and aggression, and the opposing 'being mode' of love, sharing and generosity. Fromm's personality types are described in Buddhism as the greed type (*rāga-carita*); the generous type (*cāga-carita*); the aggressive type (*dosa-carita*); and the type deluded by the ego (*moha-carita*). Then we look at the different models in ethics which are emerging in the West, such as Peter Singer's work, *The Life You Can Save*,[1] and we compare the utilitarian ethics model with that of the Buddhist model.

> The practice of giving is universally recognized as one of the most basic human virtues, a quality that testifies to the depth of one's humanity and one's capacity for self-transcendence. In the teaching of the Buddha, too, the practice of giving claims a place of special eminence, one which singles it out as being in a sense the foundation and seed of spiritual development. In the Pali *Suttas*, we read time and again that 'talk on giving' (*dānakathā*) was invariably the first topic to be discussed by the Buddha in his 'graduated exposition' of the Dhamma.[2]

Venerable Bodhi also says that whenever the Buddha delivered a sermon to an audience comprising of people who had not yet regarded him as a teacher, he would start by emphasising the value of giving. Teachings on moral excellence, the law of *kamma* and the 'renunciation' quest would be offered later. In fact, the act of giving is a miniature self-expression which leads one to make more demanding acts of self-sacrifice, and at the deepest level is considered as a '*dāna-pāramī*' (the perfection of giving) in the *saṃsāric* quest of a *Bodhisatva*.

Moral, Psychological and Spiritual Dimensions of Giving (*dāna*) and Generosity (*cāga*)

One central assumption motivating ethical theory in the analytic tradition is that the function of ethics is to combat the inherent egoism or selfishness of individuals. Indeed, many thinkers define the goal of morality as 'selflessness' or 'altruism'.[3]

> Moral behaviour is, at the most general level, altruistic behaviour, motivated by the desire to promote not only our own welfare but the welfare of others.[4]

In the West, especially due to the writings of Max Weber, there is a tendency to see in Buddhism a dichotomy between working for one's own good and that of others: 'Salvation is an absolutely personal performance of the self-reliant individual. No one and no social community can help him'.[5] But the Buddhist *Suttas* take the position, 'that by protecting oneself, one protects others; protecting others, one protects oneself'. Venerable Nyanaponika[6] developed this point in greater detail.[7] Both the good and the bad are infectious. In fact, Erich Fromm sees 'acquisitiveness' and 'generosity' as two cultural orientations manifested in the 'having mode' and the 'being mode'.

Erich Fromm, in his work *To Have Or To Be?*, makes an important distinction between character, way of living and culture, with two orientations: the acquisitive personality/the 'having mode', which concentrates on material possessions and power based on greed and aggression; the 'being mode', which manifests in the pleasure of shared experience, love, productivity, generosity and an expression of a creative and humanistic temperament.

Dāna is referred to as 'giving' and *cāga* is used in the following way: (a) abandoning, giving up, renunciation; (b) liberality, generosity. While *dāna* is basically related to almsgiving, and offering of robes, food etc., to the monks, in return the monks give back a noble gift to lay people, and that is the *dhamma* through sermons, which according to the Buddha excels all other gifts.[8] Laymen may also be involved in the production of *dhamma* books or writing books on the *dhamma*, contributions to the erection of the temple and the temple building fund is also a form of material gifts. Donating must also adhere to the rules for the *saṅgha*, offering proper gifts at the proper time. Personal qualities of generosity are associated with an inward disposition, which makes possible still more demanding acts of self-sacrifice. It is also associated with the Buddhist path for eradication of greed.

In fact, the eradication of greed is an important 'function' of giving and generosity. This disposition also helps to weaken the attachment (*upādana*) to wealth and material objects and the possessive structure of self-centred behaviour. At the level of moral excellence, the defilements of covetousness and avarice lose their power, and we build up positive emotions of liberality and compassion. At the psychological level, motivational factors develop for leading a balanced and righteous life (*sama-cariyā, dhamma-cariyā*). Both the evils of miserliness and wastefulness thin out with this lifestyle. This is developing positive character strengths, which are a base for the spiritual path. The Buddha also praises the person who earns in the righteous way and gives to the needy.[9] More than the size of the wealth or gift given, real generosity emerges from the heart. Giving security and freedom from fear is also a highest form of *dāna*.[10] The following are examples of unhealthy forms of giving, which are counter-productive and destructive: insulting a person; giving for fame and publicity; giving to obtain favours; and giving in a spirit of competition or envy of others. When some of these are practised with deception, there is an additional layer of ignorance. Practice of mental culture helps the person to have motives which are transparent to the person practising the art of generosity. Moral excellence and mental culture provide the base for spiritual upliftment. It is also an additional strength to differentiate between different varieties of giving, three important forms of *dāna* are: giving of material things (*āmisa-dāna*); the giving of fearlessness (*abhaya-dāna*) and the giving of the *dhamma* (*dhamma-dāna*).

The Humanistic Culture

Today, contexts for 'giving' have widened – not merely in terms of wealth but giving one's time, energy, creative planning, travel and so on – due to the complexities of our times: tsunami, bushfires, floods, earthquakes, people struck by dire poverty, starvation and disease. I was deeply struck by a group of kids in Melbourne who came to the platform during a fund raising musical evening, and handed over their pocket money, collected in small 'saving boxes', for the tsunami fund. They learnt for the first time that one can 'get' something by 'giving': not something tangible but a spirit of joy having done something wonderful. The factors of the donor's motive, spiritual purity of the recipient and the kind and size of the gift are the normal evaluative factors in a Buddhist setting. But the volition/motive of the donor is the most important and here, perhaps, like with the kids, an innocent, disinterested and spontaneous disposition is also to be appreciated, along with those who have a more sophisticated/mature turn of mind. During the time of the Buddha, simple folk who had a small income displayed great generosity of heart, along with the celebrated rich patrons of Buddhism who displayed great generosity.

The suffering around today is so tense that some volunteer social workers and compassionate psychologists/therapists succumb to what is described as 'compassion fatigue'.[11] The advice of the Buddha in such contexts is that compassion has to be blended with wisdom, a sense of realism and equanimity – which is the balancing principle across loving kindness, compassion and altruistic joy.

We are living at a time when there are contradictions in contemporary cultures, and we need a humanistic culture that could heal the cracks. Universities have courses on ethics, management faculties have integrated ethics into their fold and every serious research project has to satisfy an ethics committee. But in the recent economic crisis, the obvious casualties are ethics and values. These are the contradictions, when we do not have ethics integrally linked to a 'way of life'. This was the Buddha's insight, that the practice of ethics is to be blended with caring, mindfulness and wisdom.

Peter Singer on Saving Lives

There are new signs of promise to revive the humanistic culture of generosity in the West at a global level. Peter Singer, in his recent work, *The Life You can Save*, raises the question: most of us are absolutely certain that we wouldn't hesitate to save a drowning child and we would do it at considerable cost to ourselves. Yet, while thousands of children die each day, we spend money on things that we take for granted, and we would hardy miss if they were not there. Is that wrong? If so, how far do our obligations to the poor go?

Peter Singer's best reason for the benefit that is reaped by the giver is that giving in contexts like the suffering children in Africa brings meaning and fulfilment to life:

> You may have to make some adjustments to your spending, but quite possibly you will find that some of those adjustments make no difference to your well-being. Instead of having to spend money

to keep up appearances because otherwise people will think you can't afford to buy new clothes or a new car, or renovate your home, you now have a good reason for keeping things that you find comfortable and serviceable: you have better use for the money.[12]

Singer concludes that a collective effort to help the world's poorest people would give greater meaning and fulfilment to our lives. Singer was the pioneer in formulating the discipline of 'practical ethics' several decades ago, and this is one very important contribution from that discipline.

Singer does not discuss the Buddhist ethic of generosity and the present chapter illuminates the Buddhist perspective on generosity. While greatly appreciating Singer's trailblazing path to the project on saving lives, we shall try to illuminate the Buddhist perspective in terms of what has recently been described as 'an ethics of care'. Following this new dimension of caring for others, we may agree with Martin Seligman that what we need is not just ethics but ethics that we 'care for'. When a mother rushes into a burning building to save her child, she is not acting from an ethical principal but as the life of the child is important to her – because she cares about the child. Seligman, after giving this example, turns to a new perspective on ethics by the Princeton philosopher Harry Frankfurt – understanding of what we care about is the great unanswered question. This is a dimension I wish to locate in the Buddhist perspective of generosity (*dāna*).

Global Compassion: The Buddhist Perspective

Peter Singer does not examine the Buddhist perspective on 'global compassion'. He says that the 'golden rule' (to which we refer below) is found in all the major religious traditions, including Buddhism. But as we have shown in this chapter, Buddhism has its own perspective on generosity, altruism and global compassion. In a dialogue between the Dalai Lama and Paul Ekman, there is an extended discussion of the subject.[13]

The Ethics of Care

The ethics of care is a relatively new tradition in the West, which differs from the alternative moral theories of Kantian ethics, utilitarianism and virtue theory.

Virginia Held's *The Ethics of Care: Personal, Political, and Global* presents a new perspective on ethics relevant to personal relations, as well as political and global concerns.[14] It is a work which does not see a split between, on the one hand, values such as justice, equality and individual rights and, on the other hand, values such as care, trust, mutual consideration and solidarity. It is very important in the light of the concerns of the present chapter, which extends from a personal, family-based dimension to global dimensions. An ethics of care values emotions such as sympathy, empathy, sensitivity and responsiveness. Also, this ethics focuses on the relational and interdependent relations, as in family relations in Buddhism, rather than the self-interested, independent rational agents.

The ethics of care is summed up in the celebrated words of the Buddha: 'Even as a mother would risk her own life, to protect her own child, just so one should cultivate a Boundless Heart towards all living beings'.

In fact, Seligman looks at the collapse of values in the background to the current financial crisis and observes that the downturn was caused by mathematical wizards and greedy people who profited hugely in the short run by selling derivatives that they knew would crash and burn in the long run. Seligman, in a lighter vein, raises the question: would courses in ethics help?[15] It is a paradox that ethics in academia may not bring results unless people become passionate about the moral life. They are all aware of the simple lessons about honesty and integrity, which have been drowned by the pathologies of the current culture of economics. I have suggested number of diagnostic tools to reveal, diagnose and explore remedial measures.[16]

Martin Seligman has a way of bringing back 'caring' to ethics in his concept of 'character strengths', and he is also credited with the pioneering project on 'positive emotions'. In this chapter, instead of focusing on the management of emotions described as 'negative', we shall look at the place of altruistic emotions associated with 'generosity'. We will also examine the roots of greed and how we can move away from greed towards the more humanistic dimension of positive emotions. Seligman explored what he described as character strengths and virtues, and how these qualities, which are valued across China, India, Greece and Rome, apply to contemporary Western cultures. Working with a number of other psychologists, their focus was six character strengths: wisdom/knowledge, courage, humanity, justice, temperance and transcendence. Out of these virtues, no one character strength is more fundamental than others, but they have to be blended with wisdom and our sense of humanity. The background to this development is found in humanistic psychologists such as Abraham Maslow, Carl

Rogers and Erich Fromm. More recently, positive psychologists have found empirical support for humanistic psychology.

As the president of the psychological society, Seligman declared that for the last half century psychology has been consumed with a single topic – mental illness – and urged psychologists to follow the mission of the earlier humanistic psychologists for developing virtues and character strengths in normal life. This perspective falls in line with the Buddha's focus on character-strengths and virtues in normal life. The Buddha also brought ethics and psychology together. The perspective of 'positive psychology' we have described offers a meaningful basis to focus on 'generosity', and in Buddhism we have the four sublime virtues of *mettā, karuṇā, muditā, upekkhā* (loving kindness, compassion, altruistic joy and equanimity) which come under Seligman's character strength of 'humanity'. While the four sublime states we have described in the chapter on grief counselling also run through this dimension of 'humanity', in this chapter we are looking at the altruistic emotions associated with generosity and moving out of greed.

People do not, in actual life, summon a deductive calculus of moral logic to guide their lives. To reach even the most sublime impersonal truths (as in the Buddhist quest), or to act in accordance with the most desirable moral rules (as with Kant and the utilitarians) people struggle with the emotions and desires that obstruct them and generate and cultivate the most ennobling sentiments and attitudes. In the words of Parfit, 'the struggle is to live creatively, like producing a work of art'.[17] During recent times, ethics teachers have used novels and short stories to display the excitement, conflicts and creativity embedded in our moral lives, and the recent emphasis on ethical realism and moral psychology proves this point.

In fact, in the Buddhist quest, there is a threefold linkage running through the practice of giving/generosity (*dāna*), moral excellence and mental culture. When one discusses questions about the logic and ethics of generosity in general, such concerns have to be located in the mutual nourishment of three levels.

> Giving (*dāna*) can also be identified with the personal quality of generosity (*cāga*). This angle highlights the practice of giving, not as the outwardly manifest act by which an object is transferred from oneself to others, but as the inward disposition to give, a disposition which is strengthened by outwards acts of giving and which in turn makes possible still more demanding acts of self-sacrifice. Generosity is included among the essential attributes of the *sappurisa*, the

good or superior person, along with such qualities as faith, morality, learning and wisdom. Viewed as the quality of generosity, giving has a particular intimate connection to the entire movement of the Buddha's path. For the goal of the path is the destruction of greed, hate and delusion, and the cultivation of generosity directly debilitates greed and hate, while facilitating that pliancy of mind that allows for the eradication of delusion.[18]

In terms of the Buddhist path of liberation, out of the three bases for the performance of meritorious deeds (*puñña-kiriya-vatthu*), giving is the first, the other two are moral excellence and mental culture.[19] These qualities may interact. For instance, a person who practises mental culture would have an enhanced perspective on giving. Giving is also regarded as a base that can counteract greed and selfishness. When a person has moral and spiritual strength it is easy to give.[20] One has to avoid miserliness, as well as carelessness and wastefulness, and contribute to a culture of giving. It is a cultivation of character that blends *dāna* (generosity), *sīla* (moral excellence) and *paññā* (wisdom).

Apart from the functions of giving, motivation is the real nexus to discover the humanistic facet of positive emotions. Giving can be very mechanical, in fact it can degenerate, for example, one throws a coin at a beggar thinking that he is a nuisance. Also, if one gives to be known, giving for reputation can have mixed results. In line with our interest in 'patronage' and 'giving', there is a relevant image in Buddhist sermons: 'The donor is also described as one who keeps an open house for the needy (*anāvaṭa-dvāro*). He is like a wellspring (*opāna-bhūto*) for recluses, *brāhmaṇas*, the destitute, wayfarers, wonderers and beggars. Being such a one he does meritorious deeds. He is munificent (*mutta-cāgo*) and is interested in sharing his blessings with others (*dāna-saṃvibhāga-rato*). He is a philanthropist who understands the difficulties of the poor (*vadaññū*).'

From the point of view of humanistic values linked to the practice of giving (*dāna*), the most relevant criterion for evaluation of these acts should be the factor of volition (*cetanā*), as in Buddhist ethics motive/intention is the criterion for distinguishing good and bad or skilful and unskilful actions: 'Buddhist teaching devotes special attention to the psychological basis of giving, distinguishing among the different states of mind with which one may give. A fundamental distinction is made between acts of giving that lack wisdom and those that are accompanied by wisdom, the latter being superior to the former'.[21]

Acts of giving with the aim of liberation, understanding *kammic* law of cause and effect, along with the awareness that both the giver and recipient are impermanent, are considered as actions rooted in a deep understanding and having wisdom. An important feature in this process is that, by constantly making the right type of giving a disposition, one builds character, and that means the whole person undergoes positive change. I wish to focus on a special type of transformation. As my counselling work has been in the area of emotions, character building in the context of giving is linked to what Martin Seligman calls 'positive emotions'. I wish to introduce the notion of 'emotionally generous people'. It is said that such people continuously bring happiness, love and positivity to others. This is what I call the 'giving character', as opposed to the hoarding and possessing character. This giving is more than an action but a way of being which beautifully exemplified in Erich Fromm's work, *To Have or To Be*. According to Fromm, in the present period of crisis there are two ways of being: there is the 'having mode', concentrated on material possessions and power and based on greed, envy and aggressiveness; and a second alternative with the pleasure of shared experience, rooted in love. The having mode has generated a crisis around the world today, and it is the mode of gambling and risk taking which has led people and countries to the verge of bankruptcy.

Two Meanings of Altruism

Thomas Nagel says, 'altruism is any behaviour motivated merely by the belief that someone else will benefit or avoid harm by it'.[22] In fact, one sense of altruism, which is in popular usage, is giving more weight to the preferences of others than to our own. A second sense of altruism is giving equal weight to the well-being of all sentient beings, including oneself. Altruism in this second sense is found in a good deal of utilitarian philosophy, and a similar strain is found in Buddhism.

Other Meanings of Altruism

Peter Singer, in his book *The Life You Can Save*, gives other strands of altruism. One is the 'golden rule': do unto others as you would have them done to you, which implies that we should count the desires of others as if they were our own. Singer observes that, though this axiom is well-known from the words of Jesus, it is found in Buddhism, Hinduism, Confucianism, Islam, Jainism and Judaism. He also cites Bill Gates philosophy of giving – doing the most good in the world as a whole.

Personal and Impersonal Perspectives in the Buddhist Liberation Path

For a Buddhist lay person entrenched in routine life, there is an interesting tension between the concept of universal benevolence and feeling for the suffering and the good that they are obliged to do for the family, close friends, those in your village, monks and recluses, and even animals. If one goes through the *Sigālovāda Sutta*, one sees the network of relations, pointing out that they have special obligations to the elders, the aging and so on.

In giving advice to the kings, the Buddha presented a broader group – improving the living conditions of people. It is necessary to bring a sense of realism in any attempt to resolve these points of tension. 'It is important that we be clearly aware of the difference between "particular kinds of affection" and the "most extensive benevolence", which later is an expression of altruism.'

Singer followed utilitarian ethics for a long time. From my own perspective it is necessary to integrate the personal and impersonal viewpoints. On this possible integration there are different responses. Kupperman says that the utilitarian variety of 'impersonal altruism' is too hydraulic, treating concern as if it were a quantifiable and divisible liquid.[23] Yet, in its historical role as a political philosophy it was limited to a particular country and had no global appeal.

> The difficulty is to achieve some kind of integrity in human life without either overwhelming its personal core with a pervasive impersonality or bulldozing the impersonal standpoint in the name of what one must personally do…The discovery of an alternative that we can live by I take to be the task of ethical theory.[24]

Lafollette, in an article on 'Personal Relationships' (191) says that such an ethic of personal relations can empower an impersonal ethic.[25] His position is that we can neither develop moral knowledge nor the empathy necessary for an impartial morality unless we experience intimate relationships.

There is, in fact, an important difference between the 'impersonality ethic' in Buddhism and utilitarianism:

1. An ethical theory which requires the dissociating of preferences and desires from individuals, and the agglomeration of them (utilitarianism).

2. An ethical theory which recommends to individuals the restructuring of their motivational economies with the aim of transcending personal craving and desires (Buddhism).

Expanding on this distinction, Flanagan says:

> But truly living according to the tenets of Buddhism or any other very impartial, impersonal (in the second sense) or detached form requires an extremely complex and disciplined kind of character, possibly richer and more complex than required to live as a liberal individualist.[26]

What Flanagan emphasises is that being a person, an agent with a point of view, is a necessary pre-condition to moving towards the ultimate goal of *nibbāna*.[27]

It must be mentioned that even the perfected *arahant* has an enriching repertoire of positive emotions of empathy, compassion and altruism in turning the minds of people towards a way out of suffering. He does not reap any good *kamma*, as there is no need for it. But in the lives of people dominated by altruism in the world today there are many icons with a diversity of styles.

Guidelines for Readers

Buddhist/Pali Concepts: Basic Conceptual Structures of Buddhist Psychology

Pali words occurring in the book have been given English meanings, and they are best understood in the specific context of their usage. But one of our basic concerns in this appendix is the logic of Buddhist concepts and their conceptual structure in relation to some of the chapters in the book. A good Buddhist dictionary is recommended for readers: *Buddhist Dictionary* by Nyanatiloka Mahathera, Buddhist Publication Society, Sangaraja Mawatha, Kandy, Sri Lanka (an electronic version is available at http://www.budsas.org/ebud/bud-dict/dic_idx.htm [accessed 7 October 2013]); the best initial introduction to Buddhism is the Buddha's first sermon, 'Setting the Wheel in Motion' (*Dhamma-cakka-ppavattana-sutta*) and the best guide to this sermon is *The Four Noble Truths* by the Venerable Ajahn Sumedho, Amaravati Publications, Hemel Hempstead.

One of the lasting benefits of this kind of work is that it allows you to pick up certain schemes that summarise the essence of Buddhist psychology and counselling, enter these in a notebook and work them in your own mind, so that virtually you have them at your 'fingertips'. Add examples from your own experience. I have selected some basic schemes, along with some of the Pali terms. I will be more than happy to enter into an ongoing dialogue with a few readers focused on the impact of this work on their lives, which is as important to me as engaging in debates (pdesilva@alphalink.com.au); philosophical controversies have illuminated my own professional and academic life. The conceptual structures summarised below are mainly for Part I of the book, which deals with the psychology of Buddhism. For counselling, a selected number of books for readers have been recommended at the end of the Further Reading.

1. The five *khandhas* (aggregates) provide the initial basis for locating the mind and its functions: *nāma* (mind), *saññā* (perception), *vedanā* (feeling), *viññāṇa* (consciousness) and *rūpa* (body). These aggregates are important in understanding the Buddhist concept of mind and 'personality' discussed in Chapter 6, but they are also crucial in locating the three dimensions of the cognitive, volitional (*conative*) and affective. In fact, a recurring question from some readers is related to the need for clear clarification of their meanings, and it is of great interest to note that Chapters 2–6 have a relation to these three dimensions. When we look at the place of mindfulness in psychology, we also add another dimension – the 'attentional' dimension.

   Conation. Conation is a term that stems from the Latin *conatus*, meaning any natural tendency, impulse, striving or directed effort. It is one of the three parts of the mind, along with the affective and cognitive. In short, the cognitive part of the brain measures intelligence, the affective deals with emotions and the conative drives how one acts on those thoughts and feelings.

To this useful definition, it is necessary to add that 'cognition', in the context of the present work, covers 'perception' and some 'conceptual activity'. The term '*viññāṇa*' has several meanings, depending on the context of use, but in the context of the five aggregates, it represents 'sensory consciousness'. In traditional Western philosophy, 'cognition' was also associated with the rational faculty. But a more sophisticated analysis has emerged, which includes cognitive, affective and conative dimensions. 'Affect' is easy to differentiate, as it is associated with feelings and emotions and the Chapter 5 examines the relationship between emotions, cognition, desires and the will.

Motivational Cycle. The psycho-dynamics of the motivational cycle is a central feature of Buddhist psychology. Let us look at the emergence of 'anger' and its psycho-dynamics. When the uninstructed worldling is being contacted by a painful feeling, he grieves and laments; he weeps, beating his breast and becomes distraught. He feels two feelings – a bodily one and a mental one. This experience is compared to a man being hit by two darts – a bodily one and a mental one. When he is touched by painful feelings, he resists, and an underlying tendency to resistance (*paṭighānusaya*) emerges in his mind. It is also said that such a person knows no other way out of this pain but an escape into sensual pleasures and that this causes the underlying tendency towards sensual pleasures (*rāgānusaya*) (S IV, 208).

Sensory contact (*phassa*) conditions feeling, feeling (*vedanā*) conditions craving (*taṇhā*) and craving conditions clinging (*upādāna*). Pleasant feelings are fed by a subliminal proclivity for lust and painful feelings by a subliminal proclivity for aversion/reactivity/anger. The immoral bases/roots (*akusala-mūla*) of greed (*lobha*) provide the base for attachment, hatred for emotions/sentiments of aversion and delusion for an egoistic orientation and a deluded mind.

The concept of subliminal activity is very central to Buddhist motivational theory. The term '*anusaya*', which in my earlier writings was translated as the 'unconscious' (influenced by my research on Buddhist and Freudian psychology), is now being translated as 'subliminal tendencies', lying close to the day to day routine consciousness and having the potential to come within 'awareness' through the practice of mindfulness in daily life. *Anusaya-bhūmi* represents the area of dormant or sleeping passions; *pariyuṭṭhāna-bhūmi* represents the area which comes under the focus of our thoughts, and if this cannot be managed and made calm it has the potential to generate harmful physical activity (*vītikkama-bhūmi*). Chapter 4 gives more clarification of these concepts.

2. *Overcoming passions.* This is a central theme in counselling and in Chapter 16 I referred to the methods of restraint, remedying, transforming negative emotions, liberation by insight, through gratitude and living a good life. The path of purification has a scheme more directly related to our spiritual quest, and it is short and to the point:

(i) Overcoming through repression (*vikkhambhana-pahāna*): temporary suspension of the five hindrances (lust, aversion, worry and restlessness, laziness/boredom and sceptical doubt) through 'tranquillity meditation'; (ii) Overcoming by the opposite (*tadaṅga-pahāna*) through insight meditation; (iii) Overcoming by destruction (*samuccheda-pahāna*) through the noble eightfold path; (iv) Overcoming by tranquilisation (*paṭippassaddhi-pahana*) through the disappearance of fetters; (v) Overcoming by deliverance (*nissaraṇa-pahāna*), by the attainment of *nibbāna*.

What is interesting in this group is that they are within the liberation path.

3. *Ethics and the noble eightfold path.* It must be emphasised that in the background of Buddhist psychology is the eightfold noble path:

  (i) Right understanding: *sammā-diṭṭhi* (Wisdom)
 (ii) Right aspiration: *sammā-sańkappa*
(iii) Right speech: *sammā-vācā*
 (iv) Right bodily action: *sammā-kammanta* (Morality)
  (v) Right livelihood: *sammā-ājīva*
 (vi) Right effort: *sammā-vāyāma* (Concentration)
(vii) Right mindfulness: *sammā-sati*
(viii) Right concentration: *sammā-samādhi*

What is important for psychology is the integrated relation of morality to concentration and wisdom. Chapter 11 exemplifies these relations.

4. *Buddhist Psychology and the doctrine of kamma.* The doctrine of *kamma* has two facets: (i) The personal narrative of the Bodhisatta's own journey from life to life, as well as the cosmological picture of the cosmos as a whole, the life and death of beings; (ii) The mind's role in determining the moral quality of actions. The moral quality of actions depends on the 'intention' and the focus is on the 'present'. 'Essential to the Buddha's second insight, was his realization of the mind's role in determining the moral quality of actions. His analysis of the process of developing a skill showed him that skilfulness depended not so much on the physical performance of an act as on the mental qualities of perception, attention and intention that played a part in it. Of these three qualities intention formed the essence of the act' (Thanissaro).

The Pali word *kamma*, or the Sanskrit word *karma*, means 'action', but in the Buddhist context it means only 'voluntary action'. Good karma has good effects (*kusala*) and bad karma has bad effects (*akusala*). Scholars have pointed out that '*kusala*' means that you activate your path to *nibbāna*, where as '*puñña*' or '*puṇya*' means you are collecting merits for life here and after death and its opposite is '*pāpa*'. This is a good issue to discuss in class as, paradoxically, *puṇya* (rather than *kusala*) indicates that you are collecting fuel for a longer journey in *saṃsāra* (if you do not mind it) or maybe you may combine both? The results/fruits you collect are not determined by any supreme being but by the nature of the moral order in the universe.

5. *The law of dependent origination.* I have not examined this concept in the presentation of Buddhist doctrines in this book but left this perspective be learnt in the process of revision and possibly a lesson in the classroom, as it puts together a very large slice of *samsāric life.*

> We saw earlier, in the discussion of the First Noble Truth (*Dukkha*), that what we call a being or an individual is composed of the five aggregates, and that when these are analysed and examined, there is nothing left behind them which can be taken as 'I', Atman, or Self, or any unchanging

abiding substance. That is the analytical method. The same result is arrived at through the doctrine of Conditioned Genesis, which is the synthetic method, and according to this, nothing in the world is absolute. Everything is conditioned, relative, and interdependent. That is the Buddhist theory of relativity (Walpola Rahula, 1978, 52–3).

Another very important difference is that the five aggregates analysis focused on the self/mind–body relationship as a *structural map*, whereas the dependent origination and the picture of psycho-dynamics presented above is focused on the *dynamic character of the mind as a process*, and the ability to intervene at various points. For instance, the ability to slow down as 'feelings' emerge, putting our breaks on painful feelings/bodily or mental, before they get converted into negative emotions.

This theory embodies the principle of conditionality, relativity and interdependence, and it is succinctly described in the formula:

When this is, that is
This arising, that arises
When this is not, that is not
This ceasing, that ceases.
When A is, B is;
A arising B arises;
When A is not, B is not;
A ceasing, B ceases.

There are twelve links in the process of conditioned genesis.

(i) Through ignorance are conditioned volitional actions/karma formations.
(ii) Through volitional actions is conditioned consciousness.
(iii) Through consciousness are conditioned mental and physical phenomena.
(iv) Through mental and physical phenomena are conditioned the six faculties.
(v) Through six faculties is conditioned sensory and mental contact.
(vi) Through sensory and mental contact is conditioned sensation.
(vii) Through sensation is conditioned craving.
(viii) Through craving/desire is conditioned clinging.
(ix) Through clinging is conditioned the process of becoming.
(x) Through the process of becoming is conditioned birth.
(xi) Through birth are conditioned...
(xii) decay, death, lamentation and pain.

Topics for Discussion and Reflection

1. In what way does an understanding of Buddhist philosophy help you to get a deeper understanding of Buddhist psychology?

2. What are your personal reflections on the 'Buddhism and science interface', with special reference to Buddhism in general and also Buddhist psychology?

3. How does the practice of meditation lead to restraint in relation to the senses?

4. How do we 'contextualise' the different levels of cognition: (i) world of tables, chairs and trees; (ii) perceptual distortions; (iii) 'In the seen there will be just the seen; in the heard just the heard; in the sensed just the sensed; and in the cognised just the cognised' (Buddha's advice to Bāhiya).

5. What exactly is the Buddhist contribution to exploring the nature of the craving for self-annihilation (*Vibhava-taṅhā*)? How do you apply this concept into practical situations in life and counselling? Are the craving for self-annihilation and craving for ego-orientation (*Bhava-taṇhā*) opposites? (See Chapter 6)

6. Is it possible to describe the Buddhist theory of emotions as a 'componential theory'? Discuss with reference to the dialogue between Buddhist and Western theories of emotions found in Chapter 5.

7. To what extent does the philosophical analysis of the 'person' concept illuminate the issues around the psychology of personality?

8. Attempt your own analysis of 'emotional balance' with special reference to Chapter 8.

9. What are your views regarding the mind–body relationship?

10. Does the concept of 'the elegance of being your own therapist' have any attraction for you?

11. Write a long tutorial making your own evaluation of mindfulness-based therapies.

12. Divide the class into groups, each group selecting one of the 'emotion profiles' discussed in the book (grief, sadness, stress, greed/addictions, compassion, generosity); spend several sittings and come back to the teacher with (written) responses.

13. What are your visions for an ideal therapist and client relationship? How does a therapist develop his own self-knowledge and self-understanding by engaging in the process of counselling?

14. Does your engagement with counselling enrich your understanding and practice of the 'basic message of the Buddha'?

15. Illuminate the concept of mindfulness-based stress management with examples from your personal life.

16. How would you offer counselling to a person in the very early stages of 'slipping into alcohol addiction'?

17. How would you integrate the philosophy of 'altruism' into your life and that of your family? In what way does the Buddhist perspective of 'altruism' integrate Peter Singer on 'saving lives' and yet offer its own analysis of altruism, renunciation and liberation? (See Chapter 21).

Further Reading

Useful Guides

Buddhist Dictionary by Venerable Nyanatiloka
What the Buddha Taught by Venerable Walpola Rahula
Meditation in Plain English by Venerable Henepola Gunaratana Thero
Buddha's Brain by Rick Hanson and Richard Mendius
The Wings of Awakening by Venerable Thanissaro Bhikkhu
Wheel Publication Series of the Buddhist Publication Society, Kandy, Sri Lanka
Heart of Buddhist Meditation by Venerable Nyanaponika Mahathero.
Satipatthana: The Direct Path to Realisation by Venerable Bhikkhu Analayo.
The Basic Method of Meditation by Venerable Ajahn Brahmavamso
In This Life Itself: Practical Teachings on Insight Meditation, Mitirigala Nissarana Vanaya by Venerable Uda Eriyagama Dhammajiva(Consult website for regular sermons on a wide collection of the Buddhist suttas).
In This Very Life: The Liberation Teachings of the Buddha, Venerable Sayadaw U Pandita, Wisdom Publications.

Primary Sources on Buddhism

Recent translations recommended.

Bodhi Bhikkhu (2000), *The Connected Discourses of the Buddha*, Vol. I and II, Translation of the *Saṃyutta Nikāya*, Buddhist Publication Society, Kandy.
Nanamoli Bhikkhu and Bodhi Bhikkhu (1995), *Middle Length Discourses of the Buddha*, Translation of the *Majjhima Nikāya*, Buddhist Publication Society, Kandy.
Nyanaponika Mahathera and Bodhi Bhikkhu (1999), *Numerical Discourses of the Buddha*, Translation of the *Aṅguttara Nikāya* (a selection), Rowman and Littlefield, New York.
Maurice Walsh (1987), *The Long Discourses of the Buddha: A Translation of the Dīgha Nikāya*, Wisdom Publications, Boston.

Pali Texts and Translations: Pali Text Society

Aṅguttara Nikāya, H. Morris and H. Hardy (eds.), vol. I–V.
Gradual Sayings, vol. I, II, V trans. by F.l. Woodward, vol. III, IV trans. by E.M. Hare.
Dīgha Nikāya, T.W. Rhys Davids and J.E. Carpenter (eds.), vol. I, II and III.
Dialogues of the Buddha, Part I, II and III trans. by T.W. and C.A.F. Rhys Davis.
Kindred Sayings, Part I and II trans. by C.A.F. Rhys Davids, Parts III, IV and V trans. by F.L. Woodward.

Majjhima Nikāya, vol. I–V, V. Trenkner, R. Chalmers, C.A.F. Rhys Davids (eds).
Middle Length Sayings, vol. I, II and III trans. by I.B. Horner.
Saṃyutta Nikāya, vol. I–VI, L. Freer (ed.).

Basic Guides for Counselling and Psychotherapy

Colledge, Ray, 2002, *Mastering Counselling Theory*, PalgraveMacmillan, Basingstoke.

Corey, Gerald, 2005, *Theory and Practice of Counselling and Psychotherapy*, Thomson Learning, Southbank, Victoria.

de Silva, Padmasiri, *Buddhist and Freudian Psychology*, 2010, 4th edition, Shogam Publishers, Carlton North.

Eagan,Gerard, 2002, *The Skilled Helper*, 7th Edition, Thomson Learning, Wadsworth Group, Pacific Grove, CA.

Frankel, Victor, 1963, *Man's Search for Meaning*, Beacon, Boston.

Good, Glen, E. and Beitman, Bernard, D., 2006, *Counselling and Psychotherapy Essentials*, W.W.Norton and Company, New York.

Heidegger, Martin, 1962, *Being and Time*, Harper and Row, New York.

Jung, Carl, 1964, *Man and His Symbols*, Doubleday, New York.

Kieregaard, Soren, *Either/Or* Vol I & II, Anchor Books, New York.

May, Rollo, 1950, *The Meaning of Anxiety*, Ronald Press, New York.

McLeod,John, 2003, *An Introduction to Counselling*, Open University Press, Maidenhead.

Moursund, Janet and Kenny, Maureen C., 2002, *The Process and Counselling and Theory*, Prentice Hall, New Jersey.

Nelson-Jones, Richard, 2000, *Six Approaches to Counselling and Therapy*, Continuum, London, New York.

Rogers, Carl, 1980, *A Way of Being*, Boston, Houghton Mifflin

Skinner, B.F., 1971, *Beyond Human Dignity*, Knopf, New York

Sartre, Jean Paul, 1956, *Being and Nothingness*, Washington Square Press, New York.

Emotion-Focused Therapy

Greenberg, Leslie, 2010, *Emotion-Focused Therapy*, Workshop Handbook, IEFT, Sydney.

Greenberg, Leslie, and Pavio, C., 2003, *Working with Emotions in Psychotherapy*;

Greenberg, Leslie, 2008, *Emotion-Focused Therapy*, American Psychological Association, Washington, DC.

Hayes, C. Stephen, Krik, D. Stroshal and Kelly, Wilson, 1999, *Acceptance and Commitment Therapy*, Guilford Press, New York.

Hick, Steven, F. And Bien, Thomas, eds., 2010, *Mindfulness and the Therapeutic Relationship*, Guilford Press, New York, London.

Huxter, Malcolm, 2012, 'Buddhist Mindfulness Practice in Contemporary Psychology: a paradox of incompatibility and Harmony', *Psychotherapy in Australia*, 18, 2, February, 26–39.

Kabat-Zinn, John, 1990, *Full Catastrophe Living*, Dell Publishing, New York.

Kabat-Zinn, John, Segel, Zindel V., Williams,Mark and Teasdale, John, 2012, *Mindfulness-Based Cognitive Therapy for Depression*, Guilford Press, New York.

Kabat-Zinn, Jon, Williams, Mark, Teasdale, John, and Segel, Zindel, 2007, *The Mindful Way Through Depression*, Guilford Press, New York.

Kang and Whittingham, 2010, 'Mindfulness: A Dialogue Between Buddhism and Clinical Psychology', *Mindfulness*, 2010, 1, 161–173.

Kwee, Maurits, 2013, *Psychotherapy by Karma Transformation: Relational Buddhism and Rational Practice*, http://www.undv.org/vesak2012/book/buddhist_psychotherapy.pdf

Ledoux, Joseph, 1996, *The Emotional Brain*, Simon and Schuster, New York.

Milton, Ivan, 2011, 'Mindful paths to well-being and happiness', *Psychotherapy in Australia*, 17, 2, 64–69.

Prinz, Jesse, J., 2004, *Gut Reactions*, Oxford University Press, Oxford.

Pert, Candace, 1997, *The Molecules of Emotions*, Scribner, New York.

Siegel, Daniel, 2007, *The Mindful Brain*, W.W.Norton and Company, New York.

Spinoza, Benedict, 1963, *Ethics*, ed. Gutman, James, Hafner Publishing, New York.

Notes

1 Buddhist Psychology and the Revolution in Cognitive Sciences

1. George Miller, 2003, 'The Cognitive Revolution', *Trends in Cognitive Sciences*, 7(3), 141.
2. Alan B. Wallace, 2007, *Contemplative Science*, Colombia University Press, New York, p. 13.
3. Wallace, 2007, 167.
4. Richard Davidson, 2003, 'Neuroplasticity Thesis', in Goleman, Daniel, ed., *Destructive Emotions*, Bloomsbury, London, pp. 21–3.
5. Daniel Siegel, 2007, *The Mindful Brain*, W.W. Norton and Company, New York.
6. Candace Pert, 1997, *Molecules of Emotion*, Scribner, New York.
7. Evan Thompson, 2011, 'Neurophenomenology and Contemplative Experience', in Philip Clayton ed., *The Oxford Handbook of Science and Religion*, Oxford University Press.
8. Antonio Damasio, 1994, *Descartes' Error: Reason and the Human Brain*, G.P. Putnam, New York, 1994.
9. Siegel, op.cit., 322.
10. John M. Doris, (ed.), 2010, *The Moral Psychology Handbook*, Oxford University Press, pp. 1–2.

2 Basic Features of Buddhist Psychology: An Overview

1. Robert H. Thouless, 1940, *Riddell Memorial Lectures*, Oxford, p. 47.
2. Rhys Davids, C.A.F., 1914, *Buddhist Psychology*, London.
3. Rune Johanson, 1965, *The Psychology of Nirvana*, Allen and Unwin, London.
4. Padmasiri de Silva, 2008a, *An Introduction to Mindfulness-based Counselling*, Sarvodaya Vishvalekha, Ratmalana.
5. Max Weber, 1958, *Religions of India: The Sociology of Buddhism and Hinduism*, Free Press, Glencoe, NY.
6. E. F. Schumacher, 1993, *Small is Beautiful: A Study of Economics as if People Mattered*, Random House, London.
7. O.H.de A. Wijesekera, 1952, *Buddhism and Society*, Baudhya Sahitya Sabha, Colombo, p. 12.
8. D I, 12–39.
9. K.N. Jayatilleke, 1963, *Early Buddhist Theory of Knowledge*, Allen and Unwin, London.
10. Bhikkhu Analayo, 2010, *Satipaṭṭhana: The Direct Path to Realization*, Windhorse Publications, Cambridge, p. 45.

11. Mark Epstein, 2007, *Psychotherapy Without the Self: A Buddhist Perspective*, Yale University Press, New Haven, CT, p. 2.
12. Walpola Rahula, 1959, *What the Buddha Taught*, Gordon Fraser, London.
13. Padmasiri de Silva, 2008a.
14. Irwin Yalom, 2001, *The Gift of Therapy*, Piatkus, London.
15. Owen Flanagan and Ameli Rorty eds. 1990, *Identity, Character and Morality*, MIT Press, Cambridge, MA, pp. 1–15.
16. *Ibid.*
17. Kwame Anthony Appiah, 2008, *Experiments in Ethics*, Harvard University Press, Cambridge, MA.
18. *Ibid.*, 2.
19. *Ibid.*, 7.
20. Padmasiri de Silva, 2011a, 'The Pathological Features of the Culture of Economics: Does Ethics Offer a Path to Recovery'? Paper presented at the Philosophy East and West Conference, Honolulu (unpublished).
21. Siegel, 2007, 322.

3 The Psychology of Perception and Cognition

1. S II, 140.
2. Dhammajiva, 2008, 76.
3. S IV, 9.
4. Rune Johanson, 1965, 1967, *The Psychology of Nirvana*, Allen and Unwin, London, p. 125.
5. Ud 8.
6. Analayo, 2010, *Satipaṭṭhāna: The Direct Path to Realization*, Windhorse Publications, Cambridge, p. 222.
7. Analayo, 2010, 229.
8. M I, Sutta 15.
9. Sayadaw U. Panditha, 1993, *In this Very Life*, Wisdom Publications, Boston.
10. Venerable Nanananda, *Concept and Reality* (1971).
11. M I, 111.
12. P.D. Premasiri, 2006, *Studies in Buddhist Philosophy and Religion*, Buddha Dhamma Mangala Society, Singapore, p. 170.
13. Premasiri, 2006, 175.
14. In his *Early Buddhist Theory of Knowledge* Jayatilleke, 1963, pp. 422–3.
15. D I, 77.
16. D I, 79.
17. D I, 79.
18. D I, 81.
19. D I, 82.
20. D I, 83.
21. Thanissaro Bhikkhu, 1996, *The Wings to Awakening*, Dhammadāna Publications, Barre, MA, 6.
22. S XII, 70.
23. Thanissaro, 1996, 6.
24. Hick and Bien, 2010, *Mindfulness and the Therapeutic Relationship*.

25. C.R. Rogers, 1961, *On Becoming a Person*, Houghton Mifflin, Boston; A.H. Maslow, 1970, *Towards a Psychology of Being*, Van Nostrand, New York; Erich Fromm, *The Art of Listening*, 1994, Constable, London.
26. Epstein, 1995, 114; de Silva, 2010, xxiv–xxxv.

4 The Psychology of Motivation

1. Daniel Nettle, 2005, *Happiness: The Science Behind Your Smile*, Oxford University Press, Oxford, 158.
2. D II, 305.
3. Siegel, 2007, 44.
4. Padmasiri de Silva, 2010a, *Buddhist and Freudian Psychology*, Shogam Publishers, 4th edition, North Carlton.
5. Joseph Ledoux, 1998, *The Emotional Brain: The Mysterious Underpinnings of Emotional Life*, Simon and Schuster, New York.
6. Keith Oatley, 2004, *Emotions: A Brief History*, Blackwell, Oxford, p. 53.
7. Epstein, 2007.
8. M I, Sutta 2.
9. D III, 105.
10. A II,158; S II, 36–41.
11. Johanson, 1965, 1967, *The Psychology of Nirvana*, Allen and Unwin, London.
12. A I, 111.
13. Analayo, 2010, *Satipaṭṭhāna: The Direct Path to Realization*, Windhorse Publications, Cambridge, p. 159.
14. Analayo, 2010, 248.
15. The eightfold path: 1. Right Understanding 2. Right Thought; 3. Right Speech; 4. Right Bodily Action; 5. Right Livelihood; 6. Right Effort; 7. Right Mindfulness; 8. Right Concentration.
16. D II, 308.
17. De Silva, Padmasiri, 2007, *Explorers of Inner Space*, Sarvodaya Vishvalekha Ratmalana, Sri Lanka, 84–109.
18. Five aggregates: form or matter, sensation or feeling, perception or conception, mental formations, and consciousness.
19. S III, 1–5.
20. See de Silva, 2010a, 127–32.
21. de Silva, 2010a.
22. SE XIV, 252.
23. M III, Sutta 102.
24. Bhikkhu Nanananda, 1971, *Concept and Reality*, Buddhist Publication Society, Kandy, p. 57.
25. M I, 140.
26. M I, Sutta 75.
27. *Milinda Pañha*, Part I, 44, SBE XXXV, 1890.
28. Quoted in De La Vallee Poussin, 1910–27, 'Suicide Buddhist', in Hastings, James, ed., *Encyclopedia of Religion*, Edinburgh, p. 25.
29. Padmasiri de Silva, 1996, 'Suicide and Emotional Ambivalence', in Hoffman, Frank J. and Mahinda, Degale, eds., *Pali Buddhism*, Curzon Press, Richmond, VA.

30. Emile Durkheim, 1951, *Suicide*, The Free Press, Glencoe, NY.
31. Edwin Shneidman, 1985, *Definition of Suicide*, John Wiley, New York, p. 135.

5   Emotions: Western Theoretical Orientations and Buddhism

1. A. Damasio, 1994, *Descartes' Error: Reason and the Human Brain*, G.P. Putnam, New York.
2. Joseph Ledoux, 1988, *The Emotional Brain*, Weidenfeld and Nicolson, London.
3. Paul Ekman, 2003, *Emotions Revealed*, Weidenfeld and Nicolson, London.
4. Daniel Goleman, ed., 1997, *Healing Emotions*, Shambala, Boston and London.
5. Daniel Goleman, 1996, *Emotional Intelligence: Why It Can Matter More Than IQ*, Bloomsbury, London.
6. Candace Pert, 1997, *Molecules of Emotion*, Scribner, New York.
7. Solomon, R.C., 2004a, *In Defence of Sentimentality (The Passionate Life)*, Oxford University Press, Oxford; Solomon, R.C., ed., 2004b, *Thinking About Feeling: Contemporary Philosophers on Emotions*, Oxford University Press, Oxford.
8. Davidson, R.J., 2004, 'Well-being and Affective Style: Neural Substrates and Behavioural Correlates', *Philosophical Transactions Royal Society, London, B*, 359, 1395–1411.
9. Dalai Lama and Paul Ekman, 2008, *Emotional Awareness: Overcoming Obstacles to Psychological Balance and Compassion*, Times Books, Henry Holt and Company, New York.
10. Daniel, J. Siegel, 2007, *The Mindful Brain*, W.W. Norton and Company, New York.
11. Rick Hanson and Richard Mendius, 2009, *Buddha's Brain*, New Harbinger Publications, Oakland, CA.
12. C.A.F. Rhys Davids, 1914, *Buddhist Psychology*, London.
13. Averill, J.R., 1980, 'Emotion and Anxiety: Sociocultural, Biological and Psychological Determinants', in Rorty, A.O., ed., *Explaining Emotions*, University of California Press, Berkley, p. 38.
14. Averill, 1980, 68.
15. Alston, W.P., 1967, 'Emotion and Feeling', in Edwards, Paul, ed., *The Encyclopedia of Philosophy*, Vol.2, Collier Macmillan, New York, p. 480.
16. Lyons, W., 1980, *Emotion*, Oxford University Press, Oxford, ch. 8.
17. Lyons, 1980, 117.
18. Ekman, 2003.
19. William James, 1984, 'What is An Emotion?' in Calhoun, Cheshire and Solomon, Robert, eds., *What Is an Emotion? Classic Readings In Philosophical Psychology*, Oxford University Press, Oxford, 128.
20. *Ibid.*
21. Damasio 1994.
22. Jesse Prinz, 2004, *Gut Reactions: A Perceptual Theory of Emotions*, Oxford University Press, Oxford.
23. James, 1984, 131.
24. Lyons, 1980.

25. G.E. Myers, 1987, *William James, His Life and Thought*, Yale University Press, New Haven, CT, p. 240.
26. M.R. Benett, and P.M.S. Hacker, 2003, *Philosophical Foundations of Neuroscience*, Blackwell, Oxford.
27. Solomon, 2004a, 198–200.
28. James, William, 1890, 1918, 1950, *The Principles of Psychology*, Dover Publications, New York, p. 424.
29. Jon Kabbat-Zinn, 2005, *Coming To Our Senses*, Piatkus, New York, p. 115.
30. Aristotle (384–322 B.C.), in Calhoun, Cheshire and Solomon, Robert C., eds., *What is An Emotion? Classic Readings in Philosophical Psychology*, 1984, Oxford University Press, Oxford, pp. 42–52.
31. Spinoza (1632—1677), *ibid.*, 71–92.
32. Anthony Kenny, 1963, *Action, Emotion and Will*, Routledge Kegan Paul, London, p. 11.
33. Lyons, 1980, p. 209.
34. Lyons, 1980, p. 33.
35. Calhoun, 'Cognitive Emotions', in Calhoun and Solomon, 1984, p. 338.
36. Joel Marks (1986), p. 133.
37. Lyons, 1980.
38. Kraut, 1986.
39. Robert C. Solomon, 2004, *Thinking About Feeling: Contemporary Philosophers on Emotions*, Oxford University Press, Oxford.
40. Padmasiri de Silva, 2011, 'Thinking and Feeling: A Buddhist Perspective', *Sophia*, Vol. 50, Number 2, pp. 253–263. A special issue on Robert C.Solomon and the Spiritual Passions.
41. Padmasiri de Silva, 2012, 'The Lost Art of Sadness', in Kathleen Higgins and David Sherman eds. *Passion, Death and Spirituality: The Philosophy of Robert C.Solomon*, Springer, New York.
42. Solomon, 2004, 85.
43. Solomon and Calhoun, 1984, 333.
44. 1992.
45. de Silva, 2010a, xxxi–xxxv.
46. Oatley 2004, 53.
47. Epstein, 2007, 5.
48. *Ibid.*, 6.
49. Goleman, 2003, 75.
50. Danial Goleman, 1997, *Vital Lies, Simple Truths: The Psychology of Self-deception*, Bloomsbury, London. p. 237.
51. Nyanaponika, 1983, 7.
52. The concept of dependent originations needs detailed explanation, which is presented in the 'Guide for Readers' after Chapter 21.
53. (Nyanaponika, 1975, 69.
54. M I, 293.
55. M I, 111.
56. S II, 232–3.
57. Nyanavira Thero, 1987, *Clearing the Path, Path Press*, Colombo, p 9.
58. A III, 377.
59. S IV, 208.
60. Joel Marks, ed., 1986, *The Ways of Desire*, Precedent, Chicago.

61. C.C.W. Taylor, 1986, 'Emotions and Wants', in Marks, ed., *Ways of Desire*.
62. A III, 441; S I 202.
63. D III, 182.
64. A II, 144.
65. The other unwholesome roots are non-greed (*alobha*), non-hatred (*adosa*) and non-delusion (*amoha*). (generosity, compassion and wisdom).
66. 'Discourse on Forms of Thought', M I, Sutta 20.
67. Calhoun 1984, 338.
68. de Silva, 2010a, 34–75.
69. S IV, 218.
70. Leslie Greenberg, 2008, *Emotion-focused Therapy*, American Psychological Association, Washington D.C., p. 206.
71. Damasio, 1994, and Prinz, 2004.

6   Personality: Philosophical and Psychological Issues

1. C.T. Morgan and R.A. King, 1966, *Introduction to Psychology*, McGraw-Hill, London, p. 460.
2. II, 186.
3. III, sermon 33.
4. Bhadantariya Buddhaghosa, 1956,*The Path of Purification*, Trans to English by Bhikkhu Nanamoli, Singapore Buddhist Meditation Centre, Singapore, 1956.
5. *Gradual Sayings* II, 186.
6. *Gradual Sayings*, pp. 215–18.
7. Stephen Collins, 1982, *Selfless Persons: Imagery and Thought in Theravada Buddhism*, Cambridge University Press, Cambridge, p. 160.
8. *Ibid.*
9. II, 186.
10. Discourse 33.
11. *Puggala-Paññatti.*
12. Jack Engler, 2006, 'Promises and Perils of the Spiritual Path', in Unno, Mark, ed., *Buddhism and Psychotherapy Across Cultures*, Wisdom Publishers, Boston.
13. J. Rubin, 1996, *Psychoanalytical and Buddhist Concepts of Self*, Plenum Press, New York, p. 66.
14. Y. Karunadasa (1994), *Middle Way*, Volume 69:2, p.107.
15. K.N. Jayatilleke, 1967, *The Principles of International Law in Buddhist Doctrine*, Hague Lectures, Leiden, pp. 49–91.
16. M I, 323–324.
17. Rune Johanson, 1965, 1967, *The Psychology of Nirvana*, Allen and Unwin, London, p. 67.
18. *Gradual Sayings*, III, 32.
19. M III, Sutta 139.
20. D III, 289.
21. Rollo May, 1950, *The Meaning of Anxiety*, Ronald Press, New York 1950, pp. 52–5.
22. M I, 137.
23. M III, 217–21.
24. A VII, 130.

25. Deborah Bowman, 2010, 'Dispelling the Enemy Image with Clear and Compassionate Speech', in *Proceedings, 7th International UNDV Buddhist Conference*, Thailand.
26. John A. McConnell, 1995, *Mindful Mediation*, Buddhist Research Institute, Bangkok.
27. de Silva, Padmasiri, 2011b, 'Ethics for the Rough Road: Exploring New Dimensions for Inter-faith Ethics', in Cisneros, Ariane and Premawardahana, eds., *Sharing Values: A Hermeneutics of Global Ethics*, Globe Ethics Series, Geneva, pp. 101–12.
28. Glen E. Good and Bernard D. Beitman, 2006, *Counselling and Psychotherapy Essentials*, W.W. Norton, New York, p. 21.

7 Mental Health and Sickness

1. *Gradual Sayings* II, 143.
2. *Kindred Sayings*, II, 2.
3. Sigmund Freud, 1953, *Beyond the Pleasure Principle*, Volume 18, Standard Edition of the Complete Psychological Works of Sigmund Freud, Hogarth Press, London, 305.
4. Anthony Storr, 1966, 'The Concept of Cure', in C. Rycroft, ed., *Psychoanalysis*, Constable, London, p. 53.
5. Marie Jahoda, 1950, *Current Concepts of Mental Health*, Basic Books, New York, p. 13.
6. *Ibid.*
7. Erich Fromm, D.D.Suzuki and R. Martino, *Zen Buddhism and Psychoanalysis*, Harper, New York, 1960, p. 91.

8 Mental Well-being

1. Alan B. Wallace, and Shauna, L. Shapiro, 2006, 'Mental Balance and Well-Being', *American Psychologist* October, 690.
2. Padmasiri de Silva, 1998, *Environmental Philosophy and Ethics in Buddhism*, Macmillan, London, pp. 168–171.
3. Wallace and Shapiro, 2006, 694.
4. de Silva, Padmasiri, 2008a, *An Introduction to Mindfulness-based Counselling*, Sarvodaya-Vishvalekha, Ratmalana, pp. 60–61.
5. *Ibid.*, 60–81.
6. Daniel Nettle, 2005, *Happiness: The Science Behind Your Smile*, Oxford University Press, Oxford.
7. D II, 305.
8. Padmasiri de Silva, 2007, *Explorers of Inner Space: The Buddha, Krishnamurti and Kierkegaard*, Sarvodaya Vishvalekha, Ratmalana, pp. 84–110.
9. Wallace and Shapiro. 2006, 693.
10. James, quoted in Nettle, 2005.
11. Bill Devall, 1990, *Simple in Means and Rich in Ends*, Merlin Press, London.
12. Daniel Goleman, 1996, *Emotional Intelligence: Why It Can Matter More Than IQ*, Bloomsbury, London.

13. E.M. Adams, 1998, 'Emotional Intelligence and Wisdom', *Southern Journal of Philosophy*, 36.
14. Padmasiri de Silva, 2002a, *Buddhism, Ethics and Society: The Conflicts and Dilemmas of Our Times*, Monash Asia Institute, Clayton, pp. 177–200.
15. Goleman, 1996, *Emotional Intelligence*, Footnote 1, p. 315.
16. Antonio Damasio, 1994, *Descartes' Error: Emotion, Reason and the Human Brain*, Grosser/Putnam, New York.
17. Elster, Jon, 1999, *Strong Feelings: Emotion, Addiction and Human Behavior*, MIT Press, Cambridge, MA, 287–8.
18. I am also grateful to Alan Wallace for his appreciative comments on a earlier version of this present chapter.
19. Padmasiri de Silva, 2010b, 'Mental Balance and Four Dimensions of Well-being: A Buddhist Perspective', Proceedings of the UNDV Conference, Thailand, Bangkok.
20. Nussbaum, Martha, 1991, *The Therapy of Desire*, Princeton University Press, Princeton, NJ, p. 3.
21. Wallace and Shapiro, 2006, 698.
22. A viii, 153.
23. M I, 422.
24. A 10, 196.
25. Gunapala Dharmasiri, 1997, *The Nature of Medicine*, Lalith Graphics, Kandy.
26. Goleman, 1996.
27. Siegel, Daniel, J., 2007, *The Mindful Brain*, W.W. Norton and Company, New York, p. 212.
28. *Ibid*.

9 Mind–Body Relationship and Buddhist Contextualism

1. D II 337–339.
2. S II, 114.
3. M III 89–103.
4. Herbert Guenther, 1973, 'Body and Mind', *Mipham*, 15–16.
5. Eugene Herrigel, 1985, *Zen and the Art of Archery*, Penguin Books, Atkana, pp. 85–6.
6. John Searle, 1994, *The Rediscovery of the Mind*, MIT Press, Cambridge, MA, p. xiii.

10 Towards a Holistic Psychology: Blending Thinking and Feeling

1. Robert C. Solomon, ed., 2004b, *Thinking About Feeling*, Oxford University Press, Oxford.
2. John Deigh, 2004, 'Primitive Emotions', in Robert C. Solomon, ed., *Thinking About Feeling*, Oxford University Press, Oxford, p. 25.
3. Solomon, 2004b, 25.
4. Robert C. Solomon, 2001, *True to Our Feelings*, Oxford University Press, Oxford, p. 85.

5. Candace Pert, 1997, *Molecules of Emotion*, Scribner, New York.
6. Daniel Goleman, ed., 2003, *Destructive Emotions*, Bloomsbury, London.
7. Solomon, 2004b, 93.
8. J. Kabat-Zinn, 1990, *Full Catastrophe Living*, Delta, New York, 48–9.
9. Nyanaponika, Mahathero, 1983, *Contemplation of Feelings*, Buddhist Publication Society, Kandy, p. 7.
10. Padmasiri de Silva 1995, 'Theoretical Perspectives on Emotions in Buddhism', in Joel Marks and Roger Ames, eds., *Emotions in Asian Thought*, State University of New York Press, Albany, PP. 109–20.
11. Solomon, 2004b, 3.
12. *Ibid.*, 3.
13. J. R. Averill, 1980, 'Emotion and Anxiety: Sociocultural, Biological and Psychological Determinants', in Rorty, A.O., ed., *Explaining Emotions*, University of California Press, Berkley, p. 38.
14. Robert C. Solomon, 1973, 'Emotions and Choice', *Review of Metaphysics*, 27, 20–41.
15. William James, James, William, 1890, 1918, 1950, *The Principles of Psychology*, Dover Publications, New York, vol. 1, p. 424.
16. J Kabat-Zinn, 2005, *Coming to Our Senses: Healing Ourselves and the World Through Mindfulness Practice*, Piatkus, New York, p. 118.
17. S II, 114.
18. *Sutta Nipata*, 862–77.
19. Nyanaponika Mahathero, 1973, *The Heart of Buddhist Meditation*, Samuel Wiser, New York.
20. M.R. Bennett and P.M.S. Hacker, 2003, *Philosophical Foundations of Neuroscience*, Blackwell, Oxford, p. 203.
21. G.E. Myers, 1987, *William James, His Life and Thought*, Yale University Press, New Haven, CT.
22. R. M. Gordon, 1982, *The Structure of Emotions: Investigations in Cognitive Philosophy*, Cambridge University Press, Cambridge, p. 92.
23. P.E. Griffith, 1997, *What Emotions Really Are: The Problem of Psychological Categories*, Chicago University Press, Chicago, p. 100.
24. S IV, 385.
25. Pert, 1997, 187.
26. *Ibid.*, 71.
27. *Ibid.*
28. Kabat-Zinn, 1990.
29. Solomon, 2001.
30. Jerome Neu, 1977, *Emotion, Thought and Therapy*, Routledge Kegan Paul, London.
31. Jerome Neu, 2000, *An Emotion Is An Intellectual Thing*, Oxford University Press, Oxford.
32. Padmasiri de Silva, 2005a, *An Introduction to Buddhist Psychology*, 4th edition, PalgraveMacmillan, Basingstoke.
33. Sumedha, Ahahn, 1992, *The Four Noble Truths*, Amaravati Publications, Hemel, Hempstead, p. 64.
34. Paul Ekman, 2003, *Emotions Revealed*, Weidenfeld and Nicolson, London, p. 73.

35. Padmal de Silva, 1986, 'Buddhism and Behaviour Change: Implications for Therapy', in Guy Claxton, ed., *Beyond Therapy: The Impact of Eastern Religions on Psychological Theory and Practice*, Unity Press, NSW, pp. 217–31.

11   Buddhism as Contemplative Philosophy, Psychology and Ethics

1. James, William, 1890, 1918, 1950, *The Principles of Psychology*, Dover Publications, New York.
2. J. Kabat-Zinn, 2005, *Coming to Our Senses*, Piatkus, New York, p. 117.
3. J. Kabat-Zinn, 1990, *Full Catastrophe Living*, Delta, New York, p. 269.
4. M II, 197.
5. A II, 46.
6. Toby Hart, 2004, 'Opening the Contemplative Mind in the Classroom', *Journal of Transformative Education*, 2, 1, 28–46.
7. See Padmasiri de Silva, 2007, *Explorers of Inner Space: The Buddha, Krishnamurti and Kierkegaard*, Sarvodaya-Vishvalekha, Ratmalana.
8. Maria Rainer Rilke, 2001, *Letters to a Young Poet*, Trans. Stephen Michael, Modern Library, New York.
9. Jiddu Krishnamurti, 1995, *The Book of Life*, Harper Collins, New York. See, De Silva, 2007, p. 13.
10. Dalai Lama and Paul Ekman, 2008, *Emotional Awareness*, Henry Holt and Company, New York, p. ix.
11. Padmasiri De Silva, 1993, 'Buddhist Ethics', in Peter Singer, ed., *Companion to Ethics*, Basil Blackwell, Oxford; Padmasiri De Silva, 2002, *Buddhism, Ethics and Society: The Conflicts and Dilemmas of Our Times*, Monash Asia Institute, Clayton; Padmasiri de Silva, 2005b, 'Exploring Buddhist Ethics', in Daniel Kollak and Raymond Martin, eds., *Experience of Philosophy*, Oxford University Press, Oxford.
12. Padmasiri de Silva, 2011b, 'Ethics for the Rough Road: Exploring New Dimensions for Inter-faith Ethics', in Ariane Hentsch Cisneros and Shanta Premawardhana, eds., *Sharing Values*, Global Ethics Series, Geneva.
13. Ludwig Wittgenstein, 1953, *Philosophical Investigations*, Basil Blackwell, Oxford, p. 127.
14. Iris Murdoch, 1956, 'Vision and Choice in Morality', *Proceedings of the Aristotelian Society*, 30, 30–58.
15. Joseph Goldstein, 1994, *Transforming the Mind and Healing the World*, Harvard University, Wit Lectures, Paulist Press, New York, p. 32.

12   Nature of Counselling and Theoretical Orientations in Psychotherapy

1. John McLeod, 2003, *An Introduction to Counselling*, Open University Press, Maidenhead, pp. 293–4.
2. Carl Rogers, 1980, *A Way of Being*, Houghton Mifflin, Boston.
3. Padmasiri De Silva, 2010a, *Buddhist and Freudian Psychology*, 4th edition, Shogam Publishers, Carlton North.

4. Carl Jung, 1964, *Man and His Symbols*, Doubleday, New York.
5. B.F. Skinner, 1971, *Beyond Human Dignity*, Knopf, New York.
6. Gerald Corey, 2005, *Theory and Practice of Counselling and Psychotherapy*, Thomson Learning, Southbank, Victoria.
7. Soren Kierkegaard, 1959, *Either/Or*, Vols I and II, trans. D.F. Swenson and L.M. Swenson, Anchor Books, New York.
8. Martin Heidegger, 1962, *Being and Time*, Harper and Row, New York.
9. Jean Paul Sartre, 1956, *Being and Nothingness*, Washington Square Press, New York.
10. Victor Frankel, 1963, *Man's Search for Meaning*, Beacon, Boston.
11. Rollo May, 1950, *The Meaning of Anxiety*, Ronald Press, New York.

13   Mindfulness-Based Therapeutic Orientations

1. Chris Kang and Koa Whittingham, 2010, 'Mindfulness: A Dialogue Between Buddhism and Clinical Psychology', *Mindfulness*, 1, 161–73.
2. Kang and Whittingham, 2010, 161.
3. C.K. Germer, 2005, 'Mindfulness; What is It? Does it matter?', in Germer, C.K., Siegel R.D. and Fulton, P.R., eds., *Mindfulness and Psychotherapy*, Guilford Press, New York, p. 9.
4. Daniel Siegel, 2007, *The Mindful Brain*, W.W. Norton and Co, New York, pp. 12–13.
5. Jon Kabat-Zinn, 1990, *Full Catastrophe Living*, Delta Publishing, New York.
6. J. Kabat-Zinn *et al.*, 2007, *The Mindful Way Through Depression*, Guilford Press, New York, 47.
7. Zindel V. Segal, Mark Williams and John Teasdale, 2002, *Mindfulness-based Cognitive Therapy for Depression: A New Approach to Preventing Relapse*, Guilford Press, New York.
8. Jon Kabat-Zinn, Mark Williams, John Teasdale, Zindel Segal, 2007, *The Mindful Way Through Depression*, Guilford Press, New York.
9. Mark Epstein, 1995, *Thoughts Without A Thinker*, Basic Books, New York, p. 114.
10. Padmal de Silva, 1986, 'Buddhism and Behaviour Change', in Guy Claxton, ed., *Beyond Therapy*, Unity Press, NSW, pp. 217–31.
11. *Ibid.*
12. Malcolm Huxter, 2012, 'Buddhist Mindfulness Practice in Contemporary Psychology: A Paradox of Incompatibility and Harmony', *Psychotherapy in Australia*, 18, 26–39.
13. Stephen Hayes *et al.*, 1999, *Acceptance and Commitment Therapy*, Guilford Press, New York, p. 7.
14. Ivan Milton, 2011, 'Mindful Paths to Well-being and Happiness', *Psychotherapy in Australia*, 17, 66.
15. Germer, 2005, 21.
16. Epstein, 1995, 114.
17. *Ibid.*, 126.
18. *Ibid.*
19. Sigmund Freud, 1953, 'Remembering, Repeating and Working-Through (Further Recommendations on the Technique of Psycho-Analysis II)', The

Standard Edition of the Complete Psychological Works of Sigmund Freud, Volume 12, p. 148.

20. Padmasiri de Silva, 2010a, *Buddhist and Freudian Psychology*, 4th edition, Shogam Publishers, Carlton North.
21. Mark Epstein, 2007, *Psychotherapy Without a Self: A Buddhist Perspective*, Yale University Press, New Haven, CT, pp. 192–3.
22. Padmasiri de Silva, 2008a, *An Introduction to Mindfulness-based Counselling*, Sarvodaya-Vishvalekha, Ratmalana.
23. Leslie Greenberg, 2008, *Emotion-Focused Therapy*, American Psychological Association, Washington, DC, pp. 206–7.
24. Joseph Ledoux, 1996, *The Emotional Brain*, Weidenfeld and Nicolson, London.
25. Daniel Goleman, ed., 1997, *Healing Emotions*, Shambhala, Boston.
26. Richard Davidson, 2003, 'Neuroplasticity Thesis', in Daniel Goleman, ed., *Destructive Emotions*, Bloomsbury, London, pp. 21–3.
27. Candace Pert, 1997, *Molecules of Emotions*, Scribner, New York.
28. Leslie Greenberg, 2008, *Emotion Focused Therapy*, Workshop Handbook, IEFT Sydney, 22.
29. Leslie Greenberg, 2008, *Emotion-Focused Therapy*, American Psychological Association, Washington DC, 206.
30. Benedict Spinoza, 1949, *Ethics*, ed. James Gulman, Haffner, New York, iv, 195.
31. Greenberg, 2008, 206.
32. S IV, 218.
33. Jesse Prinz, 2004, *Gut Reactions*, Oxford University Press, Oxford.
34. Milton, 2011.

14   Exploring the Content and Methodology of Buddhist Meditation

1. Nyanaponika Thera, 1986a, *The Power of Mindfulness*, Buddhist Publication Society, Kandy, p. 1.
2. Sayadaw Panditha, 1993, *In this Very Life*, Wisdom Publications, Boston.
3. J. Kabat-Zinn, 2005, *Coming To Our Senses*, Piatkus, New York, p. 118.
4. Candace Pert, 1997, *Molecules of Emotion*, Scribner, New York, p. 71.
5. Kabat-Zinn, 2005, 145.

15   Stress Management and the Rhythms of Our Lives

1. Irwin Yalom, 1980, *Existential Psychotherapy*, Basic Books, New York, p. 13.
2. Glen E. Good and Bernard Beitman, 2006, *Counselling and Psychotherapy Essentials*, Norton, New York, p. 229.
3. J. Kabat-Zinn, 1990, *Full Catastrophe Living*, Delta, New York, p. 239.
4. Philippa Perry, 2012, *How to Stay Sane*, Macmillan, Basingstoke, p. 57.
5. Craig Hassad, 2006, *Know Thy Self: The Stress Release Program*, Michelle Anderson Publishers, Melbourne.
6. Guy Claxton, 1997, *Hare Brain, Tortoise Mind*, Eco Press, New York.

16 The Logic of Sadness and Its Near Allies: Depression, Melancholy and Boredom

1. Liz Sheean, 2012, 'Turning Sorrow Into Sickness: An Interview with Jon Jureidini', in, *Psychotherapy Australia*, 18, 2, 40–45.
2. Allan V. Horowitz and Jerome C. Wakefield, 2007, *The Loss of Sadness*, Oxford, Oxford University Press, p. 225.
3. Paul Biegler, 2011, *The Ethical Treatment of Depression*, MIT Press, Cambridge, MA, p. 66.
4. Sigmund Freud, 1956 (1917), 'Mourning and Melancholia', in *Collected Papers*, Volume 4, ed., Jones, E., authorised translation under the supervision of John Rivere, Hogarth Press, London, pp. 152–70.
5. Janet McCracken, 2005, 'Falsely, Sanely, Shallowly: Reflections on the Special Character of Grief', *International Journal of Applied Philosophy*, 19, 145. Also see Robert C. Solomon, 2001, 'Grief', in *True to Our Feelings*, Oxford University Press, Oxford, pp. 73–8.
6. Padmal de Silva, 2006, 'The Tsunami and its Aftermath in Sri Lanka and its Aftermath: Explorations of a Buddhist Perspective', *International Review of Psychiatry*, 18, 3, 281–7.
7. Robert Burton, 1927 (1621), *Anatomy of Melancholy*, Dell, Floyd and Jordon-Smith, Paul, eds., Farrar and Reinhart, New York.
8. Michael Ignatieff, 1987, 'Paradigm Lost', *Times Literary Supplement*, September 4.
9. Padmasiri de Silva, 2007, *Explorers of Inner Space: The Buddha, Krishnamurti and Kierkegaard*, Sarvodaya Vishvalekha, Ratmalana.
10. Lewis Wolpert, 1999, *Malignant Sadness: The Anatomy of Depression*, Faber and Faber, London.
11. Sumedho Thero, 1992, *The Four Noble Truths*, Amaravati Publications, Hemel Hempstead, 41.
12. M.O.C. Drury, 1973, *The Danger of Words*, Routledge and Kegan Paul, London, p. 22.
13. Steven C. Hayes *et al.*, 1999, *Acceptance and Commitment Therapy*, Guilford Press, New York, p. 6.
14. Padmasiri de Silva, 2008a, *An Introduction to Mindfulness-based Counselling*, Sarvodaya-Vishvalekha, Ratmalana.
15. Jennifer Radden, 2000, 'Love and Loss in Freud's "Mourning and Melancholia": A Rereading', in Michael P. Levine, ed., *The Analytic Freud: Philosophy and Psychoanalysis*, Guilford Press, New York.
16. Burton, 1927 (1621).
17. Freud, 1956 (1917), 161.
18. Hayes *et al.*, 1999, 74.
19. Erich Fromm, 1994, *The Art of Listening*, Constable, London, p. 67.
20. Cheshire Calhoun, 2011, 'Living With Boredom', *Sophia*, 50, 269–79.
21. Joseph Goldstein, 1993, *Insight Meditation: The Practice of Freedom*, Shambhala, Boston, MA, p. 80.
22. Alan B. Wallace, 2007, *Contemplative Science*, Columbia University Press, Columbia, 8.
23. Solomon, 2001, 'Grief', 74–8.

24. Leslie Greenberg and Sandra Paivio, 2003, *Working With Emotions in Psychotherapy*, Guilford Press, New York, p. 1.
25. M I, Sutta 10.
26. M I, Sutta 118.
27. Greenberg and Paivio, 2003, 163.
28. Thomas Bien, 2006, *Mindful Therapy*, Wisdom Publishers, Boston, MA, p. 69.
29. Leslie Greenberg, 2010, *Emotion-Focused Therapy*, Workshop Handbook, IEFT, Sydney, 22.
30. Leslie Greenberg, 2008, *Emotion-Focused Therapy*, American Psychological Association, Washington, DC, p. 206.
31. Benedict Spinoza, 1963 (1677), *Ethics*, ed. James Gutmann, Faffner, New York, pp. iv, 195.
32. Nyanaponika Maha Thera, 1986a, *The Power of Mindfulness*, Buddhist Publication Society Kandy, p. 55.
33. Gananath Obeyesekere, 1985, 'Depression, Buddhism, and the Work of Culture in Sri Lanka', in Kleiman, Arthur and Good, Byron, eds., *Culture and Depression, Studies in the Anthropology and Cross-cultural Psychiatry of Affect and Disorder*, University of California Press, Berkeley, p. 13.
34. Horowitz and Wakefield, 2007, 197.
35. Catherine Lutz, 1995, 'Need, Nurturance and Emotions in a Pacific Atoll', in Joel Marks and Roger T. Ames, eds., *Emotions in Asian Thought*, State University of New York Press, Albany, 235.
36. Horowitz and Wakefield, 2007, 198.
37. J. Williams, Zindel Segal and John Teasdale, 2002, *Mindfulness-based Cognitive Therapy for Depression*, Guilford Press, New York.
38. J. Williams, John Teasdale, Zindel Segal and J. Kabat-Zinn, 2007, *The Mindful Way Through Depression*, Guilford Press, New York.
39. Stephanie Morgan, 2005, 'Depression: Turning Towards Life', in Germer *et al.*, eds., *Mindfulness and Psychotherapy*, Guilford Press, New York, p. 133.
40. Jeffrey Zeig, 2008, 'Depression: A Phenomenological Approach to Assessment and Treatment', *Psychotherapy Australia*, 14, 31.
41. Wolpert, 1999.
42. Paul Ekman, 2003, *Emotions Revealed*, Weidenfeld and Nicolson, London, p. 93.
43. Cheshire Calhoun, 2011, Living With Boredom, *Sophia*, 50, 269–279.
44. Martin Seligman, 2011, 2012, *Flourish*, Random House, NSW, p. 54.
45. Mihalyi Csikszentmihalyi, 1990, *Flow: The Psychology of Optimal Experience*, Harper-Perennial, New York.
46. Katherine Higgins and David Sherman, 2012, *Passion, Death and Spirituality*, Springer, New York.
47. Elisabeth Kübler-Ross, 1975, *Death and Dying*, Harper and Row, New York.
48. Robert C. Solomon, 2001, *True to Our Feelings*, Oxford University Press, Oxford, p. 268.
49. Padmasiri de Silva, 2008a, *Introduction to Mindfulness-based Counselling*, Sarvodaya-Vishvalekha, Ratmalana.
50. Padmasiri de Silva, 2008b, 'Theories of Humour: A Buddhist Perspective', *Conference on Asian and Comparative Philosophy, A Symposium on Emotions*, University of Melbourne, Melbourne.

17   Understanding and Managing Grief: When the Desert Begins to Bloom

1. Sameet Kumar, 2005, *Grieving Mindfully*, New Harbinger, Oakland, CA, p. 9.
2. Lorne Ladner, 2004, *The Lost Art of Compassion*, HarperCollins, New York.
3. *Ibid.*, xv.
4. Martha Nussbaum, 2001, *Upheavals of Thought: The Intelligence of Emotions*, Cambridge University Press, Cambridge.
5. Sumedho Thero, 1992, *The Four Noble Truths*, Amaravati Publications, Hemel Hempstead, p. 41.
6. Acharya Buddharakkhita, 1989, *The Philosophy and Practice of Universal Love*, Buddhist Publication Society, Kandy.
7. Nyanaponika Thera, 1958, *The Four Sublime States*, Buddhist Publication Society, p. 10.

18   The Concept of Anger: Psychodynamics and Management

1. Rainer Maria Rilke, 1984, *Letters to a Young Poet*, trans. Stephen Mitchell, Modern Library, New York.
2. William James, quoted in Daniel Nettle, 2005, *Happiness*, Oxford University Press, Oxford, p. 159.
3. See Chapter 5 on emotions.
4. Padmasiri de Silva, 1984, *The Ethics of Moral indignation and the Logic of Violence: A Buddhist Perspective'*, V.F. Gunaratne, Memorial Trust Lecture, Public Trustee, Colombo.
5. Alain De Botton, 2004, *Status Anxiety*, Penguin Books, London, pp. 52–3.
6. Padmasiri de Silva, 2002, *Buddhism, Ethics and Society*, Monash University, Asia Institute, Clayton, 64.
7. William Neblett, 1979, 'Indignation: A Case Study in the Role of Feelings in Morals', *Metaphilosophy*, April.
8. Padmasiri de Silva, 2002a, *Buddhism, Ethics and Society*, Monash University, Asia Institute, Clayton, p. 77.
9. S IV, 208.
10. *Kindred Sayings*.
11. Joseph Goldstein, 1993, *Insight Meditation: The Practice of Freedom*, Shambhala Publishers, Boston.
12. Nyanaponika Thera, 1973, *The Heart of Buddhist Meditation*, Samuel Wiser, New York, p. 39.
13. Paul Ekman, 2003, *Emotions Revealed*, Weidenfeld and Nicolson, p. 73.
14. M I, Sutta 44, 59.137.
15. A IV, 190–94.

19   Addictions, Self-Control and the Puzzles Regarding Voluntary Self-Destruction

1. Gene Heyman, 2009, *Addiction: A Disorder of Choice*, Harvard University Press, Cambridge, MA.

2. Liz Sheean, 2011, '*Addiction: A Disorder of Choice*, an Interview with Gene Heyman', *Psychotherapy in Australia*, vol. 17, no. 4, 26–31.
3. Padmasiri de Silva, 2008a, *An Introduction to Mindfulness-based Counselling*, Sarvodaya-Vishvalekha, Ratmalana.
4. *Ibid.*
5. M.W. Martin, 2007, *Everyday Morality*, Thompson Wadsworth, Belmont, p. 190.
6. M. Stocker, 1979, 'Desiring the Bad: An Essay in Moral Psychology', *Journal of Philosophy*, 76, 744.
7. G.A. Marlatt, 2002, 'Buddhist Philosophy and the Treatment of Addictive Behaviour', *Cognitive and Behavioural Practice*, 9, 44–50.
8. Bien and B. Bien, 2002, *Mindful Recovery: A Spiritual Path to Healing from Addictions*, Wiley, New York.
9. A.R. Mele, 1996, 'Addiction and Self-control', *Behaviour and Philosophy*, 24, 100.
10. James Averill, 1980, 'Emotion and Anxiety: Sociocultural, Biological and Psychological Determinants', in Rorty, Amelie, ed., *Explaining Emotions*, California University Press, Berkeley, p. 38.
11. G. Ainslie, 2001, *Breakdown of Will*, Cambridge University Press, Cambridge, p. 5.
12. B. Dendo Kyokai, 1996, *The Teaching of Buddha*, Kosaido, Tokyo, pp. 228–42.
13. Bien and Bien, 2002.
14. de Silva, 2008a.
15. S. Peele, in Bien and Bien, p. ii.
16. Marlatt, 2002.
17. J. Atkinson, 1957, 'Motivational Dimension of Risk Taking Behaviour', *Psychological Review*, 64, 361, cited in Mele, 1996.
18. R. Ruden, 2000, *The Craving Brain*, HarperCollins, New York, p. 87.
19. Jon Elster, 1999, *Strong Feelings: Emotion, Addiction and Human Behaviour*, MIT Press, Cambridge, MA, p. 194.
20. Padmasiri de Silva, 2010a, *Buddhist and Freudian Psychology*, Shogum, Carlton North.
21. Sigmund Freud, 1953a, *Beyond the Pleasure Principle*, The Standard Edition of the Complete Psychological works of Sigmund Freud, Volume 18, Hogarth Press, London.
22. G.C. Flugel, 1955, *Studies in Feeling and Desire*, Duckworth, London.
23. Freud, 1953a.
24. Jon Elster, 1999, 196.
25. Stanton Peele, 1998, *The Meaning of Addiction*, Jossey Bass, San Francisco.
26. C. Caldwell, 1996, *Getting Our Bodies Back*, Shambhala, Boston, MA, p. 51.
27. Bien and Bien, 2002,37.
28. Guy Claxton, 1997, *Hare Brain, Tortoise Mind*, Eco Press, New York.
29. Mihalyi Csikszentmihalyi, 1990, *Flow: The Psychology of Optimal Experience*, Harper and Row, New York.
30. de Silva, 2008a.

20   Pride and Conceit: Emotions of Self-Assessment

1. Robert C. Solomon, 1977, *The Passions*, Doubleday, Anchor, New York.
2. *Ibid.*, 188.

3. *Ibid.*, Chapter 4.
4. Leila Tov-Ruach, 1987, 'Jealousy, Attention and Loss', in Rorty, Amelie, ed., *Explaining Emotions*, University of California Press, Berkeley, p. 477.
5. *Ibid.*, 480.
6. Gabrieli Taylor, 1985, *Pride, Shame and Guilt: Emotions of Self-Assessment*, Clarendon Press, Oxford.
7. *Ibid.*, 108.
8. Terence Penelhum, 1969, 'Self-Identity and Self-Regard', in Amelie Rorty, ed., *Identities of Persons*, University of California Press, Berkeley, pp. 253–80.
9. *Ibid.*, 253.
10. *Ibid.*, 277.
11. *Ibid.*, 275.
12. David Hume, 1989, *A Treatise of Human Nature*, ed. L.A. Selby-Bigge, Oxford University Press, London, p. 253.
13. *Ibid.*, 275–454.
14. *Ibid.*, 253.
15. Amelie Rorty, 1990, 'Pride Produces the Idea of Self: Hume on Moral Agency', *The Australasian Journal of Philosophy*, 68, 257.
16. Hume, 1989, 277.
17. Rorty, 1990, 264.
18. Penelhum, 1969.
19. Rorty, 1990, 264, n 11.
20. Steven Collins, 1982, *Selfless Persons: Imagery and Thought in Theravada Buddhism*, Cambridge University Press, Cambridge.
21. Rorty, 1990, 257.
22. Penelhum, 1969.
23. Penelhum, 1969.
24. Padmasiri de Silva, 1988, 'The Logic of Identity Profiles and the Ethic of Communal Violence', in de Silva, K.M. *et al.*, eds., *Ethnic Conflicts in Buddhist Societies*, Westview Press, Boulder, CO.
25. Collins, 1982, 19.
26. Padmasiri de Silva, 1981, *Emotion and Therapy: Three Paradigmatic Zones*, Lake House Investments, Colombo; also in Katz, Nathan ed., 1983, *Buddhist and Western Psychology*, Shambhala, Boulder, CO.
27. A I, 340.
28. Bhikkhu Nanananda, 1971, *Concept and Reality in Early Buddhist Thought*, Buddhist Publication Society, Kandy, 10.
29. Hume, 1989, 289.
30. S. Tachibana, 1943, *The Ethics of Buddhism*, Bauddha Sahitya Sabha, Colombo, p. 124.
31. Norvin Richards, 1992, *Humility*, Temple University Press, Philadelphia, p. 2.
32. Taylor, 1985, 17.
33. Richards, 1992, 3.
34. Stuart Hampshire, 1983, *Morality and Conflict*, Harvard University Press, Cambridge, MA, p. 50.
35. Iris Murdoch, 1970, *The Sovereignty of Good*, Routledge Kegan Paul, London, pp. 45, 46 and 106.
36. John Kekes, 1988, 'Purity and Judgment in Morality', *Philosophy*, 63, 460.
37. Jack Engler, 2006, 'Promises and Perils of the Spiritual Path', in Mark Unno, ed., *Buddhism and Psychotherapy Across Cultures*, Wisdom Publishers, Boston, MA.

38. Mark Epstein, 2007, *Psychotherapy Without the Self: A Buddhist Perspective*, Yale University Press, New Haven, CT, p. 15.
39. J. Rubin, 1996, *Psychoanalytic and Buddhist Conceptions of the Self*, Plenum Press, New York, p. 66.
40. Padmasiri de Silva, 2010c, 'The Current Dialogue Between Buddhism and Psychotherapy', in de Silva, 2010a, xxv–xxxi. Also see Epstein, 2007.

21 The Culture of 'Generosity' and the Ethics of Altruism

1. Peter Singer, 2009, *The Life You Can Save*, Text Publishing, Melbourne.
2. Bhikkhu Bodhi, ed., 1995, *Dana: The Practice of Giving*, Buddhist Publication Society, Kandy, p. 1.
3. W. Schroeder, 2000, 'Continental Ethics', in LaFollette, H., ed., *Blackwell Guide to Ethical Theory*, Blackwell, Oxford, p. 396.
4. J. Rachels, 2000, 'Naturalism', in LaFollette, ed., 81.
5. Max Weber, 1958, *The Religion of India*, Free Press, Glencoe, p. 213.
6. Nyanaponika Thera, 1967, *Protection Through Satipatthana*, Buddhist Publication Society, Kandy.
7. Padmasiri de Silva, 2002, *Buddhism, Ethics and Society*, Monash Asia Institute, Clayton, pp. 25–26.
8. Dhammapada 354.
9. *Sutta Nipata* 87.
10. Lily de Silva, 1995, 'Giving in the Pali Cannon', in Bodhi, ed., 13.
11. Elsa Gingold, 2005, 'Compassion Fatigue and How to Avoid It', in Marion Kostanski, ed., *The Power of Compassion*, Victoria University, Victoria, pp. 43–7.
12. Singer, 2009, 184.
13. Dalai Lama and Paul Ekman, eds., 2008, *Emotional Awareness*, Henry Holt and Company, New York, pp. 185–225.
14. Virginia Held, 2012, *The Ethics of Care, Personal, Political and Global*, Oxford University Press, Oxford.
15. Martin Seligman, 2011, 2012, *Flourish*, William Heinemann, North Sydney, p. 229.
16. Padmasiri de Silva, 2011a, 'The Pathological Facets of the Culture of Economics', Paper presented at the Philosophy East and West Conference, 2011, Honolulu (unpublished).
17. Padmasiri de Silva, 1998, *Environmental Philosophy and Ethics in Buddhism*, Macmillan, London, p. 89.
18. Bodhi, 1995, 1.
19. A IV, 241.
20. M I, 449.
21. Bodhi, ed., 1995, 4.
22. Thomas Nagel, 1970, *The Possibility of Altruism*, Clarendon Press, Oxford, p. 16, n.1; see also discussion of 'Altruism', in J.M. Doris, ed., 2010, *The Moral Psychology Handbook*, Oxford University Press, Oxford, pp. 147–205.
23. Joel Kupperman, 1995, 'The Emotions of Altruism, East and West', in Marks, Joel and Ames, Roger T., eds., *Emotions in Asian Thought*, State University of New York Press, Albany, p. 125.

24. Thomas Nagel, 1995, *Other Minds*, Oxford University Press, New York, p. 171.
25. Hugh LaFollete, 1991, 'Personal Relationships', in Singer, Peter, ed., *A Companion to Ethics*, Blackwell, Oxford, pp. 327–32.
26. Owen Flanagan, 1991, *Varieties of Moral Personality*, Harvard University Press, Cambridge, MA, p. 78.
27. *Ibid.*

References

Abbreviations for the Sutta Literature

A: *Anguttara Nikāya* (Gradual Sayings)
D: *Digha Nikāya* (Further Dialogues)
M: *Majjhima Nikāya* (Middle Length Sayings)
S: *Samyutta Nikāya* (Kindred Sayings)

Aaronson, Harvey B., 1980, *Love and Sympathy in Theravada Buddhism*, Motilal Banarsidas, Delhi.

Adams, E.M., 1998, 'Emotional Intelligence and Wisdom', *Southern Journal of Philosophy*, 36.

Ainslie, G., 2001, *Breakdown of Will*, Cambridge University Press, Cambridge.

Alston, W.P., 1967, 'Emotion and Feeling', in Edwards, Paul, ed., *The Encyclopedia of Philosophy*, Vol.2, Collier Macmillan, New York.

Analayo, 2010, *Satipaṭṭhāna: The Direct Path to Realization*, Windhorse Publications, Cambridge.

Appiah, Kwame Anthony, 2008, *Experiments in Ethics*, Harvard University Press, Cambridge, MA.

Atkinson, J, 1957, 'Motivational Dimensions of Risk-taking Behaviour', *Psychological Review*, 64, 359–372.

Averill, J.R., 1980, 'Emotion and Anxiety: Sociocultural, Biological and Psychological Determinants', in Rorty, A.O., ed., *Explaining Emotions*, University of California Press, Berkley.

Bennett, M.R. and Hacker, P.M.S., 2003, *Philosophical Foundations of Neuroscience*, Blackwell, Oxford.

Biegler, Paul, 2011, *The Ethical Treatment of Depression*, MIT Press, Cambridge, MA.

Bien, T. and Bien B., 2002, *Mindful Recovery: A Spiritual Path to Healing from Addictions*, Wiley, New York.

Bien, Thomas, 2006, *Mindful Therapy*, Wisdom Publishers, Boston.

Blum, Lawrence A., 1986, 'Iris Murdoch and the Domain of the Moral', *Philosophical Studies*, 50, 3.

Blum, Lawrence A., 1994, *Moral Perception and Particularity*, Cambridge University Press, Cambridge.

Bodhi Bhikkhu, ed., 1995, *Dana: The Practice of Giving*, Buddhist Publication Society, Kandy.

Bowman, Deborah, 2010, 'Dispelling the Enemy Image with Clear and Compassionate Speech', in *Proceedings, 7th International UNDV Buddhist Conference*, Thailand.

Brodsky, Joseph, 1995, *Listening to Boredom*: Extracts from, 'In Praise of boredom', Dartmouth College, Commencement Address, *Harper's*, March, 1995.

Buddhaghosa, Bhadantariya, 1956, *The Path of Purification*, Trans by Bhikkhu Nanamoli, Singapore Buddhist Meditation Centre, Singapore.

254

BuddhaRakkhita, Acharya, 1989, *The Philosophy and Practice of Universal Love*, Buddhist Publication Society, Kandy.

Burton, Robert, 1927 (1671), *Anatomy of Melancholy*, ed. Floyd Dell and Paul Joirdon, Farrar and Reinhart, New York.

Caldwell, C., 1996, *Getting Our Bodies Back*, Shambala, Boston.

Calhoun, Cheshire, 1984, 'Cognitive Emotions', in Solomon, Robert C., ed., *What Is An Emotion? Classic and Contemporary Readings*, Oxford University Press, Oxford.

Calhoun, Cheshire, 2011, 'Living with Boredom', *Sophia*, 50, 269–279.

Claxton, Guy, 1977, *Hare Brain, Tortoise Mind*, Eco Press, New York.

Colledge, Ray, 2002, *Mastering Counselling Theory*, PalgraveMacmillan, Basingstoke.

Collins, Stephen, 1982, *Selfless Persons: Imagery and Thought in Theravada Buddhism*, Cambridge University Press, Cambridge.

Corey, Gerald, 2005, *Theory and Practice of Counselling and Psychotherapy*, Thomson Learning, Southbank, Victoria.

Csikszentmihalyi, Mihalyi, 1990, *Flow: The Psychology of Optimal Experience*, Harper Perennial, New York.

Dalai Lama and Ekman Paul, 2008, *Emotional Awareness: Overcoming Obstacles to Psychological Balance and Compassion*, Times Books, Henry Holt and Company, New York.

Damasio, A., 1994, *Descartes' Error: Reason and the Human Brain*, G.P. Putnam, New York.

Darwin, Charles, 1998, *The Expression of Emotions in Man and Animals*, Harper Collins, London.

Davidson, Richard, 2003, 'Neuroplasticity Thesis', in Goleman, Daniel, ed., *Destructive Emotions*, Bloomsbury, London, pp. 21–3.

de Botton, Alan, 2004, *Status Anxiety*, Penguin Books, London.

de Silva, Lily, 1995, 'Giving in the Pali Canon', in Bodhi Bhikkhu, ed., *The Practice of Giving*, 11–24.

de Silva, Padmal, 1986, 'Buddhism and Behaviour Change: Implications for Therapy', in Claxton, G., ed., *Beyond Therapy: The Impact of Eastern Religions On Psychological Theory and Practice*, Unity Press, N.S.W.

de Silva, Padmal, 1984, 'The Buddhist Attitude to Alcoholism', in, Edwards, G., Ariff, A. and Jafee, J., eds., *Drug Use and Misuse, Cultural Perspectives*, pp. 33–41, Croom Helm, London.

de Silva, Padmal, 2006, 'The Tsunami and its Aftermath in Sri Lanka and its Aftermath: Explorations of a Buddhist Perspective', *International Review of Psychiatry*, 18, 3, 281–7.

de Silva, Padmasiri, 1981, *Emotion and Therapy: Three Paradigmatic Zones*, Lake House Investments, Colombo; also, in Katz, 1983, *Ethnic Conflicts*.

de Silva, Padmasiri, 1984, *The Ethics of Moral indignation and the Logic of Violence: A Buddhist Perspective*, V.F. Gunaratne, Memorial Trust Lecture, Public Trustee, Colombo.

de Silva, Padmasiri, 1988, 'The Logic of Identity Profiles and the Ethic of Communal Violence', in de Silva, K.M., Duke, Pensri, Goldberg, Ellen and Katz, Nathan, eds., *Ethnic Conflicts in Buddhist Societies*, Westview Press, Boulder, CO.

de Silva, Padmasiri, 1992a, *Twin Peaks: Compassion and Insight*, Buddhist Research Society, Singapore.

de Silva, Padmasiri, 1992b, *Buddhist and Freudian Psychology*, 4th Edition, Shogam Publishers, Melbourne.

de Silva, Padmasiri, 1993, 'Buddhist Ethics', in Singer, Peter, ed., *A Companion to Ethics*, Basil Blackwell, Oxford.

de Silva, Padmasiri, 1994, 'Emotion Profiles: The Self and the Emotion of Pride', in Ames, R.T., Dissanayake, Wimal and Kasulis, T.P., eds., *Self as Person in Asian Theory and Practice*, SUNY Press, Albany.

de Silva, Padmasiri, 1995, 'Theoretical Perspectives on Emotions in Buddhism', in Marks, J. and Ames, R.T., eds., *Emotions in Asian Thought: A Dialogue in Comparative Thought*, State University of New York Press, Albany.

de Silva, Padmasiri, 1996, 'Suicide and Emotional Ambivalence: An Early Buddhist Perspective', in Hoffman, Frank. J. and Mahinda, Deegale, eds., *Pali Buddhism*, Curzon Press, Richmond, VA.

de Silva, Padmasiri, 1998, *Environmental Philosophy and Ethics in Buddhism*, Macmillan, London.

de Silva, Padmasiri, 2002a, *Buddhism, Ethics and Society: The Conflicts and Dilemmas of Our Times*, Monash Asia Institute, Clayton.

de Silva, Padmasiri, 2002b, 'Moral Indignation and the Logic of Violence', in de Silva, Padmasiri, 2002a, *Buddhism, Ethics and Society*, Monash University, Clayton.

de Silva, Padmasiri, 2005a, *An Introduction to Buddhist Psychology*, Fourth Edition, PalgraveMacmillan, Basingstoke.

de Silva, Padmasiri, 2005b, 'Exploring Buddhist Ethics', in Kollak, Daniel and Martin, Raymond, eds., *Experience of Philosophy*, Oxford University Press, Oxford.

de Silva, Padmasiri, 2007, *Explorers of Inner Space: The Buddha, Krishnamurti and Kierkegaard*, Sarvodaya Vishvalekha, Ratmalana.

de Silva, Padmasiri, 2008a, *An Introduction to Mindfulness-based Counselling*, Sarvodaya-Vishvalekha, Ratmalana.

de Silva, Padmasiri, 2008b, 'Theories of Humour: A Buddhist Perspective', *Conference On Asian and Comparative Philosophy, A Symposium on Emotions*: Tribute to Robert Solomons, University of Melbourne, Melbourne.

de Silva, Padmasiri, 2010a, *Buddhist and Freudian Psychology*, 4th edition (with new chapter), Shogam Publishers, North Carlton.

de Silva, Padmasiri, 2010b, 'Mental Balance and Four Dimensions of Well-being: A Buddhist Perspective', Proceedings of the UNDV Conference, Thailand, Bangkok.

de Silva, Padmasiri, 2010c, 'The Current Dialogue Between Buddhism and Psychotherapy', in de Silva, *Buddhist and Freudian Psychology*, 4th edition, Shogom Publishers, North Carlton.

de Silva, Padmasiri, 2010d, 'Mental Balance and Dimensions of Well-being: A Buddhist Perspective', in *Global Recovery: A Buddhist Perspective*, UNDV Conference Proceedings, Published by Mahachulalongkorn Rajamahavidyalaya, Bangkok.

de Silva, Padmasiri, 2011a, 'The Pathological Features of the Culture of Economics: Does Ethics Offer a Path to Recovery?' Paper presented at the Philosophy East and West Conference, 2011, Honolulu (unpublished).

de Silva, Padmasiri, 2011b, 'Ethics for the Rough Road: Exploring New Dimensions for Inter-faith Ethics', in Cisneros, Ariane and Premawardahana, eds., *Sharing Values: A Hermeneutics of Global Ethics*, Globe Ethics Series, Geneva.

de Silva, Padmasiri, 2011c, 'Mindfulness-based Emotion-focused Therapy', Mahidol University Conference on The Interface Between Buddhism and Science, Nakhom Pathom, Mahidol (Unpublished paper).

de Silva, Padmasiri, 2011d, 'Tolerance and Empathy: Exploring Contemplative Methods in the Classroom', in Coleman, Elizabeth Burns and White, Kevin, eds., *Religious Tolerance Education and the Curriculum*, Sense Publishers, Rotterdam.

de Silva, Padmasiri, 2012, 'The Lost Art of Sadness and the Meaning of Love and Grief, *Buddhist Psychotherapy*, IABU, Bangkok.

Deigh, J., 2004, 'Primitive Emotions', in Solomon, R.C., ed., *Thinking About Feeling*, Oxford University Press, Oxford.

Dhammajiva Mahathero, Uda Eriyagama, 2008a, *In This Life Itself: Practical Teachings On Insight Meditation*, Nissarana Vanaya, Meethirigala.

Dhammajiva Mahathero, Uda Eriyagama, 2008b, *Talks on the Bojjhanga Sutta*, Nissarana Forest Hermitage, Meethirigala, MP3 Audio CD.

Dhammajiva, Uda Eriyagama, 2008c, *Towards Inner Peace*, Lithira Publishers, Meethirigala.

Dharmasiri, Gunapala, 1997, *The Nature of Medicine*, Lalith Graphics, Kandy.

Doris, John. M., ed., 2010, *The Moral Psychology Handbook*, Oxford University Press, Oxford.

Drury, M.O.C., 1973, *The Danger of Words*, Routledge and Kegan Paul, London.

Eagan, Gerard, 2002, *The Skilled Helper*, 7th Edition, Thomson Learning, Wadsworth Group, Pacific Grove, CA.

Ekman, Paul and Davidson, Richard, eds., 1994, *The Nature of Emotion: Fundamental Questions*, Oxford University Press, Oxford.

Ekman, Paul, 2003, *Emotions Revealed*, Weidenfeld and Nicolson, New York.

Ekman, Paul, ed., 2008, *A Conversation Between The Dalai Lama and Paul Ekman*: *Emotional Awareness*, Henry Holt and Company, New York.

Ekman, Paul, Davidson Richard, Ricardo Matthieu, Wallace, Allan B., 2005, 'Buddhist and Psychological Perspectives on Emotion and Well-Being', *American Psychological Society*, 14, Vol. Number 2.

Elster, Jon, 1990, *Alchemies of the Mind*, Cambridge University Press, Cambridge.

Elster, Jon, 1999, *Strong Feelings: Emotion, Addiction and Human Behavior*, MIT Press, Cambridge, MA.

Engler, Jack, 2006, 'Promises and Perils of the Spiritual Path', in Unno, Mark, ed., *Buddhism and Psychotherapy Across Cultures*, Wisdom Publishers, Boston.

Epstein, Mark, 1995, *Thoughts Without A Thinker*, Basic Books, New York.

Epstein, Mark, 2007, *Psychotherapy Without the Self: A Buddhist Perspective*, Yale University Press, New Haven, CT.

Fenichel, Otto, 1951, On the Psychology of Boredom, *In Organization and Pathology of Thought*, ed., Rapaport, D., 349–361, Columbia University Press, New York.

Flanagan, Owen and Rorty, Amelie Oksenberg, eds., 1990, *Identity, Character and Morality*: *Essays in Moral Psychology*, MIT Press, Cambridge, MA.

Flanagan, Owen, 1991, *Varieties of Moral Personality: Ethics and Psychological Realism*, Harvard University Press, Cambridge, MA.

Flugel, G.C., 1955, *Studies in Feeling and Desire*, Duckworth, London.

France, Peter, 1996, *Hermits: The Insights of Hermits*, Pimlico, London.

Frankel, Victor, 1963, *Man's Search for Meaning*, Beacon, Boston.

Freud, Sigmund, 1953a, *Beyond the Pleasure Principle, The Standard Edition of the Complete Psychological works of Sigmund Freud*, Volume 18, Hogarth Press, London.

Freud, Sigmund, 1953b, 'Remembering, Repeating and Working-Through (Further Recommendations on the Technique of Psycho-Analysis II)', in *The Standard Edition of the Complete Psychological Works of Sigmund Freud*, Volume 12, Hogarth Press, London.

Freud, Sigmund, 1957 (1917), 'Mourning and Melancholia', in *Collected Papers*, ed., Jones, E. Vol 4, authorised translation under the supervision of John Rivere, Hogarth Press, London, pp. 152–70.

Freud, Sigmund, and Breuer, Joseph, 1895, *Studies in Hysteria*, in *The Standard Edition of the Complete Psychological Works of Sigmund Freud*, Volume 2, Hogarth Press, London.

Fromm, Erich, 1964, *The Heart of Man*, New York.

Fromm, Erich, 1976, 2001, *To Have or To Be*, Abacus, London.

Fromm, Erich, 1994, *The Art of Listening*, Constable, London.

Fromm, Erich, Suzuki, D. D. and Martino, R., 1960, *Zen Buddhism and Psychoanalysis*, Harper, New York.

Garner, Howard, 1993, *Frames of Mind*, Basic Books, New York.

Germer, C.K., 2005, 'Mindfulness; What is It? Does it matter?' in Germer, C.K., Siegel R.D. and Fulton, P.R., eds., *Mindfulness and Psychotherapy*, Guilford Press, New York.

Goldstein, Joseph, 1993, *Insight Meditation: The Practice of Freedom*, Shambala, Boston.

Goldstein, Joseph, 1994, *Transforming the Mind, Healing the World*, The Wit Lectures, Paulist Press, New York.

Goleman, Daniel, 1996, *Emotional Intelligence: Why It Can Matter More Than IQ*, Bloomsbury, London.

Goleman, Daniel, ed., 1997, *Healing Emotions*, Shambala, Boston and London.

Goleman, Daniel, ed., 2003, *Destructive Emotions*, Bloomsbury, London.

Goleman, Daniel, 2006, *Social Intelligence*, Hutchinson, London.

Good, Glen E. and Beitman, Bernard D., 2006, *Counselling and Psychotherapy Essentials*, W.W. Norton, New York.

Gordon, R.M., 1987, *The Structure of Emotions: Investigations in Cognitive Philosophy*, Cambridge University Press, Cambridge.

Greenberg, Leslie, 2008, *Emotion-Focused Therapy*, American Psychological Association, Washington, DC.

Greenberg, Leslie, 2010, *Emotion Focused Therapy*, Workshop Handbook, IEFT, Sydney.

Greenberg, Leslie, and Paivio, Sandra, 2003, *Working With Emotions in Psychotherapy*, Guilford Press, New York.

Griffith, P.E., 1997, *What Emotions Really Are: The Problem of Psychological Categories*, Chicago University Press, Chicago.

Gringold, Elsa, 2005, 'Compassion Fatigue and How to Avoid It', in Kostanski, Marion, ed., 2005, *The Power of Compassion*, Victoria University, Melbourne.

Guenther, Herbert, 1973, 'Body and Mind', *Mipham*, pp. 15–16.

Hampshire, Stuart, 1983, *Morality and Conflict*, Harvard University Press, Cambridge, MA.

Hanson, Rick and Mendius, Richard, 2009, *Buddha's Brain*, New Harbinger Publications, Oakland, CA.

Harris, Russel, 2006, 'Embracing Your Demons: An Overview of Acceptance and Commitment Theory', *Psychotherapy in Australia*, 12, 2–8.

Hart, Toby, 2004, 'Opening the Contemplative Mind in the Classroom', *Journal of Transformative Education*, 2, 28–46.

Harvey, Peter, 2000, *An Introduction to Buddhist Ethics*, Cambridge University Press, Cambridge.

Hassed, Craig, 2006, *Know Thy Self: The Stress Release Programme*, Michelle Anderson Publishers, Melbourne.

Hayes, T. Stephen, Strosahl, Kirk D. and Wilson, Kelly, G., *Acceptance and Commitment Therapy*, Guilford Press, New York.

Heidegger, Martin, 1962, *Being and Time*, Harper and Row, New York.

Held, Virginia, 2012, *The Ethics of Care, Personal, Political and Global*, Oxford University Press, Oxford.

Herrigel, Eugene, 1985, *Zen and the Art of Archery*, Penguin Books, Atkana.

Heyman, Gene, 2010, *Addiction: A Disorder of Choice*, Harvard University Press, Cambridge, MA.

Hick, Steven, F. and Bien, Thomas, eds., 2010, *Mindfulness and the Therapeutic Relationship*, Guilford Press, New York, London.

Higgins, Katherine and Sherman, David, 2012, *Passion, Death and Spirituality*, Springer, London.

Horowitz, Allan, V. and Wakefield, Jerome, 2007, *Loss of Sadness*, Oxford University Press, Oxford.

Hume, David, 1989, *A Treatise of Human Nature*, ed. L.A. Selby-Bigge, Oxford University Press, Oxford.

Huxley, Aldous, 1998, 'Doors in the Wall', in Palmer, Hellen, ed., *Inner Knowing*, Putnam, New York.

Huxter, Malcolm, 2012, 'Buddhist Mindfulness Practice in Contemporary Psychology: a paradox of incompatibility and Harmony', *Psychotherapy in Australia*, 18, 26–39.

Ignatief, Michael, 1987, 'Paradigm Lost', *Times Literary Supplement*, 4 September 1987, 939–940.

Jahoda, Marie, 1950, *Current Concepts of Mental Health*, Basic Books, New York.

James, William, 1890, 1918, 1950, *The Principles of Psychology*, Dover Publications, New York.

James, William, 1984, 'What is An Emotion?', in Calhoun, Cheshire and Solomon, Robert, eds., *What Is an Emotion? Classic Readings in Philosophical Psychology*, Oxford University Press, Oxford.

Jayatilleke, K.N, 1963, *Early Buddhist Theory of Knowledge*, Allen and Unwin, London.

Jayatilleke, K.N., 1967, *The Principles of International Law in Buddhist Doctrine*, Hague Lectures, Leiden.

Johanson, Rune, 1965, 1967, *The Psychology of Nirvana*, Allen and Unwin, London.

Jung, Carl, 1964, *Man and His Symbols*, Doubleday, New York.

Kabat-Zinn, Jon, 1990, *Full Catastrophe Living*, Delta Publishing, New York.

Kabat-Zinn, Jon, 2005, *Coming To Our Senses: Healing Ourselves and the World Through Mindfulness*, Piatkus, New York.

Kabat-Zinn, Jon, Segel, Zindel V., Williams, Mark and Teasdale, John, 2012, *Mindfulness-Based Cognitive Therapy for Depression*, Guilford Press, New York.

Kalupahana, David, 1995, *Ethics in Early Buddhism*, University of Hawaii Press, Honolulu.

Kang, Chris and Whittingham, Koa, 2010, 'Mindfulness: A Dialogue Between Buddhism and Clinical Psychology', *Mindfulness*, 2010, 1:161–173.

Karunadasa, Y., 1994, *Middleway*, 69:2, 107.

Katz, Nathan ed., 1983, *Buddhist and Western Psychology*, Shambhala, Boulder, CO.

Kekes, John, 1988, 'Purity and Judgment in Morality', *Philosphy*, 63, 1988, 460.

Kennet, J., 2001, *Agency and Responsibility*, Oxford University Press, Oxford.

Kenny, Anthony, 1963, *Action, Emotion and Will*, Routledge and Kegan Paul, London.

Keown, Damien, 1995, *Buddhism and Bioethics*, Macmillan Press, Houndmills, Basingstoke.

Kieregaard, Soren, *Either/Or* Vol I & II, Anchor Books, New York.

Kraut, Robert, 1986, 'Feelings in Context', *Journal of Philosophy*, 83, 642–652.

Krishnamurti, J., 1995, *The Book of Life*, Harper Collins, New York.

Kubler-Ross, E., 1970, *On Death and Dying*, Tavistock, London.

Kumar, Samit, 2005, *Grieving Mindfully*, New Harbinger Publications, Oakland, CA.

Kupperman, Joel, 1995, 'The Emotions of Altruism, East and West', in Marks, Joel and Nagel, Thomas, 1995, *Other Minds*, Oxford University Press, Oxford.

Kwee, Maurits, 2013, *Psychotherapy by Karma Transformation: Relational Buddhism and Rational Practice*, http://www.undv.org/vesak2012/book/buddhist_psychotherapy.pdf.

Kyokai, B. Dendo, 1996, *The Teaching of Buddha*, Kosaido, Tokyo, pp. 228–42.

Ladner, Lome, *The Lost Art of Compassion*, Harper Collins, New York.

Ledoux, Joseph, 1988, *The Emotional Brain*, Weidenfeld and Nicolson, London.

LaFollette, H., ed., *Blackwell Guide to Ethical Theory*, Blackwell, Oxford.

Lutz, Catherine, 1995, 'Need, Nurturance and Emotions in a Pacific Atoll', in Marks, Joel and Ames, Roger T., eds., *Emotions in Asian Thought: A Dialogue in Comparative Philosophy*, State University of New York Press, Albany.

Lyons, W., 1980, *Emotion*, Oxford University Press, Oxford.

Marks, Joel, ed., 1986, *The Ways of Desire: New Essays in Philosophical Psychology on the Concept of Wanting*, Precedent, Chicago.

Marks, Joel and Ames, Roger T., eds., 1994, *Emotions in Asian Thought: A Dialogue in Comparative Philosophy*, State University of New York Press, Albany.

Marlatt, G.A, 2002, 'Buddhist Philosophy and the Treatment of Addictive Behaviour', *Cognitive and Behavioural Practice*, 9, 44–50.

Marlatt, G.A, and Chawla N., 2007, 'Meditation and Alcohol Use', *Southern Medical Journal*, 100, 451–453.

Martin, M.W., 2007, *Everyday Morality*, Thompson Wadswort, Belmont.

May, Rollo, 1950, *The Meaning of Anxiety*, Ronald Press, New York.

McConnell, John A., 1995, *Mindful Mediation*, Buddhist Research Institute, Bangkok.

McCracken, Janet, 2005, 'Falsely, Sanely, Shallowly: Reflections on Special Character of Grief', *International Journal of Applied Philosophy*, 19, 139–56.

McLeod, John, 2003, *An Introduction to Counselling*, Open University Press, Maidenhead.

Mele, A.R., 1996, 'Addiction and Self-control', *Behaviour and Philosophy*, 2, 99–117.

Miller, George, 2003, 'The Cognitive Revolution: A Historical Perspective', in *Trends in Cognitive Sciences*, 7, 3.

Milton, Ivan, 2011, 'Mindful Paths to Well-being and Happiness', *Psychotherapy in Australia*, 17, 64–69.

Morgan, C.T. and King, R.A., 1966, R.A, *Introduction to Psychology*, McGraw-Hill, London.

Morgan, Stephanie. P., 2005, 'Depression: Turning Towards Life', in Germer, C.K., Siegel R.D. and Fulton, P.R., eds., *Mindfulness and Psychotherapy*, Guilford Press, New York.

Moursund, Janet and Kenny, Maureen C., 2002, *The Process of Counselling and Therapy*, Prentice Hall, New Jersey.

Murdoch, Iris, 1956, 'Vision and Choice in Morality', *Proceedings of the Aristotelian Society*, 30, 30–58.

Murdoch, Iris, 1970, *The Sovereignty of Good*, Routledge and Kegan Paul, London.

Murdoch, Iris, 1992, *Metaphysics as a Guide to Morals*, Penguin Books, London.

Myers, G.E., 1987, *William James, His Life and Thought*, Yale University Press, New Haven, CT.

Nanananda, Bhikkhu, 1971, *Concept and Reality*, Buddhist Publication Society, Kandy.

Nanananda, Bhikkhu, ed., 1972, *Saṃyutta Nikāya Part II, An Anthology*, Buddhist Publication Society, Kandy.

Neblett, William, 1979, 'Indignation: A Case Study in the role of Feelings in Morals', *Metaphilosophy*, April, 1979.

Nelson-Jones, Richard, 2000, *Six Approaches to Counselling and Therapy*, Continuum, London, New York.

Nettle, Daniel, 2005, *Happiness: The Science Behind Your Smile*, Oxford University Press, Oxford.

Neu, Jerome, 1977, *Emotion, Thought and Therapy*, Rouledge Kegan Paul, London.

Neu, Jerome, 2000, *An Emotion Is An Intellectual Thing: The Meaning of Emotion*, Oxford University Press, Oxford.

Nussbaum, Martha, 1991, *The Therapy of Desire*, Princeton University Press, Princeton, NJ.

Nussbaum, Martha, 2001, *Upheavals of Thought: The Intelligence of Emotions*, Cambridge University Press, Cambridge.

Nussbaum, Martha, 2003, 'Compassion and Terror', *Daedalus*, 132, 10–26.

Nyanaponika, Mahathero, 1963, *The Four Sublime States*, Buddhist Publication Society, Kandy.

Nyanaponika, Mahathero, 1973, *The Heart of Buddhist Meditation*, Samuel Wiser, New York.

Nyanaponika, Mahathero, 1983, *Contemplation of Feelings*, Buddhist Publication Society, Kandy.

Nyanaponika, Thera, 1975, *The Heart of Buddhist Meditation*, Rider and Company, London.

Nyanaponika, Thera, 1986a, *The Power of Mindfulness*, Buddhist Publication Society, Kandy.

Nyanaponika Thera, 1986b, *The Contemplation of Feelings*, Buddhist Publication Society, Kandy.

Nyanavira Thera, 1987, *Clearing the Path*, Path Press, Colombo.

Oatley, Keith, 2004, *Emotions: A Brief History*, Blackwell, Oxford.

Obeyesekera, Gananath, 1985, 'Depression, Buddhism and the Work of Culture in Sri Lanka', in Kleiman, Arthur and Good, Byron, eds., *Culture and Depression, Studies in the Anthropology and Cross-cultural Psychiatry of Affect and Disorder*, University of California Press, Berkeley.

Panditha, Sayadaw. U., 1993, *In This Very Life: The Liberation Teachings of Buddhism*, Wisdom Publishers, Boston.

Peele, Stanton, 1998, *The Meaning of Addiction*, Jossey Bass, San Francisco.

Penulhum, Terence, 1969, 'Self-identity and Self-regard', in Rorty, Amelie, ed., *Identities of Persons*, University of California Press, Berkley, pp. 253–80.

Perry, Philippa, 2012, *How to Stay Sane*, Macmillan, Basingstoke.

Pert, Candace, 1997, *Molecules of Emotion*, Scribner, New York.

Poussin, De La Vallee, 1910–27, 'Suicide Buddhist', in Hastings, James, ed., *Encyclopedia of Religion*, Edinburgh, p. 25.

Premasiri, P.D, 2006, *Studies in Buddhist Philosophy and Religion*, Buddha Dhamma Mangala Society, Singapore.

Prinz, Jesse, J., 2004, *Gut Reactions*, Oxford University Press, Oxford.

Rachels, J., 2000, Naturalism, in La Folette, ed., *Blackwell Guide to Ethical Theory*, Blackwell, Oxford.

Radden, Jennifer, 2000, 'Love and Loss in Freud's "Mourning and Melancholia: A Reading", in Levine, Michael P., ed., *The Analytic Freud: Philosophy and Psychoanalysis*, Routledge, New York.

Rahula, Walpola, 1959, *What the Buddha Taught*, Gordon Fraser, London.

Rhys Davids, C.A.F., 1914, *Buddhist Psychology*, London.

Richards, Norwin, 1992, *Humility*, Temple University Press.

Rilke, Maria Rainer, 1984, *Letters to a Young Poet*, trans. Stephen Mitchell, Modern Library, New York.

Rogers, Carl, 1980, *A Way of Being*, Houghton Miffin, Boston.

Rorty, A.O., 1998, 'Political Sources of Emotion: Greed and Anger', *Midwest Studies in Philosophy*, 22, 21–33.

Rorty, Amelie, 1990, 'Pride Produces the Idea of Self: Hume on Moral Agency', *The Australian Journal of Philosophy*, 68, 3, 255–69.

Rubin, J., 1996, *Psychoanalytical and Buddhist Concepts of Self*, Plenum Press, New York.

Ruden, R., 2000, *The Craving Brain, A Bold New Approach to Breaking Free from *Drug Addiction *Overeating *Alcoholism *Gambling*, Harper Collins, New York.

Rumi, 2005, 'The Guest House', Quoted in Kabat-Zinn, Jon, 2005, *Coming to Our Senses*, p. 263, Piatkus, New York.

Salzberg, Sharon, 1995, *Loving Kindness*, Shambala Publishers, Boston.

Sartre, Jean Paul, 1956, *Being and Nothingness*, Washington Square Press, New York.

Sartre, Jean-Paul, 1962, *Sketch for a Theory of Emotions*, Methuen, London.

Sarvodaya Vishvalekha, Ratmalana, 2011, 'The Pathological Culture of Economics', East–West Philosophy Conference, Honolulu, unpublished paper.

Schroeder, W., 2000, 'Continental Ethics', in La Folette, H., ed., *Blackwell Guide to Ethical Theory*.

Schumacher, E.F, 1993, *Small is Beautiful: A Study of Economics as if People Matter*, Random House, London.

Searle, John, 1994, *The Rediscovery of the Mind*, London.

Segel, Zindel, Williams, Mark, Teasdale John, and Kabat-Zinn, Jon, 2007, *The Mindful Way Through Depression*, Guilford Press, London, New York.

Seligman, M., 2004, *Authentic Happiness: Using the New Positive Psychology to Realise Your Potential for Lasting Fulfilment*, Free Press, New York.

Seligman, Martin, 2011, 2012, *Flourish: A Visionary New Understanding of Happiness and Well-being*, Random House, NSW.

Sheean, Liz, 2011, 'Addiction: A Disorder of Choice: An Interview with Gene Hayman', *Psychotherapy in Australia*, 17, 4, 26–31.

Sheean, Liz, 2012, 'Turning Sorrow Into Sickness: An Interview with Jon Jureidini', *Psychotherapy in Australia*, 18, 2, 40–45.

Sherwood, Patricia, 2005, 'Grief and Loss Work in Buddhist Psychotherapy', *PACAWA News*, no. 33, May 2005, p. 4.

Shneidman, Edwin, 1985, *Definition of Suicide*, John Wiley, New York.

Siegel, Daniel, J., 2007, *The Mindful Brain*, W.W. Norton and Company, New York.

Singer, Peter, ed., 1991, *A Companion to Ethics*, Blackwell, Oxford.

Singer, Peter, ed., 1994 *Ethics*, Oxford University Press, Oxford.

Singer, Peter, 2009, *The Life You Can Save*, Text Publishing, Melbourne.

Skinner, B.F., 1971, *Beyond Human Dignity*, Knopf, New York.

Solomon, R.C., 1973, 'Emotions and Choice', *Review of Metaphysics*, 27, 20–41.

Solomon, R.C., 1977, *The Passions*, Doubleday, Anchor, New York.

Solomon, R.C., 2001, *True To Our Feelings: What Our Emotions are Really Telling Us*, Oxford University Press, Oxford.

Solomon, R.C., 2003, *Not Passion's Slave: Emotions and Choice*, Oxford University Press, Oxford.

Solomon, R.C., 2004a, *In Defence of Sentimentality (The Passionate Life)*, Oxford University Press, Oxford.

Solomon, R.C., ed., 2004b, *Thinking About Feeling: Contemporary Philosophers on Emotions*, Oxford University Press, Oxford.

Spinoza, Benedict, 1963 (1677), *Ethics*, ed. James Gutman, Hafner, New York.

Stocker, M., 1979, 'Desiring the Bad: An Essay in Moral Psychology', *Journal of Philosophy*, 76, 738–753

Storr, Anthony, 1966, 'The Concept of Cure', in C. Rycroft, ed., *Psychoanalysis*, Constable, London.

Sucitto, Ajahn, 1990, 'Making Peace with Despair', in Ajahn Anando, Ajahn Santacitto, Ajahn Sucitto & Ajahn Sumedho, *Peace and Kindness*, Amaravati Publications, Hemel Hempstead.

Sumedho, Ahahn, Thero, 1992, *The Four Noble Truths*, Amaravati Publications, Hemel, Hempstead.

Tachibana, S., 1943, *The Ethics of Buddhism*, Baudha Sahitya Sabha, Colombo.

Tanner, Deborah, 1998, *The Argument Culture*, Virago Press, London.

Taylor, C.C.W., 1986, 'Emotion and Wants', in Marks, Joed, ed., *Ways of Desire*, Precedent, Chicago.

Taylor, Gabrieli, 1985, *Pride, Shame and Guilt: Emotions of Self-assessment*, Clarendon Press, Oxford.

Thanissaro Bhikkhu, 1996, *The Wings to Awakening*, Dhammadāna Publications, Barre, MA.

Thanissaro Bhikkhu, 1999, *Noble Strategy*, Wisdom Audio Visual Exchange, Selangor.

Thompson, Evan, 2011, 'Neurophenomenology and Contemplative Experience', in Philip Clayton, ed., *The Oxford Handbook of Science and Religion*, Oxford University Press, Oxford.

Thouless, Robert H., 1940, *Riddell Memorial Lectures*, Oxford.

Tichtcencho, P., 1998, 'The Goals of Moral Reflection', in Evans, Martyn, ed., *Critical Reflections on Medical Ethics*, Advances in Bioethics Series, Volume 14, Jay Press, London.

Tov-Ruach, Leila, 1987, 'Jealousy, Attention and Loss', in Rorty, Amelie, ed., *Explaining Emotions*, University of California Press, Berkley and Los Angeles.

Wallace, Alan B., 2007, *Contemplative Science*, Columbia University Press, New York.

Wallace, Alan B. and Shapiro, Shauna, L., 2006, 'Mental Balance and Well-Being', *American Psychologist* October, 2006.

Watts, Jonathan, 2009, 'Exploring the Method of Socially Engaged Buddhism', INEB, The Buddhist Channe.

Weber, Max, 1958, *Religions of India: The Sociology of Buddhism and Hinduism*, Free Press, Glencoe.

Wettimuny, R.G.de S, 1978, *The Buddha's Teaching and the Ambiguity of Existence*, M.D. Gunasena, Colombo.

Wijesekera, O.H. de A., 1952, *Buddhism and Society*, Baudhya Sahitya Sabha, Colombo.

Williams, J., Teasdale, John, Segel, Zindel and Kabat-Zinn, Jon, 2007, *The Mindful Way Through Depression*, Guilford Press, New York.

Wittgenstein, Ludwig, 1953, *Philosophical Investigations*, ed., G.E.M. Anscombe and R. Rhees, Blackwell, Oxford.

Wolpert, Lewis, 1999, *Malignant Sadness: The Anatomy of Depression*, Faber and Faber, London.

Yalom, Irwin, 1980, *Existential Psychotherapy*, Basic Books, New York.

Yalom, Irwin, 2001, *The Gift of Therapy*, Piatkus, London.

Zeig, Jeffrey, K., 2008, 'Depression: A Phenomenological Approach to Assessment and Treatment', *Psychotherapy in Australia*, 14: 28–35.

Index

Adams, E.M., 242
Ainsle, George, 190, 192, 250
Alston, W.P., 238
Analayo, 12, 232, 235
Appiah, Kwami, 20, 236
Aristotle, 106, 114, 180, 189, 239
Atkinson, 194
Averil, J.R, 238, 101

behaviourism, 4; *see also* Pavlov, Ivan,
   Watson, J.B. and Skinner, B.F.
Beck, Aaron, 122
Beigler, Paul, 154
Benette, M.R. and Hacker, P.M.S,
   *Philosophical Foundations of
   Neuroscience*, 239
Bien, T. and Bien, B., 154, 250
Bien, T. and Hick, S., 236
Bodhi, Venerable, 216, 232, 252
Bowman, Deborah, 241
Brahmavamsa, Ajahn, 173, 232
Buddharakkhita, Acariya, 247
Buddhism – overview, 9–22
   ethics and moral psychology, 19–22
   mind and subliminal states, 17–19
   psychology and ethics, 11–12
   theory of knowledge, 12–13
   theory of reality, 13–14
Buddhagosha, Venerable, 240

Caldwell, C., 198
Calhoun, Cheshire, 239, 240, 247
Claxton, Guy, 110, 199
cognitive sciences, 3–7
Colledge, Ray, 233
Corey, Gerald, 233
Csikszentmihalyi, Mihalyi, 159, 250
Collins, Stephen, 70, 240
conation, 37

contemplative education, 108
   epistemology, 108–11
   ethics, 113–14
   psychology, 111–12
   spirituality, 114–15
counselling
   orientations/mindfulness-based
   therapies:
   ACT (action commitment therapy),
      131–2
   behaviour modification therapy,
      122–3
   Buddhist concept of mindfulness,
      126–8
   CEB (cultivating emotional
      balance), 140
   DEBT (dialectical behaviour therapy,
      132–3
   EFT (emotion-focused therapy),
      134–40
   existential therapy, 124–25
   MBCT (cognitive behaviour
      therapy), 129–30
   psychodynamic therapy, 131–2
   stress reduction therapy, 128–9
craving, 38–45
   craving for egoistic pursuits, 41–42
   craving for self-annihilation, 42–5
   craving for sensual pleasures, 39–41

Dalai Lama, 5, 238
Damasio, Antonio, 7, 46, 86, 235, 238
Davidson, Richard, 215, 2003,
   235, 236
de Silva, Lily, 252
de Silva, Padmal, 244, 247
de Silva, Padmasiri, 233, 235, 237,
   241, 242, 243
De Sousa, Ronald, 86
Dhammajiva, Uda Eriyagama
   Mahathero, xii, 232, 236
Dhammasiri, G., 242

Doris, John M., 7
Devall, Bill, 84, 235
Drury, M.O.C, 158
De Botton, Alain, 179
Deigh, John, 98
Durkheim, Emile, 238

Eagon, Gerard, 233
Elster, Jon, 242
emotions:
   concept, 99
   Western theories, 99
Ekman, Paul, 46, 56, 106–7, 140
Elster, Jon, 190, 195
Engler, Jack, 214, 240
Epstein, Mark, 14, 35, 111, 134, 214,
   236, 237

Flanagan, Owen, 19, 252
Freud, Sigmund, 30, 77, 97, 155,
   158–9, 185, 217, 245, 247
Fenichel, Otto, 160
Flugal, J.C., 195
Frankel, Victor, 233
Fromm, Eric, 159, 217, 237, 241

Gingold, Elsa, 252
Germer, C.K., 245
Goldstein, Joseph, 114, 160
Goleman, Daniel, 46, 86, 238, 239
Good, Glen. E., and Beltman, Bernard,
   D., 241
Gordon, R.M., 242
Greenberg, Leslie, 136, 161, 182, 233
Griffith, P.E, 242
Guenther, Herbert, 104, 242
Gunaratne, Henepola Thero, 232

Hart, Toby, 244
Hassad, Craig, 245
Heidegger, Martin, 233
Held, Virginia, 252
Herrigel, Eugene, 242
Heyman, Gene, 187, 191, 247
Hick, John, ix
Hampshire, Stuart, 251
Hanson, Rick and Mendius,
   Richard, 232
Hayes, C. Stephen, 233

Hume, David, 106, 203
Hick Stephem, 233
Higgins, Katherine and Sherman,
   David, 247
Horowitz, Allan, V and Wakefield,
   Jerome, C., 247
Huxter, Malcolm, 233

Ignatief, Michael, 247

James, William, 3, 4, 84, 97, 101,
   102, 108
Jahoda, Mary, 78, 241
Jayatilleke, K.N., 235, 236
Johanson, Rune, 235, 236
Jung, Carl, 233

Kabat-Zinn, Jon, 101, 105, 108, 148,
   233, 234, 239.
Kang Chris, and Wittingham,
   Koa, 245
Karunadasa, Y., 240
Kekes, John, 251
Kenny, Anthony, 239
Kierkegaard, Soren, 84, 113, 233
Krishnamurti, Jiddu, 110, 244
Kubler-Ross, 160, 168.
Kumar, 170
Kang and Whittingham, 234
Kwee, Maurits, 2343
Kraut, Robert, 239
Kuperman, Joel, 252
Kypkaaaai, Dendo, 250

Ladner, Lorne, 71
La Follete, Hugh, 252
Ledoux, Joseph, 46, 183, 234
Lutz, Catherine, 71, 164
Lyons, W., 238, 239

Marks, Joel, 239
Marlett, Alan, 190, 250
Martin, M.W., 250
Maslow, A.H., 237
May, Rollo, 124, 233
McConnell, John A., 241
McLeod, John, 233
McCracken, Janet, 247
Mele, Alfred, 190

mental health, 78–80
mental well-being, 79–80
Merton, Thomas, 108, 155
Milton, Ivan, 245
Miller, George, 235
moral psychology, 7, 19–22
Moral Psychology Group: (Rorty,
    Ameli, Flanagan, Owen, and
    Wong, David), 19
Morgan, C.T. and King, R.A., 240
Morsund, Janet, 233
motivation, 31–37
    subliminal motivation, 34–7
Moyers, Bill, 105
Morgan, Stephanie, 247
Murdoch, Iris, 113, 213, 251
Myers, Gerald, 104, 239

Nagel, Thomas, 252
Nanananda, Bikkhu, 28, 236
Nanamoli, Bhikkhu, 232
Naropa University, 111
Neblett,William, 180
Nelson-Jones, Richard, 233
Nettle, Daniel, 237
Neu, Jeome, 243
Nussbaum, Martha, 242
Nyanàponika, Mahathero, 164,
    182, 232
Nyanatiloka, Mahathero, 173, 232
Nyanavira, Thero, 239

Oatley, Keith, 237, 239
Obeyesekera, Gananath, 164

Pandita, Sayadaw U., Venerable,
    232, 236
Pavlov, Ivan, 4, 122
Peele, Stanton, 190
Penulhum, Terrence, 204
perception, 23–5
    extra-sensory perception, 29
    perception and thinking, 27–8
Perls, Frank, 173
Perry, Philipa, 246
personality
    personality concept, 69–72
    personality and conflicts, 73–6
    personality types, 68–9

Pert, Candace, 6, 46, 98, 104, 105, 234
Plato, 106
Premasiri, P.D.236
Prinz, Jesse, 234

Rachels, J, 252
Radden, Jennifer, 158
Rahula, Walpola, Thero, 15, 232
Richards, Norwin, 251
Rhys Davids, ix, 9, 235
Rilke, Maria Rainer, 244
Rogers, Carl, 119, 124, 233, 237
Rorty, Ameli, 197
Rubin, J., 239

Sartre, Jean-Paul, 233
Searle, John, 96, 242
Siegel, Daniel J., 5, 7, 9, 22, 234,
    235, 236
Seligman, Martin, 82, 84
Selye, Hans, 148
Sherwood, Patricia, 174
Schneidman, Edwin, 196, 238
Sheean, Liz, 247
Shroeder, W., 252
Schumacher, E.F., 235
Singer, Peter, 252
Socrates, 189
Skinner, B.F, 122, 233
Solomon, Robert. C, 105, 160, 168,
    238, 242, 250
Spinoza, 234, 239.
Stocker, Michael, 189, 250
Storr, Anthony, 241
Sumedha, Ajahn, 157

Tachibana, S, 251
Taylor, C.C.W, 240
Taylor, Gabrieli, 203
Thanissaro, Bhikkhu, 232, 236
Thompson, Evam, 6
Tov-Ruach, Leila, 202
Thouless, Robert, xi, 9, 235

Veralla, Francis, 4

Wallace, Allan, 3, 140, 156,
    235, 239
Walsh, Maurice, 232

Watson, J.B., 4, 122
Weber, Max, 11, 217, 235
Wijesekera, O.H.de A, 235
Williams, Bernard, 114,
Williams, J., Segel, Zindel V., Teasdale,
   John and Kabat-Zinn, Jon, 247

Wittgenstein, Ludwig, 113
Wolpert, Lewis, 156, 247

Yallom, Irvin, x, 16, 124, 155, 236

Zig, Jeffrey, 247

Made in the USA
San Bernardino, CA
03 September 2017